Community-based Entrepreneurship and Rural Development

How can municipalities in Central Europe create favourable conditions for local business? What and how can municipalities learn from each other? How can each individual in the local area contribute? And what requirements have to be met before know-how can successfully be transferred on a communal level? To answer all these questions, the authors of this book draw on results from a six-year research programme and comprehensively discuss the manifold opportunities, restrictions and prerequisites of establishing favourable conditions for small and medium enterprises in rural municipalities in Central Europe.

First, by using Austrian sample municipalities, the various different prerequisites for economic development in municipalities are illustrated and analysed in detail. On the basis of intensive research interviews with parties involved (mayors, opposition councillors, entrepreneurs and representatives of citizens' initiatives), two municipality portraits are developed for each of the ten different types of municipality identified. Both have started from a similar initial situation, but showed dramatically different success in economic development between 1991 and 2001. By comparing these diametrically opposed development trends, suggestions for successful intervention measures for municipality development are derived.

In the next step, it is established which measures – and under which conditions – are suitable for know-how transfer with transitional countries in Eastern Europe bordering on Austria (Czech Republic, Slovakia, Hungary and Slovenia) and which barriers have to be overcome. For this, 2,000 questionnaires were sent out to mayors in Central and Eastern Europe and more than 60 qualitative interviews were conducted. The analysis culminates in the formulation of 17 theses on the transferability of strategies successful in Austria.

This book is aimed at scholars, practitioners and policy makers interested in the development of rural areas.

Matthias Fink is Professor for International Small Business Management and Innovation at the University of Lüneburg and Head of the Research Institute for Liberal Professions at the WU Vienna University of Economics and Business.

Stephan Loidl is a Researcher at the Institute for Small Business Management and Entrepreneurship at the WU Vienna University of Economics and Business.

Richard Lang is a Senior Researcher at the Research Institute for Co-operations and Co-operatives (RiCC) and at the Institute for Small Business Management and Entrepreneurship at the WU Vienna University of Economics and Business.

Regions and Cities

Series editors:
Ron Martin, *University of Cambridge, UK;*
Gernot Grabher, *University of Bonn, Germany;*
Maryann Feldman, *University of Georgia, USA;*
Gillian Bristow, *University of Cardiff, UK.*

Regions and Cities is an international, interdisciplinary series that provides author-itative analyses of the new significance of regions and cities for economic, social and cultural development, and public policy experimentation. The series seeks to combine theoretical and empirical insights with constructive policy debate and critically engages with formative processes and policies in regional and urban studies.

Community-based Entrepreneurship and Rural Development

Creating favourable conditions for small businesses in Central Europe

Matthias Fink, Stephan Loidl and Richard Lang

Routledge
Taylor & Francis Group

LONDON AND NEW YORK

First published 2013
by Routledge
2 Park Square, Milton Park, Abingdon, Oxfordshire OX14 4RN

Simultaneously published in the USA and Canada
by Routledge
711 Third Avenue, New York, NY 10017

First issued in paperback 2014

Routledge is an imprint of the Taylor & Francis Group, an informa business

The project was funded by Jubiläumfonds der Oesterreichischen
Nationalbank, der Kommunalkredit Austria AG und des Österreichischen
Gemeindebundes.

The translation was perpared with financial support from the Austrian
Science Fund (FWF).

Der Wissensch

British Library Cataloguing in Publication Data
A catalogue record for this book is available from the British Library

Library of Congress Cataloging-in-Publication Data
Fink, Matthias.
Community-based entrepreneurship and rural development : creating
favourable conditions for small businesses in Central Europe / by Matthias
Fink, Stephan Loidl, and Richard Lang.
p. cm.
Includes bibliographical references and index.
1. Small business–Europe, Central. 2. Community development–Europe,
Central. 3. Municipal government–Europe, Central. I. Loidl, Stephan.
II. Lang, Richard. III. Title.
HD2346.C46F56 2012
338.6'420943–dc23
2012003798

ISBN: 978-0-415-61487-0 (hbk)
ISBN: 978-1-138-79223-4 (pbk)

Typeset in Times New Roman
by Taylor & Francis Books

Contents

Foreword

In this book, *Community-based Entrepreneurship and Rural Development*, the authors Matthias Fink, Stephan Loidl and Richard Lang ask the question "How can municipalities create favourable conditions for local small businesses?" They take a particular interest in rural municipalities located in the Czech Republic, Slovakia, Hungary, Slovenia and Austria, and focus their attention on the requirements of the cross-border transfer of know-how between these regions. The book is important as the creation of a favourable environment for small businesses in rural regions is a key issue in creating jobs and increasing quality of life. In this respect, small businesses located in border regions could be regarded as particularly interesting as they have access to markets on both sides of the border, are influenced by both cultures, and can adapt ideas (information and knowledge) from both countries. As a result, they could become rather dynamic – if they are given favourable conditions.

The book follows a long tradition of research interest in the regional aspects of small business development. We can go as far back as the early twentieth century and the writings of Alfred Marshall to find the first major contribution on this topic. However, Marshall's influence was rather limited, as most of the twentieth century was dominated by a belief in large-scale systems and internal economies of scale. It was not until the 1970s that the interest in the regional side of small business re-emerged. This time, the research was led by two Italian economists, Giacomo Becattini and Sebastiano Brusco, who "re-discovered" the industrial districts in the Italian economy. International recognition grew considerably as a result of Michael Porter's book *The Competitive Advantage of Nations*, published in 1990, and his introduction of the "cluster" concept that became accepted in the field. The cluster concept had a major influence, not only on researchers but also among policy makers, especially with regards to technology-oriented regions and clusters. Since these early contributions on the regional aspects of small business, the body of research has grown significantly and become more heterogeneous in character. For example, extensive interest has been shown in regional differences in business formation and the development of small businesses, but there is also interest in regional innovation systems. In this respect, the research has been heavily policy-oriented, with much discussion of how favourable conditions can be created for local and regional businesses.

It is in this context of linking regional and small business development with explicit policy implications that the study by Fink, Loidl and Lang should be seen. The authors have made an impressive empirical study that includes a longitudinal six-year research program during which they conducted in-depth interviews with a large number of key actors in the municipalities and also organized expert workshops and conducted a large-scale survey. The municipalities in the study show significantly different paths in terms of success, and these differences are analysed in a fruitful way.

There are a lot of lessons to be learnt from the study. Summarized into 17 theses, the authors, in a concrete and constructive way, discuss policy implications that could be instrumental for municipalities to create favourable conditions for local small businesses. Therefore, this book should not only be read by researchers interested in regional development and small businesses, but also by policy makers and politicians at regional and local levels.

Hans Landström
Lund University, Sweden

Introduction

Integration into the European Union (EU) poses great challenges for the new member states in Central and Eastern Europe (CEE) not only on the level of the sovereign state; also the municipalities have to support the process by means of suitable strategies. This includes creating a fruitful framework for the positive development of local small and medium enterprises (SMEs). Particularly in rural and structurally disadvantaged areas, these enterprises are the main economic drivers and are therefore the focal interest of regional development policy. The immediate economic, legal and societal environment in which SMEs are active thus deserves increased attention from politics and research alike.

By providing a favourable environment for SMEs in rural areas, communal policy can contribute significantly towards strengthening the region's economic importance and, thus, towards improving the employment situation as well as local wealth. A positive development of SMEs in rural municipalities also directly influences the local population's quality of life. On the one hand, for instance, creating jobs increases household incomes as well as living standards and also reduces the number of outward commuters. On the other hand, the increased inflow in taxes increases the municipalities' financial scope for promotional programmes and infrastructure investment. Ideally, this initiates a positive cycle of development, as the increase in local taxes continuously improves the conditions for the population as well as enterprises and so increases the overall attractiveness of the municipality.

To speed up the integration of Austria's neighbours in Central and Eastern Europe (in the present study, the Czech Republic, Slovakia, Hungary and Slovenia) into the European economic area, it is important to support municipalities in these countries in developing adequate measures of economic policy on a local level. To achieve this, intensive cross-border cooperation, as well as information and know-how transfer, between municipalities in Austria and the neighbouring countries in Central and Eastern Europe (NCCE) is required. A positive development of the NCCE economies and stable societies in these countries will benefit not only the local populations, but also the whole European economic area. This is especially true for Austria, which boasts strong trade relations with these nations.

In the present study, to create a foundation for successful cross-border know-how transfer, first, knowledge is generated about measures for a positive design for developing regional business structures in rural areas that were successful in Austria. In this study, local area denotes a municipality together with its relations with neighbouring municipalities. This leads to a particular local area being viewed differently by each given municipality, which makes a rigid definition of local areas impossible. Local areas in turn form part of a region. The more we know about the effects of key elements of communal policy on the external conditions for SMEs, the more focused we can be in supporting municipalities in Austria and abroad. This necessitates, as a *first step*, creating a functioning set of tools. In order to create such a bundle of effective elements of business-oriented communal policy, the interplay of various factors for a positive economic development in rural areas is analysed. Successful measures of economic policy at a communal level are identified that establish favourable conditions for SMEs and, thus, maintain and create jobs in Austria's rural areas.

From a holistic point of view, the reasons for the different development trends in 18 Austrian municipalities are analysed. This analysis of development trends in local areas based on configuration theory first identifies the variables relating to the characteristics of the actors and the resources available to them in the local areas and their environment. The respective values of these variables in a specific local area then have to be interpreted and their importance (weighting) in interaction has to be established. From this, eventually the causes for the development trends of particular local areas, or of particular types of local areas, can be derived. In general, these are not simple, distinct causes, but complex causal structures. For defining suggested actions for intervention in municipal systems, it is thus not sufficient just to discover individual causes. Rather, it is necessary to reconstruct the interdependencies of effects between different variables. Only based on this reconstruction of the respective configurations (*gestalts*) that have been recognized as causes for economic and societal developments both of a positive and negative nature in rural local areas, practical suggestions for intervention in the ongoing development processes are possible.

This analysis is not intended to, and indeed is not able to, provide a definite representation of local area structures existing in Austria, but aims at detecting and explaining typical development trends. For this reason, the local areas examined are not selected randomly: areas are chosen that, a priori, show (1) a significant increase or decrease in jobs and places of work in the period between the two workplace counts 1991 and 2001 and (2) characteristics typical for Austrian local areas. For each type of local area, two Austrian local areas are identified, of which one showed a positive development, the other a not so positive development, in the period under observation. Contrasting local areas that are similar in their initial situations but different in their development in this way facilitates identifying individual variables suspected of having effects, bundles of variables and forces effective between these variables or bundles.

Following the qualitative paradigm of empirical social research, the data are collected in direct field research. Up to four narrative interviews are conducted in each local area. Altogether, 65 people are interviewed in all Austrian provinces with rural areas (i.e. outside Vienna) within the first stage of the survey between September 2005 and February 2006. The selection of the interview partners is based on their social roles in the local area. By collecting perspectives and interpretations of the goings-on in the local area that are as diverse as possible, the meanings behind the statements are to be brought to the fore. To this effect, at least the mayor, a councillor with executive functions of the strongest opposition party, an entrepreneur and/or a person involved in the provision of basic amenities are interviewed in each area.

From the content analysis with a multi-stage interpretation procedure, 18 portraits of municipalities – all anonymous, out of consideration for the people involved – are created, of which contrastive pairs are built. The contrastive analysis results in bundles of measures relevant for success. Instruments of effective intervention in development processes in rural areas are evaluated anew and new instruments are developed. This all culminates in a compilation of suggested actions, formulated as theses. These theses form the foundation for the second step of the survey.

The geographical focus is then extended to Austria's neighbouring nations in Central and Eastern Europe. The measures at the communal level that have proven successful in Austria are now analysed regarding their transferability to the rural municipalities in the NCCE. Then, it is determined what is relevant for knowledge transfer under what circumstances, and which barriers have to be overcome. It has to be kept in mind that there are two types of barriers regarding the transferability of such measures. On the one hand, there are barriers to transferability that are part of the individual measures (push blockers). Such measures generally cannot be transferred to other municipalities, as they depend on resources not available in any other context; the positive effect of these measures is based on a unique constellation of success factors that cannot be replicated. Once aware of this, useless attempts at transfer can be avoided right from the start. On the other hand, there are barriers to know-how transfer due to the institutional setting and the actors' characteristics in the target municipalities. These are barriers to transferability that are part of the target municipalities (pull blockers). These barriers occur whenever measures of economic policy on a communal level are generally transferable, but the target municipality does not have the necessary prerequisites for the transfer. These barriers potentially create the need for action.

In order to be able to support the rural municipalities in the NCCE in formulating an agenda for developing a strong regional economic structure, the list of measures successful in Austria is, as a *second step*, reduced by those suggestions for action that for general reasons cannot be transferred to these target municipalities. This is based on the results of an expert workshop and a large-scale survey in the target countries.

The *third step* is the intensive evaluation of the transferability of the measures remaining in the portfolio, based on ten sample municipalities in the NCCE. In the individual countries, there is a differentiation by region based on economic indicators. In these sample municipalities, in analogy to the survey in Austria, interviews are conducted with a selection of key actors that is as diverse as possible and the data collected are then subjected to content analysis. From this analysis, a portfolio of measures, differentiated by target region, is derived, where each municipality in the target countries receives a specially prepared guideline on suggested actions to be taken. Additionally, the analysis identifies deficits in the transferability of the respective measures in the individual regions. Thus, it becomes apparent which requirements for the transfer of measures that cannot be implemented at this point have not been met yet in the municipalities in the region. This shows a need for action on the local, regional, national and EU levels.

The results of this study, summarized in 17 theses, clearly show that the focus of regional development increasingly has to be put on the cooperation of small units (municipalities). EU initiatives (e.g. LEADER+ or INTER-REG) also address this issue, and further the inclusion of civil society actors, in addition to businessmen and municipality officials, in regional development policy. The measures suggested in this study can establish the conditions for a successful development of a common economic and societal area. An important contribution to this can be made by the focused know-how transfer of successful, economically-oriented measures on a communal level. In this context, it is not enough to copy formulae for success from other areas, but the necessary knowledge on the conditions for application has to be conveyed, too, and the limits of transferability in individual cases have to be taken into account. The present study aims to contribute to such a successful and efficient know-how transfer.

1   Setting the stage

1.1 Methodological approach – narrations as a key to the configuration dilemma

1.1.1 The challenge

Business research has been dominated by the analysis of mono-causal and often uni-directional relationships between variables for a long time. A great number of studies – for instance on factors relevant for the foundation of new ventures or for business success – has been carried through with large impetus and high means (Busenitz et al. 2003, Grichnik 2006). Large samples of differing quality have hence led to many research results with restricted practical relevance (Tsang/Kwan 1999, Baldridge et al. 2004, Huw et al. 2007). Such research can hardly encompass, and most certainly cannot explain, empirically observable phenomena (Bouckenooghe et al. 2007, Diekmann 2000).

It is clear that a complete modelling of the section of the world that is relevant to business research is neither possible nor meaningful. Nevertheless, the benefit of a reductionist approach to empirical research is equally questionable, since empirical findings based on simplistic models cannot be adequately linked to everyday life (Chandler/Lyon 2001, Hitt et al. 2004). They do not present practical relevant propositions or even recommendations for action (Gopinath/Hoffman 1995, Huw et al. 2007) and are hence hardly received (Van de Ven 2002).

Conceptually, a holistic perspective may represent a possible key to this unsatisfactory situation. Thereby, empirical phenomena are tried to be pictured in their entirety by a set of variables that is as comprehensive as possible (Veliyath/Srinivasan 1995). If the values of the variables in the defined set are measured, a snapshot of the configuration results. The snapshot can be interpreted as a jigsaw piece of reality that is represented by the values of these variables at the time of measurement (Veliyath/Srinivasan 1995). By analysing the deviations between the configurations in different points in time, developments may be identified. Changes in bundles of variables may hence be related to developments. In such a structure of thought, specific variables not only affect specific other variables, but interdependencies between bundles of variables are also considered (Wiklund/Shepherd 2005). The aim is a reconstruction of the changes in the configurations and – based on that – a deduction of starting points and strategies for interventions (Harms et al. 2009).

The focus on variables that are relevant against the background of the respective research question is a fundamental principle of modern research practices. Only by using this complexity-reducing approach can the respective variables and thus the relationships between and developments of the phenomena of interest be identified from the infinite number of variables. The question is, however, which of the infinite number of possible variables are the most relevant. Due to this question, the broad application of the configuration approach as a conceptual frame for empirical surveys has failed so far (Harms et al. 2009). Attempts have been made to name the relevant jigsaw pieces of reality against the background of the research question by defining spheres following specific theoretical guidelines (Mugler 2005). However, such a procedure is affected by a high level of uncertainty and the selections can rarely be argued for stringently, which violates the criterion of scientific work regarding the transparency of the researcher's decisions.

1.1.2 *The proposed key*

It is only the choice of variables that creates the research object. The researcher constructs its object of research by choosing the aspects of reality to be measured. The choice of variables hence constitutes a decisive step in the research process (Fink 2005). If, however, the choice that follows specific theoretical guidelines cannot be argued for stringently, an empirical basis has to be used. Quantitative methods of data collection require an a priori existing structure of meaning with regard to the object of research. For that reason, such an empirical basis can only be created by qualitative data collection, since only open methods enable the collection of non-pre-structured data (Diekmann 2000). Narrations, in particular, enable data collections in the field without purporting structures by the researcher. The structuring work is then accomplished by the interviewee. The structure of the object of research may hence be developed on the basis of transcripts (Schütze 1987). Here the content analysis introduced by Mayring (2002) seems to be an appropriate method. It enables the identification of underlying structures of meaning. Hereby, the inherent structures of the field can be uncovered (Rust 1981).

With regard to the dilemma of selection, the content analysis of narrations of protagonists in the field of interest offers the possibility to use their structuring work and hence carry out a posterior choice of variables. For that reason, the scheme of categories that constitutes the empirical investigation's frame of reference evolves little by little. The persons concerned define the object of research as structures that are depicted in the configurations themselves. The variables hence constitute the section of reality under research, thus they are constitutive for the research object.

The proposed approach enables a direct application of the configuration approach in empirical studies. The answer to the key question regarding the selection decision leads to the strengthening of the holistic approach in business research due to the use of the openness of qualitative data collection and interpretative analysis methods, which therefore gains considerable relevance for the empirical social science.

1.2 Entrepreneurship and small business in Central European countries in transition

SMEs are the backbone of every developed market economy. The following survey builds on the basic thesis that a strong and prospering SME sector is an important prerequisite for the successful economic development of regions and, thus, should be focused on by regional policy (Bender 1997). It therefore makes sense to take a closer look at the situation of the SME sector and – closely connected with it – entrepreneurship in the transformation countries.

Generally, there are substantial parallels between the four countries compared as regards SMEs, which makes it logical to tackle them together. Country-specific differences or empirical studies worth mentioning will be discussed as the need arises.

1.2.1 Deficits of socialist planned economies

Criticism of capitalism started in the nineteenth century against the backdrop of a market-economy system ("Manchester capitalism"), which was characterized by enormous social differences. A minority that controlled the means of production enriched itself at the expense of the workers, who lived in atrocious conditions. The theoretical conclusion of communist thinkers was that this development based on inequality would intensify further to the proletariat's disadvantage. Private ownership of the means of production was seen as the pivotal point of this development and thus the solution was to be found in bundling means of production on a collective level.

One thing, however, which from today's perspective seems more apparent, was grossly neglected. In the nineteenth century, the market-economy system was still at its beginning. Instead of considering improvement and further development, a radical overthrow of the system was propagated. Put bluntly, "instead of providing a cure, they proposed killing the patient and creating a new organism" (Petrakov 1993: 8). The October revolution of 1917 made it possible for the first time to apply the theory – albeit with major caveats – in practice on a state level. Following the Second World War, the Soviet system spilled over to several Central and Eastern European countries. The core idea of a planned-economy model is the state's control over all means of production and its monopoly in deciding and planning on how to use them.

The planning body was the Communist Party, which, in fact, had a monopolistic position of power in the state often exerted by oligarchs (Ebel

1990: 213). Its task was to anticipate down to the last details, calculate and control, by means of the control and planning apparatus, economic processes that spontaneously emerged in the market economy (Ebel 1990: 241). This included first coordinating all areas of the economy that directly contributed towards national income: all enterprises in all sectors had to be coordinated individually and in their relationships to each other in order to optimize output. Furthermore, it was necessary to identify how and to what extent other areas of society (culture, social matters) were to be supported with resources. A decision had to be made concerning what part of national income was to be invested and what part consumed, and what was to be exported and imported. Finally, the deterioration in production facilities and infrastructure had to be calculated in advance in order to enable timely replacement and repair (Ebel 1990: 242ff).

The consequences were manifold. (1) In order to manage the immense planning effort, a strong, unwieldy bureaucratic system quickly developed, which then took up the country's important human resources (especially university graduates) to fulfil the tasks at hand (Ebel 1990: 248). (2) Central planning resulted in a seller's market, in which buyers compete for the goods on offer. Free from the market-economy pressures of a buyer's market, it was not necessary to take customers' demand into account, improve the quality of the goods offered or indeed to develop new products (Kornai 2001: 168). (3) The planners were too far removed from the actual sites of production. Their conception of what was required frequently did not match the real situation in the enterprises. In addition, the cumbersome decision mechanism reacted to events in the economic sphere only with a substantial delay. Lacking market-economy adaption mechanisms, the whole economic system was inflexible, resulting in inappropriate decisions from above that made fulfilling the plans impossible.

As a reaction to these undesirable developments, (4) total production was concentrated in a few large production sites, intended to minimize the complexity of supplier networks and the number of business units to be coordinated (Töpfer 1996: 32). Large businesses were given a certain output target that eventually resulted in (5) non-productive activity. Production became less efficient and the target was "achieved" only through (6) various types of manipulation (Indruch 1994: 19).

The seller's market ties (7) the planned economy to production. At least in the socialist planned economies under Soviet influence, the focus of production was on (heavy) industry, to the detriment of consumer-goods production. This one-sided orientation was based on the assumption that resources can be invested in production or used for consumer goods (Brenner 1993: 105f). Economic growth, however, depends on production alone. Anything used for consumer goods cannot be used for production and thus reduces economic growth. In the inter-war Soviet Union, therefore, consumption was kept on as low a level as possible. The hope that, on achieving a sufficient level of wealth, this wealth would transfer, via production, to consumption turned out to be in vain. This initial economic orientation was nonetheless continued in the socialist planned economies that emerged after the Second World War.

The economy's orientation towards industrial production rather than demand resulted in (8) an undersupply of the population. This, in turn, led to (9) a loss of trust, decreasing motivation and passive resistance. Unsurprisingly, this had a negative effect on the economy's production performance. The excellent growth rates announced regularly at the time are, with hindsight, explained by a significantly higher input of resources and manpower, as well as businesses growing autonomously, despite checks, and simple data manipulation (Brenner 1993: 110ff).

The factors mentioned resulted in (10) large-scale undersupply, which, in many cases, could only be ameliorated by taking out loans abroad. The intensive and ruthless industrial production led to environmental pollution and subsequently health problems in the population. Citizens' dissatisfaction was further amplified through Western media and communication networks (Hill/Magas 1993: 36f), until the planned-economy system finally collapsed.

Returning to the outset of our deliberations, it can be said once again: the attempt to escape from destitution actually drove people who lived in "really existing" socialist economies into destitution, both relative and absolute. Hence, this phenomenon turned out to be not an expression of the general law of capitalist accumulation, but a symptom of an underdeveloped market economy (Ebel 1990: 203).

1.2.2 Problems of transformation

Depending on the commitment with which the planned-economy concepts were applied in practice, the economy of socialist planned regimes was characterized to a greater or lesser extent by desolate infrastructure, worn-out and out-of-date facilities and machines, backward organizational and production structures, an unmotivated and passive workforce, inefficient business, high indebtedness abroad and pollution. No matter how much these burdens actually differed from transformation country to transformation country – all states faced a transformation recession and rapidly evolving regional differences within the country. The following discussion sketches out the reasons for these transformation phenomena.

The transformation process in the medium term requires making businesses autonomous (privatization), ending price and wage controls, enabling the free convertibility of the currency, lifting the international trade monopoly, redesigning the banking system, creating a real labour market and, in connection with this, setting up at least a minimum social welfare net (Indruch 1994: 13ff). There was little doubt these reforms were to be implemented, but the speed at which this was to be achieved was contentious. Proponents of shock therapy saw a massive gap in development between East and West that could only be bridged in one great leap. The gradualists made use of the metaphor of altitude difference: in order to reach the West's altitude, a slow but steady ascent with safely placed steps was required (Laski 1992: 35).

Irrespective of the strategy pursued, the more or less restrained implementation of reforms in all transformation countries resulted in a rapid decrease in economic output and – with certain exceptions – an increase in inflation, as well as higher unemployment. Naturally, the economic decline depended on the respective initial situation of the transforming country. The states of the former Soviet Union (without the Baltic countries) were hit more heavily than the Baltic and the Central and Eastern European nations (NCCE). This was because the Baltic States and the NCCE had been centrally administrated only since 1945 and – as in the case of many NCCE – applied a less rigid socialism. Hungary, for instance, had an inflation rate of just 26 per cent after transformation; in Georgia, a former Soviet republic, on the other hand, inflation went up to 56,000 per cent (Fischer/Sahay 2001).

Nevertheless, all these countries suffered an economic recession, which is due to the following mechanisms (Kornai 2001: 175ff):

- Worker protection declined. Increasing insecurity, which resulted in a higher proclivity to save, and growing unemployment led to lower domestic demand.
- As the markets opened up, pressure on producers increased, which made them reduce production and rationalize in general. Thus, more employees were set free. If – as happened in Hungary, for example – a bankruptcy law was introduced quickly, further inefficient enterprises went bankrupt, which resulted in even more job losses.
- Backward sectors and businesses oriented towards exporting to the East took a hit. Growth sectors were not able to compensate for this decline.
- After the bureaucracy was dissolved, market-economy institutions did not emerge instantaneously. The lack of coordination between market powers led to chaos, which hampered economic growth (e.g. if foreign companies refrained from investing due to legal insecurity).

Whenever the egalitarian-minded planned-economy regimes managed to inhibit social (more on this in Duke/Grime 1997: 884ff) and regional disparities, these emerged to an even greater extent with the transformation into a market economy. We now leave aside the social effects of system change and focus purely on the reasons for regional disparities.

Regarding regional differences, two clear regional patterns can be discerned (Abrhám 2007, OIR 2000: 124): in all transformation countries, the gap between the economic centres (capital and environs) and the peripheries is growing. In addition, in all transformation countries, except for the Czech Republic, a clear West–East discrepancy in favour of the West can be discerned. This is for the following reasons:

- Cities, and in particular capitals, attract foreign investors with their good infrastructure and an existing telecommunications structure, an international airport, a large municipal sales market and excellent access to public and state institutions. Moreover, (capital) cities have the advantage that no information on alternative locations in the country is available (Petrakos 1996: 7f). Cities close to a European (geographical) growth centre show additional potential.
- Regions towards Eastern markets before the transformation and – often the same – regions with little diversified business structures and a lower supply of human capital are hit harder by the transformation. Frequently, these are agricultural regions or regions focusing on old industries.
- The initial disadvantage is exacerbated through a vicious circle: foreign direct investment, essential for many countries (Radice 1996), does not flow to disadvantaged regions, as they lack the necessary structures, for the development of which the investment is required in the first place.

These disparities, however, are not due to an absolute decline in development, but rather to the capitals' prosperity (Baum/Weingarten 2004: 10). This reflects a general dilemma prevalent all over Central and Eastern Europe. In order to catch up economically, the transformation countries focus on their growth centres at the expense of already disadvantaged regions (Nagy/Turnock 2000: 262) and by neglecting regional development. Rural areas, naturally suffering from structural disadvantages, thus face additional problems.

1.2.3 The importance of SMEs and entrepreneurship in the transformation countries

SMEs (business with fewer than 250 employees) have a starring role in developed market economies. According to Mugler (1998: 38ff), this is because:

- SMEs help stabilize a pluralistic society. This is done not just by creating new jobs, but also due to the increased importance an individual typically has in an SME.
- Business diversity strengthens the mechanisms of a market economy based on competition. SMEs enrich business activity, prevent the spread of uniform customer needs through their individual product ranges, and so hamper the emergence of monopolies. SMEs' high flexibility promotes economic change and breaking up encrusted structures.
- SMEs tend to be closer to the customer than large companies producing standardized goods do. Their flexibility allows them to adjust to individual demands and to occupy market niches unattractive for larger companies. This increases the range of goods offered.
- As regards research, it can be seen that SMEs position their innovation activities closer to specific customer needs. The innovation process is much faster than with large companies.

- An economy with a broadly diverse SME sector is less prone to crises, as the economic risk is spread across many businesses and sectors.
- SMEs improve the quality of life, on the one hand, by producing personalized (niche) products. On the other hand, as employers and motors of regional development, they help increase the wealth of a society.
- SMEs, through their softer and more local processes, tend to produce in a less polluting fashion.
- SMEs play an important role in training people, especially apprentices.
- Compared to large companies, SMEs are less important for foreign trade. Yet even SMEs contribute significantly to exports because of their role as suppliers.

These factors are also valid for former socialist planned economies. In particular, the potential of SMEs to absorb workers that have lost their jobs prevented much higher unemployment figures in the early years of the transformation. The SME sector in effect replaced the barely existent social safety nets in this critical early stage of transformation. Further important functions of SMEs include:

- The command economy broke down also because of chronic supply bottlenecks. In the difficult years of system change and transformation recession, small and very small enterprises helped stabilize the availability of many important goods and services (Zapalska/Zapalska 1999: 8).
- As personification or symbols ("role models"; Forst 1996: 51) of the new economic system, the new entrepreneurs helped break up habitual values, as well as thought and behavioural patterns, in the population in the early years of the turnaround, "fostering the image of competition, risk-taking, mobility and other values essential to the successful functioning of an economic system that relies on market mechanism" (Zapalska/Zapalska 1999: 8).
- An important characteristic of planned economies was the compulsory orientation towards (heavy) industry production. With the help of new businesses, established mainly in the service sector, in only a few years, the transformation countries managed to at least reduce their structural deficits compared to the Western service economies (Smallbone/Welter 2001: 63).
- The particularly serious problem of raising capital made it essential that many small businesses finance themselves by means of private savings or loans from family and friends. Thus, SMEs indirectly contributed towards the productive mobilization of private savings (Marot 1997: 53).

1.2.4 The SME sector in the countries surveyed

1.2.4.1 Developments up to transformation

The well-developed SME structures in Czechoslovakia and Hungary fell victim to collectivization when the communists took power. Large state enterprises were promoted, while entrepreneurship was consciously suppressed, although it was never completely eradicated. In the case of Hungary – which, from 1953, time and again allowed attempts at market-economy reforms – the spirit of entrepreneurship kept burning almost throughout the whole dictatorial period. As early as in 1973, joint ventures with Western companies were condoned in the SME sector (Welter 2002). From 1980 onwards, various business constructs with market-economy characteristics emerged (see Hisrich/Fulop 1995). Nevertheless, the shift in values in society over the more than 40 years of communist rule became clear in that the entrepreneurial opportunities available in Hungary in the 1980s were not really fully utilized even within the many restrictions that prevailed. For example, quasi-private businesses did not employ the maximum numbers of employees the Party had established for them (Lagemann et al. 1994).

Entrepreneurship survived in a semi-legal or illegal form as part of a parallel shadow economy. This shadow economy was more present in rigid command economies than in other, more liberal socialist republics. In Central Europe, this was mainly the GDR and the CSSR. Until 1938, Czechoslovakia was one of the ten most important industrial nations with a strong SME sector comprising more than 400,000 businesses (Bohatá/Mládek 1999: 461ff). From 1948 onwards, private enterprise was radically erased in the CSSR, and the entrepreneurial potential then developed informally. This "second economy" included (Lagemann et al. 1994: 2000) secondary occupations in agriculture, craft activities, neighbourly help in building a house, illegal use of official working hours and state resources for private services, as well as below-the-counter sales. Only in 1982 was there some slight shift towards free enterprise, where it became possible to conduct some form of restricted trade (Ohral 1991: 2).

In many ways, the development of the Slovenian SME sector differs from the developments in the three other countries of comparison: Slovenia, as an Austro-Hungarian province, was an underdeveloped agrarian country that got rid of its structural deficits only as a member of the Kingdom of SHS and particularly within the Yugoslav Federation (Gow/Carmichael 2000: 102ff). Admittedly, the development of a modern, diversified economic structure was hampered by the prevailing planned-economy elements; but, due to the special status of communist Yugoslavia (no Soviet influence and hence no Iron Curtain), barriers to development of market-oriented behaviour were much weaker than, for example, in Czechoslovakia.

1.2.4.2 (Re-)construction of the SME sector

There were – and are – basically two ways of establishing private-economy structures in transformation countries: either by privatizing state enterprises (top down) or by setting up new businesses (bottom up) (Brezinski/Fritsch 1996). However, these two areas overlap: many new businesses were only made possible by acquiring former state property. That Czechoslovakia's entrepreneurs were able to catch up with Hungary in only a few years (despite its anti-entrepreneur history), for instance, can also be attributed to the fact that privatizations, compared to Hungary, Poland and, above all, Slovenia (for more detail, see Mencinger 2004), were conducted quickly, radically and smoothly (Lagemann et al. 1994). In 1990, the year of the turnaround, there were roughly 7,000 companies in Czechoslovakia. In 1993, the figure was 400,000 (Lagemann et al. 1994: 192). Even allowing for these statistics to be heavily distorted upwards (see Bukhval'd/Vilenskii 2003; more generally: OECD 1996: 19, 29f), this is a remarkable achievement.

There are two types of privatization: small- and large-scale, with the distinction between them fairly blurred. Large-scale privatization was mainly used for de-concentrating the many (too) large state enterprises, although SMEs were also sold (OECD 1996: 27). For the SME sector, this form of privatization brought forth roughly 2,200 companies in the Czech Republic, 440 in the Slovak Republic and approximately 500 in Hungary (OECD 1996: 27).

In small-scale privatization, small state enterprises were sold in auctions, including mainly "retail shops, services establishments (such as cafes, hotels, and smaller restaurants), handcraft establishments, and small industrial firms" (DeFillippi 1995: 4). Even though only an estimated 10 per cent of all enterprises in turnaround countries come from small-scale privatization (OECD 1996: 22), this form of privatization is particularly important in the first, chaotic phase of transformation. This is because "first they potentially form the basic stock of newly created private firms and second, the assets represented by these units can be used by future entrepreneurs as securities for generating loan finance" (OECD 1996: 21). The psychological effect of this form of privatization also must not be underestimated: transferring many small enterprises to private owners creates a much larger "aha!" effect in the population than handing over large businesses to foreign investors (OECD 1996: 22).

Similarly, the restitution of formerly collectivized private property had a mainly psychological effect: symbolically, the population's trust in property rights was gained. The return of property, however, was consistently effected only in Czechoslovakia, where up to 20,000 small businesses and roughly 100,000 other assets were restituted to the original owners or their descendants. In Hungary, on the other hand, there was financial compensation, which at least helped the population build up capital as a basis for potential investment or founding a company (OECD 1996: 24f). In Slovenia, the question of restitution was completely neglected, at least in the first few years following transformation (Rothacher 1999).

The most important factor in the revival of the SME sector in the transformation countries was the fast increase in self-employment. In 1989, there were only about 8,000 self-employed persons in the Czech part of the CSSR, but this figure rose to 925,000 in 1994. A similar picture emerged in Slovakia (1989: 2,000; 1994: 280,000). In liberal Hungary, the increase was less steep, where the 320,000 self-employed people in 1989 rose to 775,000 in 1994

(OECD 1996: 29). Owing to numerous foundations of companies as a second occupation and multiple foundations, though, these figures are too optimistic.

1.2.4.3 Founders and entrepreneurs

The high foundation rates in transformation countries raise the question of which population groups were particularly keen founders and why.

According to Benáček (1995), two opposing social groups were particularly responsible for the fast emergence of the SME sector in Czechoslovakia. He first distinguishes "operators", who held rather low positions in the social hierarchy, although these positions provided a certain entrepreneurial potential. This potential was, for instance, created through direct contact with customers or a focal position within the bureaucracy. Even people doing business in the criminal world are deemed "operators" (Benáček 1995: 48).

The second group of potential founders came from the so-called "nomenklatura", which refers to hierarchically higher-ranking civil servants in the political and/or economic areas. In contrast to, for example, simple factory workers, these two groups showed the following common features, which turned out to be an advantage for an entrepreneurial career (Benáček 1995: 48f):

- a certain degree of independent power of decision
- frequent involvement in monetary transfers
- above-average income (economic capital)
- comparatively strong integration in bureaucratic networks (social capital)
- enforcement of one's own goals by pragmatic and even unethical means
- control over state capital (financial or physical), which at times is deemed one's own property
- fascination with living standards of the Western middle classes (motivation)

These two segments of the population, which made up about a quarter of the working populace, made good use of their initial advantage. They represented a comparatively large part of the new entrepreneurial class. By contrast, in countries whose economy was less strongly interwoven with party politics (e.g. Hungary or Slovenia), the share of the political nomenklatura in foundations was much lower (Dallago 1997: 117). In Slovenia, the former management class, which in privatization – to the detriment of foreign investors – had been given significant advantages in buyouts, took a particularly large share in the newly created entrepreneurial class (Rothacher 1999).

If one takes a look at the remaining three-quarters of the population, the workers played a greater role in founding businesses. Often founding a company was the direct result of losing a job with a state enterprise fighting for survival (Dallago 1997: 117). The motive for founding a company thus was not a Schumpeterian urge, but the necessity to improve one's socio-economic position or to find an alternative source of income (Ivy 1997). More recent empirical data for the Czech Republic, on the other hand, show that looming unemployment is mentioned less often as a reason for founding a business than, for instance, seizing a market opportunity or having a good idea for a product (Kessler 2003: 137).

Finally, the role of foreign entrepreneurs and foundations is worth mentioning, which in the first years of the turnaround, particularly in Hungary, significantly contributed towards the re-creation of the SME sector in the form of direct investment.

1.2.4.4 Specifics of the SME sector in transformation countries

The rapidly re-created SME sector in transformation countries differs from SME sectors in Western European market economies in certain respects. Specific differences can be found on the structural and psychological levels.

In contrast to Western European countries, where the SME sector had a few decades to develop properly, in transformation countries, this important area for the economy developed more or less overnight. The inverted pyramid of company size (many large companies, few small businesses), which is typical for centrally planned countries (Berko/Gueullette 2003), was rapidly turned on its head again. Still, this happened mostly by establishing micro-businesses in the service sector, as there are generally few barriers to entry here (and, above all, little start-up capital is required) (Arzeni 1996, Bateman 2000). In the Slovak region of Nitra, for example, the service sector accounted for 74 per cent of all business founded (Ivy 1997). In this regard, industrial SMEs in transformation countries – compared to Western market economies – are heavily underrepresented.

Specific barriers inhibit the growth of SMEs in transformation countries. This is reflected by a gap in the size structure of the SME sector: there is a dearth of medium enterprises (Gibb 1993: 464, Kremser 1991), with Hungary being closest to the Western "norm", mainly due to foreign investment (OECD 1996: 38). Together with the strong tilt towards services, mainly in traditional areas, this undermines the industrial structure in transformation countries, resulting in a general weakening of the SME sector (Bateman 2000: 278). There are consequences: many positive external effects ascribed to SMEs fail to materialize: "a weak SME sector is unlikely to lead, inter alia, to inter-enterprise networking, subcontracting, exports, technology transfer, a local R&d culture, local product and process innovation, high quality training institutions, and so on" (Bateman 2000: 278).

In fact, a lack of innovation in the SME sector of transformation countries has been diagnosed (Berko/Gueullette 2003, Marot 1997). In contrast to "old" market economies, where many important innovations would have been impossible without SMEs, in transformation countries most innovations are initiated by large, often foreign companies. All said, the economies of transformation countries show a clear shortage of innovation with all the related negative effects.

Several decades of propaganda against the entrepreneur as the archetype of the exploitative capitalist left their mark on the population's attitude. The bad reputation entrepreneurs had to battle in the years of planned economies, on a psychological level, was approached with a behaviour distinct from that of Western European entrepreneurs: "[h]e became individualistic and disinclined to co-operate or to communicate, compared with his equivalent in the West" (Berko/Gueullette 2003: 248). Such behavioural attributes, however, are detrimental to entrepreneurial growth in an ever more closely linked world economy. One effect, for instance, is the poor links between SMEs and research institutions, which further weaken the poor innovation performance (Marot 1997: 58).

In most transformation countries, entrepreneurship took place in a semi-legal or even illegal shadow area, with the corresponding techniques in use to achieve one's goals: theft of state property and, in particular, bribery were part of the day-to-day business for entrepreneurs. The change in the political system in 1989/1990 brought forward a new one, but the tradition of corruption remained (on the part of both the entrepreneurs and the authorities) (Arzeni 1996). This resulted in a very weak sense of business ethics and little quality awareness (Lagemann et al. 1994). The latter vanished within just a few years, due to pressure from the markets and the foreign competition, but corruption is a medium-term problem that – also against the background of the low salaries in the public sector – is very difficult to overcome.

1.2.5 Problems of SMEs in transformation countries

In conclusion, we will now address barriers and problems that have emerged particularly for SMEs in transformation countries or still appear relevant. These are problem areas that make both establishing a business and SME growth more difficult.

1.2.5.1 Financing

Raising capital in the case of SMEs is particularly difficult in former command economies. In addition to the problems encountered by SMEs requiring capital in the old market economies, transformation-related structural difficulties also arise. Communist economies had a one-tier banking system (the central bank and nothing else), which does not meet the requirements of market economies (two-tier: central bank and commercial banks). Formally, the transition happened fast, as the banking monopoly was broken up. In Hungary, this happened as early as in 1987, when five commercial banks were introduced (Zapalska/Zapalska 1999: 15). In fact, these newly positioned two-tier banking systems were in dire need of improvement. The banks lacked liquidity as well as practical experience in assessing loan requests. Systematically, the (well-known) state enterprises were preferred to the new SMEs and little competition between the few large banks hampered the development of new products and the reduction of bureaucracy for the clients' sake (DeFillippi 1995, Hisrich/Fulop 1995, OECD 1996).

In the first few years as a market economy, the weakly developed capital market was one of the biggest hurdles for establishing a business and business growth, as empirical studies show for the Czech Republic (Bohatá/Mládek 1999, Kessler 2003), Slovakia (Ivy 1997), Hungary (Fogel 2001) and Slovenia (Bukvic/Bartlett 2003). Only in the transformation countries is the capital market seen as one of the three major hurdles for creating and developing SMEs (Pissarides 1999). If one's own savings are not sufficient, the capital required is raised within the family (informal capital) (Ivy 1997, Růžička 1996). Kessler (2003: 175) shows that, for newly established companies in the Czech Republic, more than 55 per cent of respondents answer the question whether it was difficult to get a bank loan with "don't know". This suggests that these respondents never tried to take out a loan with a bank (Kessler 2003: 175). The fact they did not try might indicate that the idea of borrowing money from the banks seemed quite absurd. All remaining answers underlined the difficulty of getting a bank loan.

Despite the further development of the banking system, not least because of Austrian direct investment, financing is still a comparatively big problem for the SME sector (Bukvic/Bartlett 2003, Hutchinson/Xavier 2006) and therefore also for the economies of the transformation countries. Phenomena found in the economic structures of transformation countries such as the lack of medium enterprises, innovative SMEs or SMEs in industry are certainly partly due to the weak capital markets.

1.2.5.2 *State institutions*

Particularly in the first few years of transformation, state institutions were too out of their depth to develop sensible rules for conducting business – this was understandable as there was too much to do at the same time. In Czechoslovakia, this was reflected in a drastic decrease in business crimes, with other forms of crime rising rapidly. This statistical anomaly could be explained by the fact that it was generally not clear what was forbidden and what was allowed and legal texts were not able to give clear answers either (Gibb 1993: 69).

In this context, for example, there were no instruments or methods to tackle small legal disputes. Such "minor cases" mainly concerned SMEs, as in the case of non-paying customers (DeFillippi 1995, Ivy 1997). There were also no clear property rights and property transfer rights (Hisrich/Fulop 1995), nor was there a functioning market regulator. A decade after transformation, Czech founders still see the legal situation as restrictive and chaotic (Kessler 2003: 166).

Finally, the burdens of the post-communist bureaucracy have to be mentioned, which systematically made founding a business more difficult.

Artificial barriers were erected not just by authorities, but also mainly by large companies owned by the state (e.g. municipal utilities), which were able to exploit their monopoly position for making extra gains (see Růžička 1996: 222 for a practical example).

1.2.5.3 Human resources

In the area of human resources, two aspects concerned and concern the sector of SMEs in particular. Firstly – in reference to Max Weber's protestant ethics (Weber 2000 [1905]) – the so-called socialist work ethic (Pissarides 1999): the planned economy had made full employment into an ideological constant. Everyone had the right to work, even if no extra workplace was required (which resulted in over-employment). As there was no threat of job losses, the motivation to perform was limited, particularly in rigid Czechoslovakia. Often, the means of production at work were used for one's own activities in the shadow economy. These working habits learned over the years were a particular burden to the burgeoning entrepreneurial class and had to be unlearned in the first years after transformation (Růžička 1996).

Secondly, in transformation countries, there were – and are – few opportunities to train and educate entrepreneurs. In socialist planned-economy systems, private entrepreneurs were not provided for, as training took place for specific units of the large companies (Vértesi 1991), and practical training opportunities were lacking (OECD 1996). In this respect, trainings for entrepreneurs, but also consulting services, are growing more and more important in transformation countries, in order to make better use of the growth potentials unused because of a lack of expert knowledge in the respective SME sectors.

1.2.5.4 Psychological barriers

In the first few years after system change, "[t]he entrenched and lingering logic of egalitarianism, still ingrained in the minds of people" (Arzeni 1996: 53) posed a considerable barrier in the heads of potential founders. Apart from the unwillingness to become active as an entrepreneur ("envy and hostility against entrepreneurial spirit", Růžička 1996: 221), it was the founders' environment, in particular, that was characterized by incomprehension regarding the consequence of economy thinking – such as that price is determined by supply and demand – that went as far as accusations of usury (Růžička 1996: 221).

2   An action framework for rural municipalities

2.1 Design of the empirical study

2.1.1 Data collection

Between September 2005 and February 2006, we conducted 4,157 minutes of interviews and created 1,473 pages of transcript with a total of 65 interviewees in 18 local areas in all provinces of Austria with rural areas (that is, all but Vienna). As no full representation of local-area structures in Austria was intended, but an explanation of typical development trends, no randomly selected local areas were analysed, except those for which (1) in the period between the two job counts, 1991 and 2001, a significant increase or decrease in jobs and other indicators was recorded and (2) a clearly discernible category was determined a priori that showed an influence on the (positive or negative) development of local areas. The following categories of characteristics were, for instance, considered: region for which a particular product is well known, social cohesion, drastic change in the economic structure or inter-communal business zone. For each of these categories, two local areas were identified, of which one developed well and the other less so in the period surveyed.

In the NCCE, the survey took place a year later. The data were collected in direct field studies. The narrative interviews were conducted in the respective national languages. Altogether, in the NCCEs interviews with a total length of 3,812 minutes were conducted with 61 interviewees, which resulted in 1,142 pages of transcripts.

The territorial distribution of the local areas surveyed was effected proportionally to the nation's geographical area, with each country to be represented by at least two local areas. Hence, three Czech and three Hungarian, as well as two Slovak and two Slovene local areas were analysed. In order to record the influence of different rules on the level of local administration, the specific selection of local areas made sure that the individual places selected were in different areas regarding the categorization of the countries surveyed based on NUTS II. As Slovenia consists of only one region on this level, national administrative regions were used. Additionally, the influence of the distance from the area surveyed to the Austrian border was to be made transparent. Therefore, the selection process ensured that in each country there was at least one area close to the Austrian border and one further away.

Thus narrowed down, the specific local areas were selected for analysis together with experts from the respective countries. In order to safeguard a broad scope of the assertions generated, the selected areas, particularly regarding their key demographic and economic data, were to be typical of the respective NUTS II region. Also concerning qualitative criteria such as historical development and social situation, the areas selected were to differ as little as possible from other local areas in the region.

Within the local areas, following a holistic view developed above, in discussing the research questions, the perspectives of various actors on different levels of administration and from different walks of life were recorded. By including points of view on and interpretations of what was going on in the municipalities surveyed that were as contrary to each other as possible, the meanings behind the statements made were to emerge. The minimum people interviewed were the mayor, a councillor from the biggest opposition party, an entrepreneur and a representative from the institution in charge of regional development on an inter-communal or regional level.

2.1.2 Data analysis

The transcripts of the recorded interviews were content analysed. In order to reduce distorted perceptions, interpretation took place on two levels and was conducted by four different teams. On the first level, the interviews were interpreted independently by the interviewers themselves, in group work within a seminar by qualified students specializing in small-business management and entrepreneurship at WU Vienna University of Economics and Business, and by the authors. These three interpretations were then, on a second level (interpretation of the interpretations), brought together in a discursive process into a final interpretation. In the case of discrepancies between the interpretations, a feedback loop was inserted.

During interpretation work, the categorization scheme illustrated in part in Table 2.1 was established.

2.2 For starters: statements from the interviews

IDEAS AND INITIATIVES

"Each town designs itself; it depends on the respective conditions. You can't say you take the concept from one town and transfer it to another, one for one. You can only transfer ideas!"

"Everybody says something has to happen in the region, but no one takes the initiative. And if you do start something and there are start-up costs, nobody dares provide the money!"

Table 2.1 Excerpt from the categorization scheme with encoding examples

Categories scheme			Questions to the text	Encoding examples
Field of action: Integrative municipal development	*Measure 1: The individual activities in the municipality are part of a comprehensive development concept*			
Affected	Favoured groups		Who gains what advantage from this measure?	*"Groups without a lobby are the winners of well-balanced planning."*
	Disadvantaged groups		Who suffers what disadvantage from this measure?	*"The powers that be naturally do not like a long-term development plan. Because it restrains them in what they want to do for themselves."*
Implementation	Type of application		How is the measure applied?	*"The municipality only does what it has to do. What can be done by others is done by others."*
				"Entrepreneurs in the town centre cooperate and don't see themselves as competitors. Where people live, there's frequency, after all. And so they all live off one another!"
Barriers	Personal barriers	Within the municipality	What personal barriers are there to the measure?	*"The mayor is a local emperor. Other ideas are blocked."*
		Outside the municipality		*"Inter-communal tourist agencies cannot be run from the mayors of the municipalities involved, as they often dislike each other and aren't experts in this matter."*

Table 2.1 (continued)

Categories scheme			Questions to the text	Encoding examples
Field of action: *Integrative municipal development*	*Measure 1: The individual activities in the municipality are part of a comprehensive development concept*			
	Factual barriers	Within the municipality	What factual barriers are there to the measure?	"Partly there is not even a basis for discussion in our town."
		Outside the municipality		"There are constantly new ideas brought in from outside the municipality, from all sorts of levels and they mostly contradict each other."
				"Well, there IS a development concept for our region. And the municipality is trying to squeeze what they want into what they should do. Of course that doesn't go together."
	Legal barriers	Within the municipality	What legal barriers are there to the measure?	"We need a well-considered zoning plan in our municipality. Also because of regional planning."
		Outside the municipality		"Sometimes the rules have to be seen more flexibly. Naturally that's difficult for me outside the municipality. And so it is blocked by a rule that doesn't make any sense here."
Need for action	Personal need for action	Within the municipality	What need for action is there in the personal area?	"In implementing projects it is important that the mayor integrates the people."

Table 2.1 (continued)

Categories scheme		Questions to the text	Encoding examples
Field of action: Integrative municipal development	Measure 1: The individual activities in the municipality are part of a comprehensive development concept		
	Outside the municipality		"Those gents from the Province should learn that you can't plan a whole region on the drawing board. You need time for preparation and coordination. But we have no such structures here yet!"
Factual need for action	Within the municipality	What need for action is there in the factual area?	"You have to communicate the value of shops in our municipality to the people"
			"Only who looks at the whole picture will take future generations into account"
	Outside the municipality		"A local area needs a common voice!"
			"There's no point in poaching each other's people in the local area. We have to get in someone from outside!"
Legal need for action	Within the municipality	What need for action is there in the legal area?	"We must not turn every bit of our municipality into a building plot."
			"The municipality should only provide the framework, but step in when there's no other way."
	Outside the municipality		"Provincial money for larger projects should only be available if several municipalities develop them together."

"The tourists are the only ones making us aware how beautiful it is here!"

"Citizens and municipal staff identify with the municipality if there is personal involvement and people know each other. Then they identify themselves and bring in a lot of commitment and initiative for the community!"

"You have to change something every year; I can clearly see that in our business. People really want to see something new every time. So the visitors can see: something's going on!"

"Our main idea right from the start was: we have to take matters in our hands, because there's no outside sponsor that will conjure up an attraction out of thin air! It's always been important for us to have something authentic for our people. Only then the whole town will support it!"

IMPLEMENTATION

"On paper it's easy to design things, but in practice things usually look very different!"

"Every project needs a central figure. If there's no one at the front propelling the project, it will soon wither away!"

"It's often like this: there are good ideas never put into practice because there's no one there to take care of things. A good idea is good, but someone implementing it is just as important!"

SUBSIDIES

"As long as non-wage labour costs are that high, no businesses will come – even if we built an eight-lane motorway!"

"We don't see ourselves as the authorities but as service providers for people and businesses. We are trying to support everyone in some way, even if it's just a tax return or something!"

"We always try to handle planning and licensing procedures unbureaucratically and transparently when new businesses want to locate here, as especially SMEs have difficulties in this area. If there are a lot of administrative hurdles, they don't even try!"

"There is no concept behind the municipality's subsidy policy. It all depends on the applicant's initiative. If you apply and provide good arguments, you will get some money. And if you have a friend on the council, you'll get more. What I'm saying is that who meets certain criteria should have a right to receive a certain subsidy!"

"There's something wrong with project promotion: first they support a venture and then there's no support in the first few years. Unless you're financially independent straight away, that's really hard and kills off many projects immediately!"

"I am against one-off subsidies, as they don't achieve anything. He pockets the money and stays for exactly the time he has to; and then the trek moves on!"

RELATIONS TO FEDERAL AND PROVINCIAL AUTHORITIES

"Infrastructure measures are only taken in regions relevant for electoral reasons!"

"You do get the feeling we are a forgotten region!"

"Those above keep creating new regions! No wonder people don't even know which region they belong to any more!"

"The federal government keeps adding to the municipalities' tasks. Officially to strengthen their autonomy, but in reality they just want to pass on the costs!"

POLITICS

"If you address the wrong party with your suggestions, they simply vote you down – it's like hitting a brick wall!"

"In the old days the municipality did what is now being done by the provinces and the feds, and that is selling everything. Now the municipality has no land to build on left and so they can't influence the town's development any more!"

"You have to know: we have the Socialists and the Conservatives. There are pensioners here and there who would quite like to do something together occasionally, but then they'll get an earful from their party friends!"

"In municipalities where a party has an absolute majority and there is no citizens' initiative in the council, the local politicians fix what's to be done down the pub and then it happens. They needn't talk to or ask anyone!"

"Regional planning should follow the criteria for regional planning and not the principle of: that's Mister X and Mister Y and Mister Z!"

MAYOR

"You can't really do this job on the side any more, it's a full-time task – my predecessors were all employed by the municipality!"

"Partly there is not even a basis for discussion in our town. Everything is killed off right from the start. He is the local emperor: other ideas are blocked and, if they still happen to be implemented, they were naturally his ideas in the first place. In the end nothing ever gets anywhere!"

"Especially in the early stages of a project it is important that the mayor comes along to begging trips to authorities and other decision-makers. It doesn't matter whether he knows these people or not, as a mayor he is our representative and if he supports something it is quite different to just Joe Public turning up and saying: 'I've got something interesting here!'"

LIFE IN THE MUNICIPALITY

"The town hall must not be a service desert. If a citizen turns up, he must feel he is being taken care of and supported, as he'll only come when he needs something or requires information. Nobody enjoys going to the authorities anyway!"

"We have a home for the disabled in the middle of town, where the handicapped sit in the Town Square. Fifteen years ago they would have run me as the mayor out of town. But today these people are integrated and cordially accepted by everybody!"

"Then they want planning permission for every corner of the municipality to build a house there. Well, I told them we certainly wouldn't do that. First, as it is against regional planning rules, second because there will be nothing but needless quarrel with a house next to a farm, and third because it causes massive infrastructure costs for the municipality!"

"When I started out as the mayor a few years back, it was quite often the case they called me from town: 'Hey, mayor, we have a stranger in town! What does he want here?' Today we have a few thousand overnight stays in town per year."

COMMUNITY AND BUSINESS

"The Chamber of Commerce helps us with problems we would never have if there weren't the Chamber!"

"Many small businesses are always better than a large one. The risk for the municipality is smaller and they can't blackmail you that much."

"The municipality should only do what it has to do. What can be done by others should be done by others. The municipality should only provide the framework and step in when there's no other way."

"If the municipality builds a municipal centre in the middle of town, where there is a baker's, a grocer, a doctor and a bank, they must not see themselves as competitors. Where people live, there's frequency, after all. And so they all live off one another!"

"On their own, the product range would be much too small, that's not attractive for customers any more. But if there are several shops, everybody benefits. Competitive thinking is always wrong here. Basically everybody survives because there are several of them. Together they offer a broad and attractive range."

LOCAL AMENITIES

"The only thing you can't take into account is time, the working hours, because, if I had a 40-hour week, I'd have to stop Wednesday afternoon!"

"A local lady was very happy her daughter got a job at the local retailer, but she never ever shops there. People just don't see the connection."

"If a businessman in town wants to open a sorely needed local shop, people say: 'He just can't get enough.' They actually prefer an outsider doing it!"

"People say: 'Municipality, go and make our shops stay in town!' And the same lot then goes shopping in the discount store!"

"Business has its own momentum. At the moment the trend is towards supermarkets and shopping malls with a broad range and sufficient parking. This can't be stopped by just paying lip service, it takes specific measures in order to keep and promote local amenities in town!"

"Many local shops don't invest anything any more these days but do nothing but complain. That's a disaster. Nobody depends on these ramshackle places any more!"

"Not everybody has to buy everything at the corner shop, but if a few people buy a lot that also amounts to something!"

"You have to communicate the value of shops in our municipality to the people, as they are not just shops but also local jobs, local amenities. As long as local amenities work, the town works better and tourism, too!"

COOPERATION

"A local area needs a common voice!"

"Along the hiking path people get to a variety of businesses. That can't be seen as competition, it's interesting for tourists only that way and so it's a mutual advantage."

"If coordination in the municipality already fails due to everybody's fixation on their own part of town, how is a local area ever to function?"

"We have to market ourselves together as a region. When a tourist comes to the region, he does not do it just because of us."

"There's no point in poaching each other's people in the local area. We have to get in someone from outside!"

"Inter-communal tourist agencies cannot be run from the mayors of the municipalities involved, as they often dislike each other and aren't experts in this matter. Politicians can only initiate things, implementation is not their business. Because they get involved every time, often everything comes to a standstill!"

"Not municipalities but regions should decide which tourism activities to pursue, as tourism is only interested in the region, not the municipal boundaries!"

2.3 Comparative analysis of municipality development

2.3.1 Region known for a particular product: the dynamic vs. the traumatized municipality

The dynamic municipality was characterized by agricultural mass production, the traumatized municipality by artisan large-batch production. Both sectors have lost a lot of significance across Austria in the last few decades. Nonetheless, the two municipalities have developed very differently.

In the dynamic municipality, the crisis led to a focus on its own core competence and the product with the highest potential in the product range was identified, integrated forward from mere production to finishing, and its marketing was adapted to the changed market requirements. The relaunch of the selected agricultural product as a high-quality product was implemented by means of an active supraregional cooperation of entrepreneurs and municipalities. What was important for the project's success was that entrepreneurship was traditionally strong in the region, which has deeply entrenched entrepreneurial creativity, spotting and utilizing opportunities, as well as the connected openness for new things in the community. The municipal administration has, with pronounced business sense, always taken care to create a supportive environment for entrepreneurial activities. It also helped that many mayors were themselves entrepreneurs.

As entrepreneurial thinking met the attitude that communal business policies always have to aim at supporting the people's and businesses' own initiative, the dynamic municipality managed to turn the potentially threatening drastic change in business structures into an opportunity and to see the crisis as a reason for re-orienting the regional economy. Infused with regional identity, the agricultural product turned into a medium to convey the region's image internationally. This provides benefits for all businesses located there and, in particular, for the tourism sector. At the same time, the entrepreneurial attitude made people and municipal representatives believe in the concept's success from early in the project. This new spirit kept people from leaving and resulted in lively investment activity, particularly of young entrepreneurs, which in turn was a requirement for the project's success. The effect was fast structural change with little friction. By integrating agriculture into a modern and productive business structure, the job losses in the primary sector were kept low and more than compensated for by the rising secondary and tertiary sectors.

The development in the traumatized municipality was decidedly different. The slow decline of the industry dominant in the region was passively accepted by people and officials alike. For decades, all regional-policy decisions and measures focused only on the leading enterprise in the municipality, and the emergence and development of small-business structures were inhibited. Given these unfavourable conditions, potential entrepreneurs gave up and refrained from independent business activities. Resignation and passivity resulted in the desolation of regional business structures. Gradual job cuts right up to the closure of the local bellwether business led to a massive trend to leave the area, particularly among the young, as no substitute jobs became available. This left mainly pensioners, who tend to be more interested in quiet surroundings than economic growth.

A well-balanced mix of business sizes and sectors, prevented for decades, is now difficult to achieve in the time frame required. The small number of people employed in the municipality creates accordingly little tax revenue, resulting in little room for communal business policies, and even the little room available is not sufficiently utilized.

Personal grudges between the two remaining artisan businesses kept alive over generations, as well as general tension among people from different parts of town, do not produce the momentum necessary for a positive economic development of the municipality. Activities of individual small businesses are not integrated in an overall development concept and, therefore, do not reach the critical mass required to set impulses for the regional economy. Suprar-egional cooperation of artisan businesses and municipalities exists on paper only and is seen by many businesses as a threat rather than an opportunity.

FACTORS TO BE CONSIDERED FOR THIS CATEGORY OF CHARACTERISTICS

- Regional cooperation must be actively lived. In doing so, a bottom-up approach is generally preferable to a top-down design.
- In designing and implementing supraregional cooperation to market regional products, it has to be kept in mind that ideally all sectors already important or to become important in the region should be included. Only thus can the advertised product be used to successfully convey an image for the whole regional economy.
- To spread risks, special emphasis is to be put on an even mix of business sizes and sectors.
- Imminent crises must be tackled proactively through a broad discussion for developing innovative future concepts.

2.3.2 Social cohesion: the traumatized vs. the community-oriented municipality

Both in the traumatized and the community-oriented municipality, social cohesion in the population and businesses is a factor critical for success. Based on the diverging developments in the municipalities, insight is to be provided into how a lack of a sense of togetherness can lead to little economic development, while strong social cohesion can promote the municipality's progress.

In the traumatized municipality, originally an agriculturally active part of town was dominant, until industrial enterprises emerged in the region at the turn of the nineteenth century. One of these industrial enterprises was established in a part of the municipality that was of little importance at the time, and with the growth of this business the immediate area also gained importance. Communal policy was now almost exclusively focused on this emerging large enterprise. Due to this firm's increasingly dominant role as employer and local taxpayer, the municipality became more and more dependent on it. This was exacerbated by the fact that mayors regularly came from this enterprise.

With about 1,000 employees, staff numbers reached their peak in the 1960s. In order to safeguard a sufficient number of workers for the firm, the municipality discouraged the development and relocation of small businesses. This prevented the emergence of business structures as an economic basis for other parts of town. At the same time, the primary sector's importance as a source of income and employer gradually decreased, which dramatically turned on its head the wealth gap between the individual parts of town. The changed social circumstances created envy and jealousy, resulting in distance and estrangement.

As a reaction to the slow decline of the major enterprise since the 1960s, communal policies were centred even more on its needs, which in turn made people in other parts of town feel more and more discriminated against and the resulting tension thus further eroded social cohesion. This was reflected in a clear separation of social activities between the individual parts.

The bad atmosphere in the municipality had grave consequences: the low social cohesion and lack of solidarity, in view of the depressing job-market situation, increased the tendency to leave town especially among the young. At the same time, potential entrepreneurs were frightened off as they could not rely on goodwill and understanding of either people or the few other entrepreneurs. As people show no initiative, there is no basis for economic activity and this hampers the emergence of – now sorely needed – structures of small and medium enterprises in the municipality.

In the community-oriented municipality, in contrast, there is strong social cohesion. Social life in the municipality is characterized by active involvement in all sorts of clubs and societies by practically everybody. By installing a common funding scheme, the clubs are motivated to cooperate ever more closely and to coordinate activities and events. The members of the individual clubs – often the same people anyway – discuss matters of municipal development intensively. This creates a tight network of social relationships.

The mayor of the community-oriented municipality managed to reduce the influence of party-political considerations on decisions in the town council in favour of objective debate. From the start, he initiated a comprehensive discussion process across all parties in order to be able to effectively implement the communal-policy measures resulting from it based on broad consensus. The belief in putting the common before any differences became the leitmotif of the municipality's officials and sent a strong signal to the people and the businesses.

A formal cooperation of the local businesses represents the organizational framework for inter-business exchange and cooperation. This association gives the entrepreneurs from the community-oriented municipality a feeling of strength. Coordinating their advertising and presenting at fairs together creates an innovative and dynamic image for the businesses, and hence also for the municipality to the outside world and internally strengthens the feeling of togetherness.

In general, the dynamics of the people and the entrepreneurs in the community-oriented municipality are held up by their pronounced own initiative and the willingness to render services for the community. People identify with the town community and its development. As citizens they donate money; as club members they provide voluntary work; and as entrepreneurs they make investments. In this manner, they actively design their environment and lives. The individual gains strength from the conviction of being able to stand up to any challenge together. The citizens are further emboldened by the experience of having successfully implemented very ambitious projects as a town community. Thus, the pronounced social cohesion results in a feeling of power, which in the people's and entrepreneurs' perception makes opportunities outweigh risks. At the same time, this improves the information flow between the individual actors as well as the courage required for innovation and so increases the level of economic activity and the municipality's performance potential.

FACTORS TO BE CONSIDERED FOR THIS CATEGORY OF CHARACTERISTICS

- The strength of social cohesion is the main influence on the municipality's sentiment. Close social ties create a pleasant atmosphere. As an important part of the quality of life, this atmosphere is the basis for migration, establishing a family as well as the willingness to work, choice of profession and decision to found a business.
- Soft pressure to cooperate can initiate the emergence of social cohesion.
- In order to promote social cohesion in the population, municipal representatives have to set an example in communitarian thinking. Party-political tactics are hence to be avoided.
- With communal measures of economic policy, a balanced promotion of individual parts of town is essential in the long term. Strong imbalances bring the risk of envy and jealousies eroding social cohesion in the municipality.
- Places to meet are important incubators for people and entrepreneurs to create and intensify a dynamic social structure. In designing the town's appearance and erecting public buildings, the people's needs for interaction and communication are to be taken into account. For example, it seems useful to have social meeting rooms in fire service buildings or a municipal centre in the town hall. In this context, a town square with little or no traffic is also very important.
- Not just the people, but also entrepreneurs are to be motivated to cooperate. If the entrepreneurs see themselves as a community, they can make use of synergies and coordinate their behaviour to save resources in marketing and create an effective image. This strengthens their position in supraregional competition.
- If people can rely on the citizens and the other entrepreneurs, they are more willing to take risks. Social cohesion, therefore, is a major influential factor for the willingness to embrace opportunities and initiate entrepreneurial activities.

2.3.3 Traditional economic structure: the linked wine-growing community vs. the ambitious laggard municipality

These two small municipalities, traditionally growing wine, are both in economically weak border regions of Austria. In both municipalities, generational change at the wineries has provided a positive economic stimulus. The linked wine-growing community managed to set off a dynamic economic development as early as the mid-1980s, both by improving wine quality tremendously and by opening up to tourism, while the ambitious laggard municipality remained inward-oriented well into the 1990s. Good wine and lovely scenery are the major tourist attractions here, too, but these are advertised in isolation to the outside. Tourists mainly visit the ambitious laggard municipality for the wine and the scenery.

The linked wine-growing community, on the other hand, managed to integrate interesting scenery and quality wine into one touristic whole, enriched with regional identity. In addition, the aspect of speciality foods of the region was included in the image of the linked wine-growing community. Tourists go to the linked wine-growing community for a whole package of pleasant things.

In both municipalities, people do a lot of voluntary works in societies and clubs and are socially well linked. In the ambitious laggard municipality, however, people's strong social cohesion is opposed to the cooperation-averse attitude of entrepreneurs, while social ties in the linked wine-growing community include the businesses. Numerous smaller and larger cooperations on all levels of wine-producing result in synergetic links between all individual activities and a dynamic and highly differentiated local business structure characterized by creativity and initiative.

Interestingly, local politicians did not further this development in the linked wine-growing community by creating an open and supportive climate. On the contrary, it was exactly the quite conservative stance of some municipal officials and the sometimes quite antagonistic relationship between local parties that made entrepreneurs realize their ideas and innovative project with the support of friends and acquaintances. This led to an overlap of business and private life that, in turn, promoted the integration of private and entrepreneurial objectives. Citizens thus developed a strong feeling of responsibility for the municipality's development.

This combination of initiative and responsibility can only rarely be found in the ambitious laggard municipality. Here, most initiatives are not implemented in the private or business spheres, but are taken to the municipal authorities, who willingly offer assistance. However, the openness and impartiality of the mayor and councillors, although generally a good thing, have also prevented entrepreneurs from creating strong links among each other. The practically non-existent links between economic actors make coordinating individual activities and formulating a common development strategy difficult. The municipality was not able to develop a clear image.

Yet this deficit might clearly diminish in the next few years. The positive impulses from the fall of the Iron Curtain on economic development, but also on the sentiment in the ambitious laggard municipality, as well as suprar-egional integration of the local area, pushed significantly in recent years, might lead to the emergence of cross-border, inter-regional relationship net-works, triggering a dynamic development of the local area's economy. In this case, establishing an image for the whole local area would decisively strengthen tourism and the area as a business location.

In particular, the reaction of the linked wine-growing community to the opening to the East is a threat to positive future development. While the links between businesses within the municipality are exceptionally strong, there is no interest at all in creating links to the numerous wine and tourism busi-nesses across the border. Similar business sizes and sectoral structure in the neighbouring towns abroad are seen as a threat by the entrepreneurs rather than an opportunity. The same holds true, in a slightly less pronounced form, for relations between local entrepreneurs and entrepreneurs from neighbouring municipalities within the borders. This isolationism is the greatest danger to the linked wine-growing community's successful socio-economic system.

FACTORS TO BE CONSIDERED FOR THIS CATEGORY OF CHARACTERISTICS

- In order to initiate dynamic development in regions with traditional eco-nomic structures (e.g. wine-growing regions), it can be advantageous to infuse the dominant product with regional identity and, if possible, integrate it into one overall experience with complementary products.
- In order not to inhibit the emergence of relationship networks between entrepreneurs, the municipal administration should only play an active role in the implementation of those initiatives that cannot be implemented within a business cooperation. If the latter is possible, the municipal administration has to provide supportive conditions for successfully implementing the common entrepreneurial activities to the best of its ability. If need be, the municipal authorities can bring together potential cooperation partners or mediate in disputes.
- The overlap between private and business spheres, common in rural areas, can result in the emergence of a socio-economic system that promotes initia-tive and responsibility among both people and entrepreneurs. Particularly common entrepreneurial activity among friends and acquaintances can inte-grate private and entrepreneurial objectives. The municipal administration is to promote such initiatives by providing advice and administrative support.
- In case of similar business sizes and sectoral structures, cross-border cooperation is a great opportunity to get established as an attractive, inter-communal location for business. Using the respective locational advantages together can strengthen the whole region's competitiveness. In cross-border cooperations, businesses from the respective countries can mutually open up new markets in the immediate vicinity.

2.3.4 Proximity to conurbations: the two-class municipality vs. the quarrelling loner municipality

Both municipalities are in the immediate vicinity of conurbations. Nevertheless, the two-class municipality developed into an attractive place to live with an active social life and a booming business location, while the quarrelling loner municipality was not able to benefit significantly from the proximity to a conurbation.

At first glance, the two municipalities look similar even beyond proximity to a conurbation: both the dominant personality of the mayor and the influx of wealthy people from the conurbation with the corresponding hike in land prices characterize the two towns. The town centres of both municipalities are quiet and tidy, local amenities in town are adequate but – due to the overwhelming competition in the close conurbation – unremarkable. In both places, people can get hold of daily shopping even without having to use a car.

Yet, regarding infrastructure and economic development, there are significant differences. For example, the two-class municipality is conveniently connected to the supraregional road network. In the near future, there will even be a motorway close by. The quarrelling loner municipality, on the other hand, is connected to the conurbation and the major road network only via an A-road in need of repair that is difficult to negotiate for lorries. Additionally, the bad mood among the population and a municipal policy that tends to go against the interests of businesses lower the attractiveness of the quarrelling loner municipality as a business location.

While the two-class municipality established a business zone with excellent infrastructure links, in the quarrelling loner municipality the province had to acquire a former business site and rent out the old buildings to local businesses in order to create some supply of building land for business. The municipal itself was not willing or able to do so. There are hardly any other measures to stimulate the regional economy.

The differences regarding business promotion are particularly striking. In the quarrelling loner municipality, the only support is financial subsidies that can be applied for to be approved by the council. Organizational help such as administrative support or procedural help, which in the two-class municipality are the mainstay of business promotion, are not offered at all in the quarrelling loner municipality. What is more, businesses there face bureaucratic procedures and partly subjective decisions that create envy and jealousy among entrepreneurs. Many years of inactivity by tourist businesses have led to out-of-date tourism infrastructure in the town and a resulting dramatic decrease in revenues. Only a hill situated within the municipality is popular with day tourists, without businesses in the municipality benefiting economically. The unfavourable socio-climatic and infrastructural conditions have prevented the decline of local tourism being compensated for by the development of local businesses or the relocation here of new ones. There is no overall concept and no vision for municipal development.

At the same time, tourism in the two-class municipality was expanded. A great number of new attractions were created in order to consequently broaden the product range, which originally focused exclusively on wine tourism. Early success motivated people, officials and entrepreneurs to engage in further projects, resulting in a virtuous circle of renewal, which, controlled by the mayor, brought dynamic development to the municipality. The mayor uses his authority not for preventing but for enabling new projects. Local taxes from the business zone, established as an extension to the town area, provide the financial leeway required.

Although both mayors orient their municipal policies on target groups, the mayor of the two-class municipality focuses on economically relevant parts of the population (vintners and trades people, as well as wealthy incomers), while his counterpart in the quarrelling loner municipality uses personal, discriminatory criteria. The effects are, in one case, the emergence of a two-class society and, in the other, the split of the population into rival factions: cronies and critics of the mayor. Even though the effects on society are similar in both cases, the behavioural pattern of the mayor in the quarrelling loner municipality provides much more unfavourable conditions for economic activity in the municipality.

FACTORS TO BE CONSIDERED FOR THIS CATEGORY OF CHARACTERISTICS

- Proximity to a conurbation alone is no guarantee of positive economic development for a rural municipality. To make use of the favourable location, conditions in the municipality have to be adapted to those businesses that relocate from the conurbation.
- Particularly in rural municipalities close to conurbations, an infrastructural link to the centre close by is a major locational factor. Entrepreneurs tend to locate in areas that enable them to efficiently work the urban market due to good traffic links, with low land prices and fewer conflicts of interest with the people living there.
- When creating business zones and attracting enterprises for relocation, it is important to keep in mind the need to maintain the townspeople's quality of life, in order to remain attractive for incomers from the conurbation. The provision of public amenities should focus mainly on young families to counteract an overageing population.
- In view of the comparatively high land prices close to the city, municipalities close to conurbations in particular have to take measures to make it possible for the young people in town to acquire flats and houses in their home town. A sufficient supply of land for building on at affordable prices has to be provided by means of an appropriate model to secure building land. Another option is social housing.
- Rural municipalities close to conurbations, by combining comparatively low infrastructure costs, easy reach of a big market and a large supply of highly qualified workers, are an attractive location for establishing new

businesses that offer highly qualified services. In order to reduce such initiatives' high susceptibility to failure, some supportive measures and grants should be provided.

- Making economic use of the tourist potential of conurbations requires a modern, steadily expanding range of recreational activities. If you do not make renewal investments and adapt your products to the constantly changing needs of the urban day tourists, the customers will react negatively and revenues will fall. City-dwellers no longer demand week-long stays in rural towns, but short stays offering as much entertainment as possible or a few days of relaxation in accommodation of a high standard.

2.3.5 Drastic change in economic structure: the quarrelling loner municipality vs. the revived grab-the-chance municipality

In the quarrelling loner municipality, tourism as the sole economic pillar has collapsed in the last few decades. The revived grab-the-chance municipality lost its local economic structure, consisting of two medium enterprises, at about the same time. Thus, both municipalities faced a drastic change in economic structure. While the revived grab-the-chance municipality actively set measures in order to create a new business structure with a more balanced mix of business sizes in future-oriented sectors, the quarrelling loner municipality, entangled in personally motivated bickering and paralysed by mutual distrust and envy, is in deep slumber.

As a reason for the very different reaction of the municipalities to the massive change in local economic structure and the clearly diverging developments arising from it, the first thing coming to mind is the uneven infrastructure situation in the municipalities. While the revived grab-the-chance municipality is situated directly on the railway and bus lines, as well as a wide A-road and close to the motorway, the quarrelling loner municipality is linked to supraregional centres and the motorway, some distance away, only via a narrow A-lane in need of repairs. Therefore, the two towns have a quite different attraction as a business location. Getting businesses to relocate, which in times of the decline of traditional economic structures enables the creation of an alternative business structure, is much more difficult for the quarrelling loner municipality.

In both municipalities, people reacted to the economic decline with passivity and resignation. In the revived grab-the-chance municipality, however, the mayor succeeded in actively grabbing the chance arising from the lucky break of an innovative business relocating there. This positive impulse was taken as the starting point for redesigning the area zoning plan, where a business and industrial zone was developed. The crisis turned into an opportunity, as the mayor cleverly created a new supply of attractive land to locate businesses by acquiring the plots of the run-down businesses, as well as by swapping land and using option contracts. Even if there was some luck in having the new flagship business relocate here, due to the entrepreneur's personal preferences, the people took it as a signal for a new revival. The municipal administration and the population started to re-create local business structures. In the revived grab-the-chance municipality, positive dynamics emerged, which, starting from the establishment of favourable conditions for small and medium enterprises, included the business relocation, building homes and creating public amenities.

In the quarrelling loner municipality, positive impulses, such as a successful international sports event and the mountain-bike track built for it, were not made use of on a long-term basis, as they were not integrated into a comprehensive development plan with a long-term perspective. In the perception of people and town officials, not the opportunities but the risks prevailed. A lack of initiative and visions, as well as the sluggish and inflexible administration, further dampen business activity in the municipality and prevent any positive dynamics from emerging. Instead of developing holistic future concepts, the municipality bets on selective business promotion and hopes for an improvement of the conditions in its macro-environment.

FACTORS TO BE CONSIDERED FOR THIS CATEGORY OF CHARACTERISTICS

- If traditional economic structures collapse due to a change in the overall economic situation, a radical shift in orientation is needed for communal economic policy. Openness to new things and the willingness to support entrepreneurial activities in new sectors are in such a case important success factors for the municipality.
- If individual strokes of luck influence the developments of municipalities, on the other hand, it is necessary to include these single events in a comprehensive development concept in order to transform the positive impulses thus arising into sustainable economic development.
- In times of crisis and when traditional local economic structures collapse, it is one of the major tasks of municipal representatives to keep the population from getting stuck in passivity and resignation. Focused initiatives must show perspectives for the future and their implementation in a convincing manner.
- Apart from financial considerations, enterprises' decisions to relocate depend on the mood in the municipality, the quality of personal relationships with municipal representatives and mainly the offer of support in administrative matters. If entrepreneurs willing to relocate have the feeling of being welcome in a municipality and receiving professional support, they even accept higher land prices and lower subsidies.

2.3.6 Innovative leading enterprise: the imaginative enabler municipality vs. the inept resource municipality

Both the imaginative enabler municipality and the inept resource municipality are characterized by a very weak business structure. The economic basis of both municipalities is really only one single firm in each case. This makes local tax revenue from these companies the major source of the towns' budgets. Similarly, practically all jobs available in both places are at these enterprises.

The two leading enterprises produce food. While the leading enterprise in the inept resource municipality has existed for decades and has offered its products practically unchanged for many years, the leading enterprise in the imaginative enabler municipality in its current form and orientation emerged only a few years ago from a family business that was taken over. By means of a consistently pursued specialization strategy, the firm in the imaginative enabler municipality managed to establish itself at the top end of the market nationally and partly even internationally within just a few years, using innovative product variation and an unconventional marketing concept.

Some years ago, the leading enterprise in the inept resource municipality also started to get an angle on direct competitors through product innovations and thereby to secure its market position. An unusual marketing strategy accompanies the successful process of image creation. The traditional firm can today be called an internationally active innovative leading enterprise.

Albeit for different reasons, the local nature of both the leading enterprise in the inept resource municipality and the leading enterprise in the imaginative enabler municipality is very pronounced. The inept resource municipality has natural resources that can only be processed locally. Thus, the company's production is tied to the location. The local nature of the leading enterprise in the imaginative enabler municipality comes from the marketing concept and image of the product. The attributes "individualist" and "different", which are associated with the region, have been transferred to the leading enterprise's products. Now the product has been infused so strongly with the regional image that moving the production site would massively devalue the product.

Therefore, both the inept resource municipality and the imaginative enabler municipality are lucky to have a leading enterprise tied to the locality in their municipality. In addition, the two towns can sleep safely as the two leading enterprises are set to expand in the next few years.

Yet the two municipalities surveyed make very different use of this favourable situation. The imaginative enabler municipality, for instance, managed to utilize the positive impulse from the creation of the innovative leading enterprise as a starting point for designing a development concept that is embedded in a supraregional concept and coordinated with the activities of other municipalities in the region. This initiated an economic development mainly focused on establishing a tourism industry that is based on agricultural production as an identity-creating element and uses the local leading enterprise as an attraction. Given this dynamic situation, there is an optimistic spirit in the municipality and the people are again beginning to show initiative.

The situation is very different in the inept resource municipality: here, everybody is used to the local leading enterprise providing local taxes to the municipality and jobs to the people. The leading enterprise's dynamic development and its new positioning through innovative products and marketing are not even registered in the municipality. As long as there are no problems, nobody is very much interested in the leading enterprise. Moreover, so far no strategies have been developed to use the positive signal sent out by the existence of the leading enterprise or the local taxes paid by the firm for developing a local small-business structure. The priorities in creating public amenities in the inept resource municipality seem similarly questionable. A fairly oversized farm, for example, and a mortuary have indeed been built, but there is still no hall for events or any youth centre. The municipality seems to rely completely on the status quo and the positive development of the leading enterprise, without considering building up an alternative or complementary business structure.

FACTORS TO BE CONSIDERED FOR THIS CATEGORY OF CHARACTERISTICS

- Innovative ideas by the people can make the overall economic development of a local area more dynamic. Therefore, initiatives should be actively supported in their entrepreneurial implementation. Often, it is not so much financial help these entrepreneurs need to realize their visions. Rather, the task of municipal representatives is to actively design favourable conditions that further a positive development of innovative businesses. Little things such as erecting signposts or organizational matters such as coordinating the marketing between business and municipality can be of help here.
- It is much more likely for citizens to turn into entrepreneurs who realize their visions in the municipality if there is a high quality of life there. By taking measures to improve the quality of life, the municipality can stem the outflow of entrepreneurial people or induce their return to their home town. Apart from good local infrastructure, an active social life with intensive links between clubs and societies, and attractive public amenities, openness to new things and the willingness to support entrepreneurial activities also in young industries are also of great importance.
- Leading enterprises make the surrounding economic structure more dynamic. Their success proves that businesses in the region can take a positive development. This good example encourages other citizens to realize their entrepreneurial plans. If the municipality succeeds in communicating the success of its leading enterprise as a best-practice example to the population, initiative and entrepreneurial activities in the municipality can be promoted.
- If entrepreneurial activities are made dynamic in such a manner in rural municipalities, agriculture also has to be included. It can be advantageous to integrate agricultural products into the municipality's image as identity-creating elements. Hence, farmers also have to be included in the

image-creating process. Offering holidays on the farm can support such a strategy.

- Unfavourable locations can be compensated for mainly by innovative businesses. If the unconventional business locations can be used for creating a likeable corporate image and/or a valuable brand, the higher costs of logistics will be offset by higher sales prices.
- If there are flourishing leading enterprises in the municipality, it is the municipal representatives' task to use the positive signal sent out and local tax revenues for establishing alternative business structures. This also holds for leading enterprises tied to the location, as legal and economic conditions can change rapidly and it does not make sense from a risk point of view for local economic development to depend on one company alone.

2.3.7 Actively attracting businesses: the arty entrepreneur municipality vs. the self-related traditional municipality

Both municipalities have created successful local business structures. They started from different initial situations, followed contrary strategies and now face different structural deficits. Both municipalities have a favourable geographical location and a good connection to the road network. The potential of well-educated workers is sufficient in both regions. While there is strong social cohesion in the population of both towns, there are hardly any links beyond the municipal borders. Likewise, entrepreneurs within either of the municipalities are hardly linked with each other.

As regards business promotion, financial incentives are not the major means of doing so, neither in the arty entrepreneur municipality nor in the self-related traditional municipality. Rather, the focus is put on non-monetary support. Local businesses and those that want to locate there are offered assistance in administrative matters.

The initial situations in the municipalities regarding local business structures differ mainly in the businesses' distribution within the municipalities and the local infrastructure. In the self-related traditional municipality, businesses are concentrated in the town centre, while, in the arty entrepreneur municipality, they have always been spread out throughout town, so that there is no business centre in the middle of town.

The self-related traditional municipality has customarily had diverse local amenities in the town centre. In the arty entrepreneur municipality, on the other hand, the already weak local infrastructure has been reduced to one little food store within the last few decades.

At the beginning of the economic recovery that set in when the municipalities created their own business zones, the quality of life was strikingly different in the two places. Decision-makers in the arty entrepreneur municipality had to deal with the problem that, although one large company and a few small businesses provided sufficient jobs, the bad infrastructural situation and the fairly desolate town centre resulted in a bad mood, little social cohesion and little entrepreneurial activity in the population. In the self-related traditional municipality, on the other hand, the quality of life and social cohesion were fine, mainly due to the manifold very small local businesses offering a broad range. As most businesses were run as family enterprises, though, there were hardly any jobs in the self-related traditional municipality.

Motivated by the different problems, the municipalities followed different strategies, which, in both cases, still included establishing a business zone within the municipality's boundaries: the arty entrepreneur municipality managed to create a community spirit through a massive range of social and cultural activities and, at the same time, to position itself as an innovative, modern municipality of culture. The image of a municipality is a major factor in assessing the location's attractiveness, as the location of a business sends out a signal in the form of positive or negative connotations with the municipality's name. The self-related traditional municipality, in contrast, was not able to establish a clearly defined image. In developing the business zone, decision-makers relied on the geographical location favourable for the businesses and the good infrastructural links. The intention was to increase local tax revenue significantly by relocating large enterprises there.

The arty entrepreneur municipality's strategy is more sustainable in that, on the one hand, not only business relocations but mainly new business foundations are specifically promoted and, on the other hand, emphasis was put on a balanced mix of business sizes and a good sectoral structure when relocating businesses here. This creates a strong link to the location that inhibits businesses from relocating elsewhere.

FACTORS TO BE CONSIDERED FOR THIS CATEGORY OF CHARACTERISTICS

- Planning a business zone always has to take into account the municipality's resources. In particular, factors such as a good link to high-performance transport routes, a favourable geographic location regarding the strategic orientation of businesses and a sufficient supply of qualified workers influence the success of such a project.
- In developing a business zone, a well-balanced mix of business sizes and sectoral structure has to be kept in mind, in order to provide stability in economic downturns and to enable synergies between the businesses.
- If the municipality supports the local population in founding or expanding businesses, a local economic structure can develop that remains devoted to the location in the long term.
- In assessing the attractiveness of a location, companies also take into consideration the image of and the mood in the municipality to be selected. In order to successfully get businesses to locate, a sensible development in these areas also has to be focused on.
- If the mayor is elected directly, the losing candidate, as long as he received a sizeable number of votes, should be included in the political leadership

structure, possibly as deputy mayor, in order to prevent tension and the building of factions.

- For the sake of a good and cooperative atmosphere among people and entrepreneurs, the municipal administration must not neglect their customer orientation towards their citizens, as this dampens people's and entrepreneurs' own initiative.
- The municipality is to support formal cooperations between local businesses or provide a professional mediator in order to facilitate coordination between entrepreneurs. Cooperations can make local businesses more competitive through synergies and so strengthen the business location as a whole.

2.3.8 Inter-communal business zone: the manager-driven pioneer municipality vs. the debt-laden optimist municipality

In the debt-laden optimist municipality, the main pillar of the local economy collapsed with the decline of the brick works. Mining in the manager-driven pioneer municipality has taken a steadily negative turn in the last few years and will end in the next few years, which means that also in this municipality the majority of local tax receipts and jobs are gone and more are yet to disappear. Both municipalities thus have, compared to their size, very few jobs to offer. Both in the manager-driven pioneer municipality and the debt-laden optimist municipality, almost the entire employed working population has to commute to the conurbations nearby. By establishing business zones, the municipalities are aiming at locating businesses there in order to create local jobs for the people and reduce the commuting problem.

Encouraged by the province's new promotion policy, which favours inter-communal initiatives, and driven by the insight that competition between locations within the local area hampers the development of the local economy, both municipalities decided to include their neighbours in these projects.

Although the municipalities are located fairly close to each other, their inter-communal initiatives have shown very different degrees of success. While quite a sizeable number of businesses has already located in the inter-communal business zone in the manager-driven pioneer municipality, only three building plots have been sold in the inter-communal business zone of the debt-laden optimist municipality, and nothing has been built there yet.

The reason for this is, firstly, that the business zone in the manager-driven pioneer municipality has better infrastructure links. Although the inter-communal business zone of the debt-laden optimist municipality is linked to the hubs in the region and the major road network via a broad A-road, there is no connection to the motorway in order to keep up with the manager-driven pioneer municipality's initiative in direct competition. It becomes clear that creating inter-communal business zones prevents competition between locations at the level of municipalities, but, at the same time, new and fierce competition at the local-area level arises.

By pooling resources, commonly developed and financed building zones for businesses can be provided with a far better infrastructure than could be achieved by a single municipality. For this reason, individual initiatives are increasingly inferior to inter-communal business zones, which forces municipalities to develop common initiatives. In future, it will not be municipalities vying for businesses, but local areas competing for relocating firms. The concept of inter-communal business building zones has been a first step towards creating a coordinated and thus sustainable development of a viable economic structure in rural areas. However, competitive thinking can only give way to the idea of constructive cooperation once the flows of money from the businesses back to the municipalities are no longer tied to the location of the business.

Secondly, the manager-driven pioneer municipality has a special bonus: the mayor, personally in charge of locating businesses here, is also an official on the provincial and even federal level. His special know-how and political clout definitely were an advantage for project development and the location of businesses. In the debt-laden optimist municipality, on the other hand, until recently, a broker was in charge of locating businesses there, employed on the basis of an exclusive exploitation agreement. Due to the lack of success, this contract was terminated a short while ago and the mayor has taken over this matter. Nevertheless, he cannot resort to such a large and influential network.

Thirdly, the manager-driven pioneer municipality was assisted in project development by a consulting agency, which helped avoid several mistakes from the start. For instance, the plots intended for the business zone were not purchased but secured in advance by means of option contracts. This reduced the capital required and the pressure to realize the inter-communal business zone significantly, and more resources could be used for infrastructure links and advertising. In the debt-laden optimist municipality, large amounts were invested for the purchase of plots. Now, with no businesses locating and no revenues from local taxes, the pressure on the mayor is enormous.

FACTORS TO BE CONSIDERED FOR THIS CATEGORY OF CHARACTERISTICS

- Creating business zones in isolation by individual municipalities, in view of the emergence of numerous inter-communal business zones and their competitive advantages, makes little sense today. Rather, municipalities intending to develop a business zone should include their neighbours in the projects and develop an optimum solution for the whole region together. In this way, a single municipality can prevent competing business zones from cropping up in the immediate vicinity.
- In general, when developing business zones, it has to be taken into account that, by making use of the experiences of other municipalities, relevant institutions and consultants, mistakes can be avoided and a schedule ideal for the respective project can be developed. A particularly critical question

in this context is when the venture is to be communicated to the public. An announcement before having secured the intended plots can lead to real estate speculation and make project implementation more expensive. Waiting too long might anger the population and result in an unpleasant atmosphere in the municipality.

• A business zone only makes sense if the location has excellent infrastructure links. A connection to the motorway is a major success factor. Insecurity about the future situation in this respect hurts the location of businesses, as firms want security in their planning. In addition, frequent changes in the qualities of the location hurt the credibility of the people in charge of locating.

• It makes sense to put personalities in charge of locating businesses who, apart from the required openness, ability to communicate, persuasiveness and business background, have a personal network that gives them privileged access to relevant personalities in business and decision-makers at higher levels of administration. Such a person sends a signal to business looking for a location that this particular municipality can provide optimum support in administrative matters and with subsidies.

• Often, financing the relocation of a business and erecting a new business object is a barrier to locating. Frequently, it is not the bad economic situation of the businesses that lets debt financing fail, but the lack of suitably prepared documents. Small businesses, in particular, are often unable to produce balance sheets or plans that meet the financiers' requirements, as they lack the time and/or know-how to draw up these documents. Suitable support in creating presentation documents would be particularly useful for these businesses.

2.3.9 Tourist attraction: the aimless adjunct municipality vs. the sleepy future-plan municipality

Both the aimless adjunct municipality and the sleepy future-plan municipality are located at a bathing lake in middle Austria. In fact, the two municipalities surveyed are quite close to each other geographically. As traditional tourist towns, they have to fight unstable weather, strong competition from cheap air travel and the visitors' change in needs, often translating into more demands. Both municipalities recorded a clear decline in the number of stays over the last two decades.

The two municipalities reacted very differently to the lack of competitiveness of the local tourist industry. While the aimless adjunct municipality is trying to reduce the importance of tourism for the municipality by the intensive and mostly random location of businesses in town, the sleepy future-plan municipality is making a real effort to reposition itself as a tourist destination.

The favourable location of the aimless adjunct municipality next to the motorway and the support measures offered have lured a number of trades businesses to the municipality in recent years. That these are mostly businesses poached from neighbouring towns and whose tie to their location is apparently very weak seems to be of no concern in this strategy. Nor is there any selection according to sector. Nevertheless, some firms have developed very well in the municipality in the last few years, and the decline in tourism was mostly compensated for. The question remains how many of the new businesses will keep their location in the municipality once the support ends. There is the danger that some other neighbouring town will then poach these businesses by making attractive offers. Thus, the business-promotion measures of the municipalities in the region are, from an inter-communal perspective, almost exclusively deadweight effects. Inter-communal coordination of measures aimed at attracting businesses and business promotion is urgently required.

In the sleepy future-plan municipality, on the other hand, no efforts are made to attract businesses. The unfavourable transport links and the confined geographical situation make the municipality fairly unattractive as a business location. Nonetheless, a large enterprise has been in the municipality for decades and provides important jobs in the community. The municipality's economic mainstay, though, is tourism. As in the aimless adjunct municipality, it is mainly visitors staying for a prolonged period that have become increasingly scarce in the sleepy future-plan municipality in recent years. However, here it was decided to adapt to the changes in visitors' needs and habits by specifically extending the touristic product range. In coordination with the other members of the inter-communal tourism association, the dependence on the weather is to be countered by focusing less on the bathing lake and more on attractions, such as diving or the lake stage. By putting special emphasis on diving, these municipalities were able to get an angle on other municipalities around the lake and establish a competitive advantage. The planned stage on the lake is intended to extend the product range for tourists by the cultural aspect and tap new types of visitors for local tourism.

Such clear strategies are almost completely missing in the aimless adjunct municipality. Although attempts have been made to develop major projects, those include, for example, oversized hotel complexes that are not part of any overall concept. In general, there is no clear future strategy in the aimless adjunct municipality. Even though in the sleepy future-plan municipality a certain part of the population has not realized yet that active steps must be taken now to safeguard the citizens' wealth for the future, the decision-makers and a few active citizens have already agreed on a clear development strategy in coordination with the other municipalities in the tourism association. Additionally, participation in a highly active and efficiently run inter-communal tourism association helps the touristic repositioning of the sleepy future-plan municipality, as individual activities are coordinated with a general cross-municipality development concept and are embedded in a general marketing concept.

A further barrier to the touristic development of the aimless adjunct municipality is the lack of a town centre. The scattered settlement also uses the town centre of a neighbouring municipality. Positioning as a separate tourist town is hence almost impossible, and municipal development depends on the strategic orientation of this neighbouring town. This constellation would not be problematic if this dependency were used to gain a more competitive position by coordinated behaviour. Unfortunately, instead of a cooperative strategy, a competitive strategy is pursued. The combination of dependence and competition, however, makes constructive cooperation next to impossible.

FACTORS TO BE CONSIDERED FOR THIS CATEGORY OF CHARACTERISTICS

- Particularly in sectors with intense competition such as tourism, it is of great importance to position oneself clearly in the market by pursuing an unambiguous and consistent specialization strategy. This strategy has to be communicated to decision-makers, citizens and entrepreneurs in order to receive widespread backing.
- For such a positioning, coordinated behaviour within an inter-communal cooperation is an advantage. In particular, communicating the positioning efficiently to the outside world can only work on the basis of concerted marketing efforts.
- In traditional sectors, innovative marketing strategies can lead to surprise effects and thus have a greater impact on the public. If such strategies are not undermined by conservative forces, the relaunch of a tourism region as a young and trendy tourist destination can work.
- If there are strong dependences between municipalities, for example, if one municipality also uses the infrastructure of another, the two municipalities should coordinate their activities in cooperation. A competitive situation inevitably results in a further weakening of the dependent municipality and reduces the attractiveness of the whole region as a business location.
- Also regarding the location of businesses, interdependencies on an inter-communal level are to be taken into account. Poaching businesses from each other and a competitive attitude in the location of businesses from outside have to be avoided. Such behaviour only results in dead-weight effects and unfavourable self-selection of the businesses locating in the region. It will attract mainly those firms that relocate to another municipality offering support once the subsidies are gone. In the interest of a positive economic development of the region, inter-communal coordination of locating activities of the individual municipalities is very important.

2.3.10 In the sticks: the rural activist municipality vs. the Far-East ex-mining municipality

Both the rural activist municipality and the Far-East ex-mining municipality are located far away from high-performance transport routes in geographical isolation. In the rural activist municipality, the negative trend in agriculture means that the most important economic sector and provider of jobs is about to disappear. With the end of mining in the Far-East ex-mining municipality, practically all economic structures have gone. The only chance for positive development of the local economy in both municipalities is creating and using tourist attractions.

Although there has been need for action in the Far-East ex-mining municipality for about 30 years, the development of concepts to make the municipality a tourist town started only recently, while the rural activist municipality became active when there were the first signs of need for action. In developing tourism, neither of the municipalities can rely on natural attractions such as bathing lakes or ski slopes. Both the rural activist municipality and the Far-East ex-mining municipality realized that a positioning as a normal holiday destination would not make any sense given the heavy national competition and the fall in prices for air travel. Therefore, both towns are betting on creating a unique tourist appeal.

The two municipalities' strategies, however, differ as regards their development process, their anchoring in economic, social and public structures, and the role of the municipal administration and the mayor.

While the mayor in the rural activist municipality as an enabler provides the administrative and organizational basis for activities developed by the people and gives the activists free rein to realize their visions, the mayor in the Far-East ex-mining municipality pulls all the strings in town. Projects are developed in the inner circle of selected councillors. In implementation, too, neither the local businesses nor the people are in any way involved as they are in the rural activist municipality. Hence, it remains questionable whether local businesses and people in the Far-East ex-mining municipality can be included to the desired extent later.

In the rural activist municipality, the touristic orientation has been identified as the optimum future development strategy within the village renewal process. This process was initiated by the municipality and supported by the province, which financed a facilitator, but was ultimately carried by people and entrepreneurs. All creativity in the municipality, for example, went into strategy development and the needs of all stakeholders were taken into consideration. During strategy development and implementation, a tight social network was created as a productive basis for dynamic economic development. Individuals contribute ideas to the network, allies are found quickly and a lot of commitment is put into implementation. Some ideas that were realized give positive impulses to the whole network and further the emergence of new initiatives. This resulted in a self-strengthening, organic village renewal process in the rural activist municipality, which includes all parts of the population and where every citizen can contribute actively to the extent and at any time he wants.

In the Far-East ex-mining municipality, in contrast, the project is quite isolated from any other business structures or the people. The mayor advances project development, keeps in contact with the investors and organizes subsidies, as well as providing the content for the planned Far-East culture and therapy centre. So far, these activities have had hardly any effect on the future expectations and the planning world of the people and the entrepreneurs. The municipality's planned tourism measures have resulted in neither a common initiative nor economic momentum.

The rural activist municipality is also more successful in using existing resources for implementing the development strategy. For instance, existing buildings and the traditional local trades, as well as the equally traditional strong social cohesion, have been recognized as the basis for developing tourism. In the Far-East ex-mining municipality, on the other hand, it was not possible to make sustainable touristic use of the mining ruins that had already been prepared for tourism for the Provincial Exhibition, which took place in the region a few years ago. Years of passivity of council and people alike made the originally excellent public infrastructure crumble away. In the rural activist municipality, in contrast, with the massive help of volunteers, starting from a very low level, an attractive range of public amenities has been created in the last few years. So the whole population can partake in the success of the village renewal process and activists see confirmation that their efforts have paid off.

FACTORS TO BE CONSIDERED FOR THIS CATEGORY OF CHARACTERISTICS

- As soon as there are signs that the established economic structure might take a turn for the worse, the municipal representatives should think about developing an alternative structure. The sooner there is a strategy for reorienting the local economy, the better the local infrastructure's condition will be and the more favourable conditions will be for implementing the new development strategies.
- When identifying possible new orientations of municipal development, sensible starting points are the existing infrastructure and resources, on the one hand, and social structure and the abilities and skills of the population, on the other. A development based on the existing infrastructure that is in harmony with the people's way of life is much more likely to induce sustainable economic development than an isolated project.
- In developing strategies for the future economic development of a municipality, including all parts of the population in the sense of considering as many individual interests as possible and making use of the total creative potential of the citizens is a major success factor. Centrally controlled development processes are problematic, particularly in financially weak municipalities, as the voluntary and free cooperation of the population is essential there in order to implement the development strategies. If the people are not included in devising the initiatives and projects, there will be little willingness to make an effort in implementation.
- Including the population, and particularly the local entrepreneurs, is also advisable against the background of a broad economic utilization of the development initiatives. Only if initiatives and projects are developed in a transparent manner and are communicated openly can they be anticipated when building up future expectations and included in individual planning.

- For strategy development and implementation, the mayor and municipal representatives have the task of creating supportive conditions. Initiative and creativity are to be woken from slumber and strengthened. Once enough initiative has built up in the population, controlling intervention or even manipulative intrusion are to be avoided if at all possible, as such behaviour could frustrate active and committed citizens and inhibit the emergence of a dynamic discussion process.
- Measures that can be realized and presented in the short term ought to take second place to a long-term development strategy. Given the scarcity of public funding, a far-sighted use of funds and setting priorities accordingly are crucial in order to, for example, avoid misinvestment in public buildings for which no other use can be found any time soon. If public buildings are no longer used for their original function, a decision has to be made on alternative use in line with a long-term development strategy.

3 An agenda for cross-border know-how exchange

A two-step selection process served to identify those measures of economic policy presented in the study conducted on Austria, which should be further examined with a view to their transferability to the municipalities of the Central and Eastern European neighbouring countries.

3.1 First step in the selection process – workshop

In a workshop with mayors, municipal councillors and parliamentarians, 60 measures for creating favourable conditions for SMEs in rural areas, developed in Chapter 2, were evaluated with a view to their general transferability to other municipalities. It was possible to condense their number to 31 measures generally transferable to other municipalities.

The results of the evaluation workshop will be presented in this section. The 31 measures that had been identified as generally transferable will be discussed briefly against the backdrop of the Austrian part of this study.

Suggested measure 1: Population and businesses are actively integrated into the process of municipal development.

The timing of integrating the population into the process of municipal development is particularly critical. Where the population is integrated before the municipal officials have formulated a clear perspective of the possible directions of development and/or before the necessary information is available, there is a danger that the population will feel overburdened or will be frustrated by lacking or contradictory information and will consequently withdraw from the process. Where this happens repeatedly, interest in municipal development may be lost. On the other hand, where the population is integrated only after the municipal officials have made fundamental decisions, there is the danger that the population will feel left out and will impulsively refuse to get involved. Therefore, it appears optimal that municipal officials obtain information relevant to decision-making (e.g. appraisals, planning documents, option contracts) beforehand in order to be able to present concrete alternative proposals to the general public. The population can subsequently express their views on the alternatives suggested and become involved in the decision-making process.

Suggested measure 2: The individual municipal activities form part of a comprehensive development concept.

Many Austrian municipalities already coordinate individual projects and activities, which results in tangible advantages, even though it entails substantial coordination effort. For instance, local agricultural products together with the offering provided by local gastronomic venues are integrated into municipalities' efforts to build a unique image as destinations for tourism. Where all actors involved share a common understanding of the development perspective for the municipality, the individual can act in line with the desired overall development. This can also foster the cooperation among those participants who pursue identical sub-goals within the overall plan or who can at least proceed jointly part of the way – despite different objectives. This helps bundle resources and coordinate activities. This way, it becomes easier to generate synergy within which the municipal citizens contribute to implementing the overall strategy. Joint efforts lead to sustainable community development being realized more efficiently.

Suggested measure 3: Involving all interest groups of the municipality leads to identifying conflicting objectives already at the stage of strategy definition and to the development of possible solutions.

It cannot be refuted that not every concrete solution can satisfy all interests. It is important, however, that all interest groups can live with the consensus that has eventually been reached. In this context, it is relevant to ensure a solution that balances the needs of all interest groups in the long term. Where an individual interest group renounces its claims at least partially, it may be confident that in later decisions another interest group in the municipality will hold back in turn.

Suggested measure 4: Achieving a balanced structure in terms of business size is a principle guiding the development of the local economic structure (e.g. attracting businesses to locate, promoting young entrepreneurs).

On the one hand, large companies can act as leaders that generate positive impulses for the local economy. On the other hand, the dominance of a large company can easily lead to a relationship of dependence of the local municipality on the company that is influential in the local economic structure. A mixed portfolio of company sizes leaves more room for the municipality to decide on economic policy. Additionally, risk can be spread where a larger number of smaller enterprises are present. Enterprises of varying size can interact synergistically, which leads to the disadvantages of the individual company sizes cancelling each other out. Austrian municipalities that actively engage in inducing companies to locate in their areas are already paying very close attention to the objective of attracting enterprises that harmonize with respect to size.

Suggested measure 5: Achieving a balanced industry mix is a principle guiding the development of the local economic structure (e.g. attracting businesses to locate, promoting young entrepreneurs).

Just like monocultures, economic structures that are unbalanced are more prone to distortions compared to a balanced mix. Where an industry faces a crisis, only individual companies will be affected rather than the entire local economy. Many regions in Austria have already become aware of the dangers of economic structures that are homogeneous regarding industry. Hence, municipalities that actively engage in inducing companies to locate in their areas pay attention to achieving an industry mix that is as broad as possible.

Suggested measure 6: If external influences (e.g. changes in the general economic conditions) threaten the existence of established companies, these are supported by the municipality.

As long as the entrepreneurs and the municipality maintain a dialogue, the needs of local enterprises can be considered. However, one-off measures such as the municipality granting a loan or placing an order with a local enterprise are limited by competition regulations and make sense only where changes in the business environment threaten businesses acutely. Where the local industries face lasting deterioration of their business environment, the municipality would be called upon to mitigate the negative social consequences of the structural change by establishing an alternative local business structure.

Suggested measure 7: Strengthening social cohesion within the municipality by creating meeting places (e.g. club rooms, reducing traffic on the village square).

Club rooms and premises compete with local inns. Therefore, the municipality should only make such facilities available to societies that do not directly compete with the local gastronomic venues. Wherever possible, the municipality should also strive to counteract a direct rivalry when it comes to supporting individual societies in their establishment of club premises. In such cases, the municipality should employ an active information policy and should subsidize club celebrations held at the local inns. Where a municipality has no inn, it does make sense for the municipality to actively participate in the establishment of a club room, which includes municipal funding. Generally, municipalities should see to it that the catering for club facilities is in the hands of local gastronomic venues.

Suggested measure 8: The municipality actively supports networking between individual groups within the population (e.g. Christmas markets, village fetes, sports celebrations).

Celebrations and other occasions that bring together the population of the municipality, and also those living in neighbouring municipalities, boost social cohesion in the local area. In addition, issues relevant to the development of the municipality and the region are discussed in an informal setting on such occasions. Views on concrete projects are compared, and possibilities for compromise are considered. Private conversations held in the course of such events also frequently lead to business cooperations. Other entrepreneurs report how their business is doing, which problems they are currently facing, and where they anticipate threats and opportunities for the future. An informal exchange of views and ideas facilitates identifying possible starting points for future cooperations. Most Austrian municipalities already engage in activities that bring together different groups of the population.

Suggested measure 9: It does not make a difference which group puts forward suggestions or initiatives; these are discussed and evaluated in an objective manner.

Party politics or personal dependence block the road to optimal decisions for the municipality or the local area as a whole, as they crowd out objective selection criteria. Suggestions that are viewed as motivated by party politics are not included in the portfolio of possible activities available for the purpose of ensuring a positive municipal development. Viewed holistically, this may lead to suboptimal decisions and, in turn, to suboptimal municipal development. Consequently, decision-making processes at the municipal level are to be designed in a manner that ensures an objective basis for decision-making. Where oppositional forces are seriously involved in the decision-making process, this will operate as a voluntary monitoring mechanism and will signal dedicated commitment to the cause. It is also predominantly the personality of the mayor that will determine whether the majority tolerates different views and is open to suggestions and initiatives put forward by other groups. What is relevant is the individual's willingness and capacity to enter into a dialogue, together with the conviction that the political process is about the welfare of the municipality.

Suggested measure 10: Concrete projects (e.g. inter-communal industrial zones, initiatives in tourism, infrastructural measures) are financed jointly with neighbouring municipalities.

Many aspects of municipal development are effective beyond the boundaries of the municipality. They concern the local area, some even the entire region. Even though coordinating one's behaviour with cooperation partners first of all amounts to losing autonomy, bundling resources enables municipalities to realize attractive new options and eventually increases their management scope. This reflects the general paradox of the cooperation phenomenon: renouncing some freedom will make resources available, which eventually leads to more freedom. In order to facilitate synergies from the activities of individual municipalities, it is necessary for the municipalities to coordinate at least their planning and implementation measures. However, as the useful implementation of numerous measures goes together with investments, which frequently exceed the financial capacity of individual municipalities, an inter-communal coordination of resources also appears appropriate. Nevertheless, Austrian municipalities only rarely finance projects jointly.

Suggested measure 11: Efforts to attract companies are coordinated with other municipalities in the region.

Currently, municipalities hardly ever cooperate with other municipalities when trying to attract businesses to locate in their area. As the municipalities receive communal taxes that are contingent on the number of jobs in the respective municipal territory, every municipality tries to induce businesses to locate within its own municipal area wherever possible. As long as municipal financing is organized according to this principle, it will be very difficult to advocate inter-communal locating efforts. In some Austrian provinces, federal subsidies and zoning plans were made contingent on the existence of inter-communal industrial zones. Apart from the problem of opportunism, inter-communal location initiatives would not only make sense for every municipality, but would also be advantageous from the perspective of the individual municipality and the local area as a whole.

Suggested measure 12: Municipal officials align the extension of infrastructure with the development plan for the municipality.

In Austria, decisions on superordinate traffic infrastructure rest with the pro-vincial or the federal government. Such decisions are not made on the muni-cipal level. Municipal officials can, therefore, only attempt to influence these decisions in an informal manner. This will be all the more successful the more such interventions have been coordinated within the local area. How-ever, the infrastructure on the municipal territory can also be influenced by the municipality. To a large extent, the success of a comprehensive strategy for municipal development will depend on whether the individual measure is aligned with the development objectives defined for the municipality.

Suggested measure 13: The municipality provides entrepreneurs willing to locate in the area with detailed information about location possibilities and costs.

As location decisions are characterized by high complexity, which accounts for fairly inaccurate prognoses, companies are forced to make such decisions under great uncertainty. Every reduction of the risk perceived by the company willing to locate in the area increases the attractiveness of a given munici-pality as a potential location for business. Measures intended to reduce per-ceived uncertainty include offers of property for construction at fixed prices or additional services provided by the municipality, such as consulting services on obtaining subsidies or on dealing with the authorities. However, this depends on the ownership of the property intended for the construction of business premises. The same applies to the municipality's capacity to provide entrepreneurs willing to locate in the area with detailed price information.

Only where the municipality already owns the property or has entered into appropriate option agreements for the property can it offer more detailed information to entrepreneurs.

Suggested measure 14: The municipality offers consulting services regarding dealings with the authorities (e.g. permits and approval procedures) and available subsidies to companies willing to locate in the area.

Beyond the measures intended to reduce uncertainty for companies willing to locate in the area that were outlined above, every municipality should be able to direct companies in need of information to other competent bodies. The expert network of the federal province, the chamber of commerce or specialist institutions, such as the Regionalmanagement or the regional innovation centres (RIZ), is already very closely knit in Austria. A contact person in the municipality responsible for businesses intending to locate in the area will further reduce uncertainty, as such a person signals competence and commitment.

Suggested measure 15: The image of a remote region serves to market products from this region as something special. These products fetch a price premium on the market compared to similar rival products.

In recent years, modern consumer behaviour has increasingly shaped a buyer segment that demands high-quality products with local origin. Municipalities and regions situated in geographically unfavourable areas can draw on this trend and position their products as antitheses to mass products. A characteristic of the municipality that had previously been perceived as a weakness can now be turned into a competitive advantage. Before a municipality can use this advantage, however, it must have created a unique image.

Suggested measure 16: The municipality actively ensures the availability of property for construction (e.g. by means of option agreements, the purchase of construction plots put up for sale, or property exchange) to safeguard affordability of premises for residential and business construction.

Younger individuals, in particular, are more willing to engage in new entrepreneurial activity or to take over and expand an existing business. The younger generation, backed by the achievements and experience of their parents' generation, is the force driving the local economic structure. Young entrepreneurs, in turn, need motivated employees capable of entrepreneurial thinking. Municipalities can only achieve a balanced age structure among their populations when they manage to keep young citizens in the municipality and/or to motivate young individuals to move there. Besides attractive jobs, one necessary prerequisite is the availability of housing at affordable prices. This can be effected either by means of models of securing property for construction or by social housing projects.

Suggested measure 17: The municipality actively communicates its particular qualities (e.g. by means of articles on municipality projects published in regional papers) and consequently has an authentic image also at the supraregional level.

One approach available to rural municipalities wishing to create competitive advantage lies in linking the dominant products and services provided by its local enterprises with regional identity. The customer or guest enjoys an overall experience where this effect is enhanced through integration of complementary products (e.g. food products and tourist services) and the local *Lebenswelt*. This marketing strategy facilitates augmenting the products with additional qualities that help the local offering stand out from rival products or services. A municipality can obtain clear market positioning and the corresponding competitive advantages, where it consistently pursues a strategy for municipal development that aims at the lasting establishment and effective, authentic communication of a regional identity and that is backed by the local business community. In recent years, almost all Austrian municipalities/regions have started positioning themselves on the market by specifically communicating certain characteristics and differentiating themselves from other municipalities/regions in the perception of the public. This measure aims to achieve a unique positioning as a location for production in the perception of customers.

Suggested measure 18: The mayor acts as facilitator who listens to the population, responds to suggestions, promotes initiatives and withdraws from ongoing projects in due time.

Municipalities that are well equipped for positive municipal development can fail because of their own mayor. At the same time, mayors can lead municipalities in very troublesome settings to a dynamic economic development. This is especially successful when it is possible to change the perception of the population and business community so that municipal characteristics that had previously been viewed as unfavourable are now seen as important resources. Very often, it is not so much what the mayor does, but what he does not do. Success factors include showing commitment and withdrawing at the right moment, initiating and facilitating without claiming the outcome for himself, as well as openness to new ideas and the tolerance involved in accepting contrary opinions and seriously submitting them to discussion procedures. A mayor who is open to suggestions from all members of a municipality and who keeps a clear holistic view on the development of the municipality is better suited to acting as a facilitator than somebody who only follows his own desires or those of one group. In the short term, this measure is contingent on the personal qualities of the respective mayor currently in office. Projected beyond the current term of legislature, the measure indicates a profile of a mayor's qualifications, which makes the measure transferable to all municipalities in the medium term.

Suggested measure 19: In the long term, all parts of the municipality are promoted equally in order to prevent envy and ill will.

To a large extent, the atmosphere in the municipality is a consequence of the strength of social cohesion. Close social ties create a positive general atmosphere among the population. Forming a relevant element of the quality of life, the general atmosphere in the municipality has an effect on the population's attitude towards migration, building a family and willingness to work, choice of occupation and setting up businesses. The general atmosphere in the municipality also depends on the ties that populations from different parts of the municipality maintain with each other. The municipality's investment policy is decisive for maintaining harmony among the individual parts of the municipality. In the short term, however, budget restrictions will make it almost impossible to make parallel investments in all parts of the municipality. In the longer term, measures of economic policy at the communal level need to be employed with a view to promoting individual parts of the municipality in a balanced way. A strong imbalance with regard to investments and funding entails the danger that envy and ill will will erode the social cohesion within the municipality. So far, an equal promotion of all parts of a given community in the long term has only rarely been realized in Austria.

Suggested measure 20: The municipality supports the formation of businesses in industries previously not established in order to be prepared for the future (e.g. start-up centres, cheap office space for young entrepreneurs).

Guided by the requirement of a broad mix of industries and business sizes, the municipality must consider which companies are set up or locate in the municipality when it promotes the location or incorporation of businesses. Not every additional business is equally suitable for the development of the local economic structure. In Austria, this requirement has hardly been considered so far. Where new industries are developed, the municipality should strive to coordinate the start-up initiatives with the existing local economic structure so that balance is maintained in the municipality. In particular, the effects that the businesses will have on the population of the municipality need to be considered. The promotion efforts should, therefore, be designed in such a way that projects that distort the "balance" within the municipality are prevented.

Suggested measure 21: Where an industrial zone is created, the municipality acts jointly with the neighbouring communities, and the location objectively most attractive is selected.

In the past few years, almost all municipalities have designated their own construction plots for business premises. Municipalities situated in favourable areas have done so with much success, those situated in unfavourable zones less so. Slowly, it is being acknowledged that not every geographic location manages to attract businesses – regardless of the direct and indirect financial support granted to companies willing to locate. As developing an industrial zone is associated with considerable costs, the public sector would save many resources if it were possible to establish industrial zones only in municipalities that represent promising locations. Inter-communal cooperation should enable the municipalities that do not dispose of an attractive location to participate in these industrial zones. This also entails the positive effect of spreading risk for those municipalities that represent attractive locations. Not only can such a measure be implemented in all municipalities, rather, it must be implemented so that this policy can develop a lasting effect. As inter-communal industrial zones frequently fail owing to the parish-pump politics of individual municipal officials, the superior level is called upon to install an incentive system. For instance, municipalities can only obtain funds for creating industrial zones where these are established jointly by several municipalities.

Suggested measure 22: Establishing a productive local economic sector includes the possibilities for tourism available in the municipality/region.

Already today, many municipalities are adept at identifying and specifically utilizing the existing potential for tourism in the municipality or region, respectively. Moreover, a functioning network of municipal cooperations in tourism has developed in recent years. Numerous supraregional tourism projects, such as theme routes or regions jointly marketing their specialities, have been implemented and have strengthened the respective local economy. Inter-communal associations of municipalities that also integrate several industries are especially effective (e.g. cooperations between agricultural and commercial enterprises).

Suggested measure 23: Tourism is not developed separately in the municipality, but in close coordination with the municipalities of the region.

Organizational structures in tourism are increasingly being determined by attractions and potential shared by municipalities rather than by politically defined boundaries. Thinking in terms of regions encourages the development of tourism initiatives that range across different municipalities. Thinking beyond the administrative boundaries of a municipality can be established in any municipality and is especially important in the context of tourism, because the guest does not visit the individual municipality, but the region as a whole.

Suggested measure 24: In municipalities that are poorly connected to transport infrastructure, the development concept is oriented towards those businesses that do not require efficient transport routes (e.g. call centres, telework).

The services sector is increasingly crowding out the manufacturing sector. This structural change is particularly noticeable in rural municipalities. In order to enable these municipalities to participate in the rise of the third sector and in this way to compensate for the loss of jobs, a communication infrastructure required by service enterprises (e.g. broadband internet, wireless network) needs to be established. In general, the unfavourable locations of many rural municipalities are less relevant in connection with business models that do not rely on conventional logistics or personal contact with customers.

Suggested measure 25: The municipality positions itself as a tourist destination by establishing a common theme under which its activities are offered and by integrating its efforts into a comprehensive concept (e.g. theme paths, brand).

Both the existing infrastructure and the capabilities and skills of the residents provide useful starting points for identifying possible perspectives for municipal development. A development strategy that builds on what is already established and accords with the way the residents live can be implemented with fewer resources and is more conducive to initiating sustainable economic development than an isolated project. Existing facilities (e.g. municipal museum) need to be adapted in accordance with the tourism perspective (e.g. conversion into a theme park) and integrated into an overall concept. In this context, it needs to be considered that, whenever possible, tourist facilities should be usable all year round.

Suggested measure 26: The municipality has a club house shared by several clubs and associations.

This measure facilitates improved communication and in this way strengthens the cohesion among the individual clubs and associations. By the same token, it promotes mutual assistance (e.g. at functions and events) and reduces costs for both the municipality and the individual club or association. This measure also promotes networking and social cohesion among the residents. It is especially advantageous if such club houses are established by means of contributions from the individual club members because this increases lasting identification with the project, the clubs and associations, and ultimately with the municipality.

Suggested measure 27: Club houses are only supported where no local inns exist.

This measure prevents town centres becoming desolate. In order to be able to offer the clubs and associations meeting points throughout the entire year, the municipality is to ensure that inn-keepers coordinate their opening and closing times among each other.

Suggested measure 28: In order to free town centres, businesses that generate high emissions are relocated to the outskirts or to industrial zones.

Relocating to an industrial zone situated outside the town centre generates high costs for businesses. These businesses will not be prepared to bear these costs alone. For this reason, it appears necessary to reimburse the businesses for the direct and indirect relocation costs. However, the budgets of rural municipalities are too small, which is why this measure can hardly be applied directly. Nevertheless, the municipality should see to it that businesses that expand or new companies that wish to locate in the municipality choose sites in suitable industrial zones rather than in the town centre. In this way, it becomes possible to establish separate residential areas and industrial zones in the long term.

Suggested measure 29: In order to free the town centre from heavy traffic, a bypass is or has already been established.

Contrary to the misgivings that reduced frequency would negatively affect the sales of shops located in the town centre, which were voiced in many rural municipalities prior to the establishment of a bypass, the calm and quiet has created a pleasant atmosphere in the municipal centre in most of the cases. Frequently, the establishment of the bypass marked the beginning of efforts to redesign the village. Subsequently, the town centre, which had been freed from traffic and other disturbances (e.g. noise, harmful substances), served as a centre of communication. In many municipalities, industrial areas well connected to transport routes were developed on the other side of the bypass without impairment to the quality of life for the municipal citizens.

Suggested measure 30: Appropriate childcare is provided so that already existing companies or new businesses willing to locate in the municipality can be offered sufficient labour supply from the municipality.

Owing to the long commuting distances, especially in rural areas, it is frequently difficult for working parents to have their needs for child care exclusively covered by their respective families. In rural areas, in particular, facilities that provide all-day child care are insufficient, which is why many parents (predominantly women) relinquish their participation in gainful employment. If sufficient day-care facilities for children are offered, the rate at which women participate in the labour force can be considerably increased and, thus, the potential labour supply can be augmented.

Suggested measure 31: The municipality encourages the local and regional businesses to form networks (e.g. organizing information events, personal discussions or appearances at trade fairs).

Establishing networks among businesses encourages the exchange of information and the coordination of the activities undertaken by the individual businesses. If businesses are mutually informed about the steps other businesses are planning to take, they can anticipate these when defining their own strategy. This raises the clout, and by the same token the probability of success, of the regional business sector.

3.2 Second step in the selection process – quantitative survey

Mayors of rural municipalities in the target countries were interviewed by means of a large survey by questionnaire. The survey pursued two objectives: firstly, to approach the field of study for the purpose of preparing the qualitative survey, and, secondly, to arrive at an empirically substantiated selection of measures that were to be evaluated with a view to their transferability to other geographic contexts.

3.2.1 Key data of the survey by questionnaire

In the spring of 2007, the Institute for Small Business Management and Entrepreneurship at the Vienna University of Economics and Business conducted a survey by questionnaire among the mayors of rural municipalities located in the Czech Republic, Slovakia, Hungary and Slovenia, respectively. The questionnaires and the cover letter were translated into the respective national languages. The sample size was 1,710 municipalities. The sample comprised 210 Slovenian (full count), 500 Czech (random sample, universe 6,244), 500 Slovakian (random sample, universe 2,891) and 500 Hungarian (random sample, universe 3,154) municipalities.

No measures were taken to enhance response. Nevertheless, 211 questionnaires were available for analysis. This corresponds to a response rate of 12.3 per cent.

3.2.2 Description of the municipalities that participated in the survey

The municipalities in the Czech sample mostly consist in only one district and on average have 425 inhabitants on a territory of 6.5 square kilometres. On average, the municipalities surveyed house four business enterprises and approximately forty places of employment. The three most important industries are agriculture and forestry, construction and trade. In the Czech municipalities surveyed, the largest local business enterprise on average employs 20 persons, the second largest 12 and the third largest 9. As much as 22 per cent of the residents of the municipalities surveyed are under 20 years old; almost 58 per cent are aged between 20 and 60; and the remaining 20 per cent are older than 60.

The Slovak sample comprises municipalities that on average have two districts, 906 inhabitants and a territory of almost 21 square kilometres. In the municipalities surveyed, on average there are six business enterprises with approximately 162 places of employment. The three most important industries are agriculture and forestry, wood processing and commerce. In the Slovak municipalities surveyed, the largest local business enterprise on average employs 66 persons, the second largest 24 and the third largest 20. Almost 24 per cent of the inhabitants in the Slovak municipalities surveyed are under 20 years old; 52 per cent are aged between 20 and 60; and the remaining 24 per cent are older than 60.

On average, the municipalities in the Hungarian sample have two districts, roughly 2,000 inhabitants and a territory of 27 square kilometres. The municipalities surveyed on average house 12 business enterprises and 107 places of employment. The three most important industries are agriculture and forestry, wood processing and personal services. In the Hungarian municipalities surveyed, the largest local business enterprise on average employs 60 individuals, the second largest 32 and the third largest 20. In the municipalities surveyed, approximately 23 per cent of the residents are under 20 years old; 56 per cent are aged between 20 and 60; and the remaining 21 per cent are over 60.

In the Slovenian sample, the municipalities on average have 18 districts, more than 5,300 residents and a territory of almost 90 square kilometres. On average, the municipalities surveyed house 125 business enterprises with approximately 1,000 places of employment. The three most important industries are agriculture and forestry, construction and tourism. In the Slovak municipalities surveyed, the largest local business enterprise on average employs 268 individuals, the second largest 207 and the third largest 147. In the municipalities surveyed, approximately 21 per cent of the residents are under 20 years old; 58 per cent are aged 20 to 60; and the remaining 21 per cent are over 60.

Moreover, the survey assessed the infrastructure available in the individual municipalities. The results for all four country samples are summarized in Table 3.1.

Table 3.1 Overview of infrastructure available in the municipalities surveyed (in per cent)

Facility	Czech Republic	Slovakia	Hungary	Slovenia
elementary school	50	53	26	100
Hauptschule (secondary compulsory school)	28	0	97	13
kindergarten	69	68	100	100
Höhere Schule (secondary school with university entrance qualification)	8	0	0	9
music school	11	7	13	43
retirement home	11	76	32	26
parish	44	85	77	100
post office	53	50	100	100
police	11	9	39	26
fire brigade	75	40	13	96
sports ground	89	81	97	7
event hall	97	38	90	96
swimming pool	33	74	0	30
hiking path	78	59	52	91
neighbourhood shops	81	97	100	100
railway connection	36	19	41	48
motorway connection	19	7	16	57
bus connection	94	100	100	96
inn	89	87	71	100
clubs and associations	89	69	87	87
industrial zone	28	24	55	96

3.2.3 *Results of the survey by questionnaire*

In the analysis of the questionnaires, first the number of positive responses to the individual items (suggested measures) was added up for the topics "responsible for implementing the measure", "measure is applied" and "measure would be applicable", respectively. The sums corresponding to the individual items were subsequently sorted in ascending order and each item was assigned a rank (from 1 to 31). After this step had been completed, the topics were weighted, with the topic "responsible for implementing the measure" being assigned the factor three, the topic "measure is applied" the factor two, and "measure would be applicable" the factor one. After the weighted rank scores had been added up, the sums were again sorted in ascending order. This was performed for all four countries. The results of these analyses per country are reported in columns two to five in Table 3.2.

In the next step, the results per country were consolidated into an overall ranking. The three sections of the overall ranking were drawn up according to the criteria (1) perceived responsibility, (2) assessment of viability and (3) assessment of the degree to which a measure has already been realized.

Against the backdrop of the experience gathered in the expert workshop and the study in Austria, four especially interesting measures were selected from each of the three defined sections. These selected measures are shaded in dark in Table 3.2 and address the following issues:

- strengthening social cohesion by creating meeting places
- democratic and pluralist decision-making processes
- integrating the individual measures into a comprehensive development concept of the municipality
- consulting services provided for businesses willing to locate in the municipality
- resolving conflicting goals of municipal development through involvement of all interest groups
- actively securing land for construction
- joint financing of inter-communal projects
- inter-communal coordination of efforts to attract new companies
- communication policy and creating a supraregional image
- promoting new businesses in industries previously not well established
- competitive products by virtue of local origin
- freeing town centres by relocating businesses that generate high emissions

This list comprises measures of economic policy at the municipal level that are conducive to providing favourable conditions for small and medium enterprises. Moreover, these measures have been successful in Austria and basically can be transferred to other municipalities as well. Consequently, the list represents a selection that covers the entire spectrum of measures and of probabilities with which these will be implemented successfully in the target municipalities in the Czech Republic, Slovakia, Hungary and Slovenia.

Table 3.2 Selection of measures

Suggested measure	Ranking of measures according to relevance for the municipalities surveyed				
	CZ	SLO	HU	SK	Overall
Section 1					
Creating meeting places (e.g. club rooms, reducing traffic on the village square) strengthens social cohesion within the municipality.	4	7	4	12	1
The municipality actively supports networking between individual groups within the population (e.g. Christmas markets, village fetes, sports celebrations).	3	1	3	24	2
The municipality provides entrepreneurs willing to locate in the area with detailed information about location possibilities and costs.	10	13	6	11	3
In the long term, all parts of the municipality are promoted equally in order to prevent envy and ill will.	7	4	2	29	4
Population and businesses are actively integrated in the process of municipal development.	1	3	9	30	5
The mayor acts as facilitator who listens to the population, responds to suggestions, promotes initiatives and withdraws from ongoing projects in due time.	2	2	19	20	6
No matter which group puts forward suggestions or initiatives: these are discussed and evaluated in an objective manner.	5	5	8	28	7
Municipal officials align the extension of infrastructure with the development plan for the municipality.	8	6	7	25	8
Tourism is not developed separately in the municipality, but in close coordination with the municipalities of the region.	6	11	14	18	9
The individual municipal activities form part of a comprehensive development concept.	11	8	1	31	10
The municipality offers consulting on dealings with the authorities (e.g. permits and approval procedures) and on available subsidies to companies willing to locate in the area.	17	10	18	9	11

Table 3.2 (continued)

Suggested measure	Ranking of measures according to relevance for the municipalities surveyed				
	CZ	SLO	HU	SK	Overall
Section 2					
Appropriate child care is provided so that already existing companies or new businesses willing to locate in the municipality can be offered sufficient labour supply from the municipality.	15	17	21	6	12
Involving all interest groups of the municipality leads to identifying conflicting objectives already at the stage of strategy definition and to the development of possible solutions.	14	16	10	23	13
The municipality actively ensures the availability of property for construction (e.g. by means of option agreements, the purchase of construction plots put up for sale, or property exchange) to safeguard affordability of premises for residential and business construction.	9	12	16	26	14
Concrete projects (e.g. inter-communal industrial zones, initiatives in tourism, infrastructural measures) are financed jointly with the neighbouring municipalities.	12	18	12	22	15
Where an industrial zone is created, the municipality acts jointly with the neighbouring municipalities, and the location objectively most attractive is selected.	20	24	13	7	16
The municipality encourages the local and regional businesses to form networks (e.g. information events, in personal discussions or appearances at trade fairs/functions).	19	21	5	19	17
The municipality actively communicates its particular qualities (e.g. by means of articles on municipality projects published in regional papers) and consequently has created an authentic image also at the supraregional level.	16	9	26	15	18
In municipalities which are poorly connected to transport infrastructure, the development concept is oriented towards those businesses that do not require efficient transport routes (e.g. call centres).	27	23	17	2	19
Achieving a balanced structure in terms of business size is a principle guiding the development of the local economic structure (e.g. attracting businesses to locate, promoting young entrepreneurs).	30	20	15	8	20

Table 3.2 (continued)

Suggested measure	Ranking of measures according to relevance for the municipalities surveyed				
	CZ	SLO	HU	SK	Overall
Section 3					
Establishing a productive local economic sector includes the possibilities for tourism available in the municipality/region.	13	15	24	21	21
If external influences (e.g. changes in the general economic conditions) threaten the existence of established companies, these are supported by the municipality.	26	31	11	10	22
Achieving a balanced industry mix is a principle guiding the development of the local economic structure (e.g. attracting businesses to locate, promoting young entrepreneurs).	25	26	23	5	23
The municipality supports the formation of businesses in industries previously not well established in order to be prepared for the future (e.g. start-up centres, cheap office space for young entrepreneurs).	18	22	25	16	24
Club houses are only supported where no local inns exist in a municipality.	31	27	22	1	25
Efforts to attract companies are coordinated with other municipalities in the region.	23	25	31	4	26
The image of a remote region serves to market products from this region as something special. These products fetch a price premium on the market compared to similar rival products.	24	29	27	3	27
The municipality positions itself as tourist destination by establishing a common theme under which its activities are offered and by integrating its efforts into a comprehensive concept (e.g. theme paths, brand).	21	19	30	17	28
In order to free town centres, businesses that generate high emissions are relocated to the outskirts or to industrial zones.	28	28	20	14	29
In order to free the town centre from heavy traffic, a bypass is or has already been established.	22	30	28	13	30
The municipality has established a club house shared by several clubs and associations.	29	14	29	27	31

It does not represent an exhaustive enumeration of those measures that would be transferable, but rather a selection of those measures the transferability of which those concerned consider particularly important. Contrary to expectations, those concerned did not mention issues that are currently being discussed, such as public–private partnerships or forming cooperatives for the purpose of completing municipal tasks.

The transferability of the measures selected is examined in exemplary municipalities in the qualitative study described in the next chapter.

4 The evaluation of the transferability of the proposed agenda

4.1 Design of the study

The present study analyses the transferability of the measures outlined above to Austria's Central and Eastern European neighbouring countries by means of qualitative methods of empirical research on the basis of a selection of local areas. In this context, local area denotes a municipality together with its relations with neighbouring municipalities. This leads to a particular local area being viewed differently by each given municipality, which makes a rigid definition of local areas impossible. Local areas, in turn, form part of a region.

Selecting the cases surveyed according to specified rules represents an important criterion for the soundness of qualitative research. For this purpose, the selection procedure comprised several stages.

The study focuses on local areas in rural settings. Consequently, only such regions in the respective countries surveyed that are to be rated as rural according to the OECD definition were considered (OECD 1993: 13, OECD 1995: 15). Ten local areas were analysed.

The number of local areas to be examined per country surveyed was determined in proportion to the size of the national territories of the eligible countries. Moreover, each country was to be represented by at least two local areas. Consequently, three Czech and three Hungarian local areas were examined together with two Slovak and two Slovenian local areas. In order to consider the influences of different regulations at the regional administrative level, the concrete local areas selected all had to correspond to a different NUTS II level in the individual countries surveyed. As Slovenia only consists of one region according to this level of classification, in this case, national administrative units were taken as a basis. Moreover, the effect of the distance of each local area surveyed from the Austrian border was to be controlled for. Therefore, the cases for analysis were selected in such a manner that, in each country surveyed, at least one local area is situated close to the Austrian border, and at least one other local area is situated further away.

Based on this specification, the concrete local areas were selected for analysis together with experts from the individual countries. In order to ensure that the findings generated could be generalized to as large an extent as possible, the local areas selected had to be typical of their respective NUTS II region, in particular with regard to their demographic and economic parameters. Moreover, the local areas selected were to be as similar as possible to other local areas in the same region regarding qualitative criteria, such as the historical development and the social situation.

In accordance with the holistic perspective developed at the beginning, within the local areas, the research questions were explored with a view to capturing the perspectives of different agents at diverse administrative levels and different aspects of their outlook on the world. The intention was to reveal the sensemaking structures that underlie the individual statements gathered. For this purpose, opposing views were to be gathered to as large an extent as possible and what is happening in the municipalities surveyed was to be interpreted. Accordingly, the actors interviewed in each case included at least the mayor, one municipal councillor representing the strongest oppositional group, one entrepreneur, as well as one representative of the institution in charge of regional development at the inter-communal or regional level.

The data were gathered by means of primary research. The problem-centred interviews were conducted in the respective national language. The research instrument was an interview guide including the 12 suggested measures selected previously. In total, interviews with an overall duration of 3,812 minutes were held with 61 interview partners, which resulted in a transcript comprising 1,142 pages.

The transcripts of the interviews captured on audio recordings were subjected to a content analysis. In order to limit distorted perception, the interpretation was effected four times and at two levels. On the first level, the interviews were interpreted separately by the interviewers themselves, by qualified students of the specialist business administration master programme on SME-Management and Entrepreneurship at the Vienna University of Economics and Business working in groups in the course of a seminar, and by the authors, respectively. Subsequently, at the second level (interpretation of the interpretations), these three interpretations were integrated into a final interpretation in a process of discourse. In the case of discrepancies of interpretations, a feedback loop was introduced.

This process of interpretation led to discussions of the suggested measures against the backdrop of the municipalities selected. Following the enumeration of several typical statements from the interviews, in the following section, the discussions will be presented according to the country surveyed. All twelve measures suggested will be analysed from the perspective of the research questions in the respective contexts of the three Czech, two Slovak, three Hungarian and two Slovenian municipalities.

4.2 For starters: statements from the interviews

"In my opinion, meeting places by themselves do not have a significant effect on the development of the municipality."

"In the municipality, we have two kinds of citizens: those that live here and those that only have their home address here. If the number of those that only have their home address here exceeds the number of those that live here, this marks the beginning of the end of the municipality."

"The public internet access draws many young people to the 'house of culture', as they cannot access the internet from their homes."

"On the weekend, after mass, the men of the village go to the inn and discuss the incidents of the previous week."

"The rigidly organized youth associations abruptly vanished at the time of the turnaround. Formerly, this all somewhat reeked of coercion. Nowadays, the young people come together casually in the youth club."

"The young think differently from the old. The village community should give the young their chance, the old ones can be safely written off."

"One misses space for young people. Formerly, there was enough, now there is no room for them any more."

POLITICS

"As mayor, I also take the opposition seriously. When they have a good idea, I support it, because every good idea should be realized."

"A mayor told me that he does not like to see a large discount supermarket being constructed in his municipality. He'd rather promote smaller shops in the town centre instead. But he fears that the supermarket may move to the neighbouring municipality then and that his residents will punish him for it."

"If an investor turns up somewhere in a municipality, the mayor will grab him with both hands. If he releases him, he will not be re-elected because he has failed to create new jobs."

"Resistance from the population brought the plans of a large company to move to the municipality to nothing, because the pros and cons were not openly discussed with the residents."

"The older decision-makers have forgotten to delegate leadership responsibility to the young. There are the 50- to 60-year-old municipal representatives, but no 20- to 30-year-olds."

"I don't attend municipal assemblies. Mostly, it does not concern me anyway and I cannot influence anything. Let them do what they believe – and that's that."

"I don't know how these decisions are made. That they are discussed is clear, but what happens exactly I wouldn't know, as I have not been to an assembly for more than ten years already."

"There are no coalition contracts put down in writing. Everything is agreed orally."

"Democracy has its limits somewhere. Once a matter has been decided, one cannot ask time and again if somebody has changed their mind."

"If you ask a citizen from this municipality today, he will not even know what happens in our municipality, let alone what's going on in the neighbouring municipality."

"I think that in the future there will not be a full-time mayor in every little municipality. I also dare say that it is unnecessary that in a small municipality mayor and staff are present every day so that two citizens a day can complete their business. This is a luxury that the country cannot afford any more. Instead, there will be one main mayor and one deputy mayor in the local area."

"Formally, the municipal council is the highest decision-making institution. In reality, however, it is the mayor who has the leading role."

"First, they don't want to hear anything about a project. I have advertised it again and again. Later, when they see it in the media, they would like to be part of it."

BUSINESS COMMUNITY

"There are no start-up entrepreneurs who do not know who to turn to with their questions. Those that don't know anything about it do not get started in the first place."

"I think that new companies are established spontaneously. We as a municipality cannot do anything to influence that one way or the other."

"We entrepreneurs do not ask anything of the municipality, and the municipality does not ask anything of us. There is no reason why we should communicate with them."

"Once we had the first cinema in the region, the first public pool and telephone. We have become somewhat lazy since then."

"For three years, we have been working on expanding the industrial zone and integrating an investor. The municipal councillors support the project by maintaining secrecy about it. Confidentiality is very important nowadays; an indiscretion can upset the project even when it is close to its implementation."

"In the small residential estates, future technologies at best take the form of a garage door operated by remote control."

"Instead of talking about problems, nowadays the revenue authority arrives by helicopter and you are immediately fined if a friend helps you harvest the crops."

"The entrepreneurs pay their taxes here, so I as the mayor feel obliged to award them municipal contracts."

"I have often witnessed that the municipality has not awarded a contract to the local entrepreneurs for personal reasons."

"Two years ago, we were approached by a young man who wanted to establish a small business and had not been able to obtain a site in the neighbouring industrial zone for years. We got into my car and I showed him a piece of land at the outskirts of the town. Two days later, the contract had been concluded. The hall has already been erected."

"Healthy competition for attracting companies among the municipalities is only positive. Let them communicate the advantages of their locations!"

"When a large investor turns up in the municipality, the mayor personally takes charge of the matter and assists him in every way. But no municipal official can be bothered to lift a finger for an entrepreneur that wants to establish a small business."

TOURISM

"Tourism is no business. This is definitely not a way to get rich."

"As we are in such a remote location, knowledge and traditions that have long been lost elsewhere have persisted here. In the information age, such locations are extremely interesting, because what is more beautiful than living in nature and working creatively."

"Many municipalities do not even know what they have to offer in terms of tourist attractions. When I as a city person go there, I see natural and cultural treasures that they themselves do not see because they are used to them."

"We are no tourism municipality, but just a destination for excursions."

"Many municipalities imitate something that already exists somewhere else in a much more original form."

INTER-COMMUNAL COOPERATION

"The neighbouring municipalities have schools with a handful of pupils. I have suggested that we pool our resources. But that doesn't work. A mayor who closes down a school is not re-elected."

"Attracting companies jointly? The time when municipalities consider such activities has not come yet."

"I am critical of municipal cooperation. I am not keen on managing other municipalities and having to solve their problems."

"In the local area, cycling paths have been established, but these do not intersect at the individual municipal borders."

"The zoning plans of the individual municipalities are developed strictly independently. On the one side, you will then find an industrial zone, on the other side, one and a half metres away, a housing estate."

"Apparently, people only come to appreciate the problems of others once they have reached a certain development stage. Until then, you can only make them cooperate using 'force' or financial incentives."

"Now that a regional association of schools has been established, cooperation has improved. Such small hamlets need to stick together after all."

"As long as it's only about discussing shared visions for the future, it works beautifully. As soon as the whole thing is to be agreed, the contrasts reappear all of a sudden."

"There is no long-standing tradition of cooperation here. In the past, when two municipalities wanted to do something for themselves together, the central government got scared that there might be dissenters at work."

"The small municipalities cooperate when it is about environmental protection or education. I could not name a single example that addresses the domain of economic development. In this respect, the municipalities see each other as competitors, not as partners."

COMMUNICATION

"Every month, I get the village paper from the mayor of the neighbouring municipality. That's as colourful and huge as the New York Times. It always reports what is happening in the municipalities of the local area owing to the LEADER programme."

"We have developed a programme for the municipality. In our latest workshop, suddenly a gentleman rises and argues that something has not been considered. It was the same measure, only put differently. We do not understand each other any longer, because we do not communicate any more."

TRANSFORMATION

"One cannot blame the people for not showing any initiative of their own. They have lived in a certain way for 40 years. For 40 years, the rule applied: whoever exposes themselves will be destroyed."

"An internet room was established for young people. But the people have not yet come to appreciate the public property, so these computers were damaged. They don't care about what's going to happen tomorrow."

"In the past, there were large factories in the region. Like everywhere else, these have now been privatized more or less and have made workers redundant. We need to compensate for that with smaller businesses."

"Today, many citizens are not even willing to mow the lawn in front of their own houses. In the past 40 years, they were accustomed to services simply being provided. Now this does not work like that any more. One has to educate them so that they redevelop more initiative of their own."

"We have already come so far that the municipality has its own homepage. But not that far that this is also regularly updated."

"Somehow, it is not in our mentality that we are proud of our own products. If something comes from abroad, we are completely fascinated."

"In the past, the municipalities were units of bureaucratic administration, now they are also asked to perform development functions. The municipalities are still learning, but we are making progress."

"No, I'm no optimist; this is still going to take a long time."

INFRASTRUCTURE

"Just like many others, we have no school in our municipality any more. For lack of funds. Yes, it is true that there are too few pupils here. But then, when is a municipality attractive to families with children? When the surroundings are lively and the municipality is worth living in. Without school and infrastructure, the young move away."

"Those people that are forced to go home through the mud find it hard to understand why there are already paved streets in the neighbouring village. The mayors should have a fundamental interest in ensuring that every citizen has a paved street and is connected to the sewer system and has cable TV and access to the internet."

REGION

"Frequently, entrepreneurs play the municipalities against each other. Finally, the municipality offering the highest tax relief is selected from among 20 locations."

"The companies that pollute the environment are ultimately always located where they generate least attention and least resistance. There will always be a few small municipalities where the location can be arranged."

"Slowly, also here the time is coming when demand for regional products increases. Already now many consumers are afraid of the meat offered cheaply by the discount store, when you don't know where it comes from."

"Good communication would finally show the people that domestic products are a hundred times better than imported goods. The tomatoes from Spain have as little taste in December as they had in August. With our ignorance we are killing our own agricultural producers."

"There are many who have turned crazy for 'organically grown' stuff and buy everything only because it features a label that says 'organic'. It is not questioned whether this really is organic after all, they do that for reasons of fashion. So whoever is clever is trying to ride with this trend."

"We live from one day to the next, we buy the cheapest food products and later pay three times as much for the doctor."

"Sometimes, you get the impression that the old state control is still determining the way people think. Of late, the state has made decisions like municipality A gets a school, municipality B 200 metres of pavement.

The things are distributed like Christmas presents and this is why mutual envy is returning."

"I see the LEADER programme as a strong catalyst of rural development."

"These regional development agencies contribute a lot to realizing locations of new companies. The municipalities need to pull their weight more."

STRATEGIC MUNICIPAL DEVELOPMENT

"The municipality advertises itself to new companies, but fails to consider the needs of the population and of the local companies."

"Today, it is very fashionable in municipalities to develop ten-year plans, which I find very bizarre. We have had this already in the past. Frequently, you do not know what is going to happen tomorrow, never mind what will happen in five or ten years' time."

"If a municipality applies for support from the EU fund, it needs a development plan. This accounts for 75 per cent of the reasons why such a plan is drawn up."

"I could not argue that the residents involve themselves very strongly in the development of the municipality. They always expect the municipality to provide solutions."

"If somebody has an idea or shows initiative, it is up to the mayor to act on this. When the proposals are ignored repeatedly, then the population will lose interest in getting involved in the future."

"If the municipality carries out initiatives on its own, they come to nothing. The entire community must be interested in it and must work on a concrete project."

"If we beautify our municipality – put the squares in order, improve the condition of the old buildings – then I hope that settling down here will become attractive again and we will find prospects for our construction plots."

"So far, the municipalities have relied on the exceptional competitive advantage that nature has given them, so that it is not seriously considered what could be offered in addition to that."

"Measures to be prepared for the future? In this context, I have my doubts whether anybody knows what the future should look like in this country."

"In this budget situation, talking about foresighted economic policy sounds ridiculous. I fill one hole by opening up another."

"My experience tells me that development plans are usually limited to promises in election times and rarely intend to fulfil these."

"The municipalities do not develop strategies unless they are forced to do so."

"Experts and specialists should increasingly work in the municipalities. The mayor has little time, because his office hours are taken up by trivia."

SECURING LAND FOR CONSTRUCTION

"There are many young adults who are forced to continue to live with their parents because they cannot afford a place of their own as the prices of land have risen owing to foreign private investment."

"A few years ago, foreigners bought houses here. Now many try to sell again because they have come to the conclusion that the municipality is too remote and it would be plain luxury to maintain a house that they use three weeks per year."

"When an Englishwoman bought a plot, the mayor was afraid that domestic property would be sold out. But she is a European citizen. We are part of Europe and could also buy property in England – if we had the money."

"The problem is that zoning is not regulated. Even if somebody possessed capital, he would not obtain a construction permit."

"Many municipalities in the region have designated an industrial zone, and many of these are vacant nowadays. It is not enough to designate an industrial zone, one also has to arrange for the appropriate infrastructure. This is not coordinated at all."

4.3 Analysis of the sample municipalities

4.3.1 The municipality located in the southwest of the Czech Republic

The municipality of medium size located in the southwest of the Czech Republic was first mentioned in records in the fourteenth century. However, numerous archaeological finds in its surroundings suggest that settlements in the area date back much longer. The municipality benefits from its favourable geographic location in two ways: on the one hand, it is situated not far from the border with Germany and, on the other hand, a national park known and popular beyond the region is situated in its immediate surroundings. Consequently, substantial foreign investment in the tourism infrastructure on the municipal territory had already been made soon after the turnaround of 1989. This is manifested in the freshly renovated buildings and hotels visible in the municipality today.

4.3.1.1 Strengthening social cohesion by creating meeting places

SITUATION

Few clubs and societies exist in the municipality surveyed. The most important societies include the Feuerwehrverein and the village renewal society. The latter represents a pool for active and oppositional citizens of the municipality. In the most recent elections, this group obtained one seat in the municipal council. Despite the efforts of the active municipal citizens, there is still a dearth of venues for social activities in the municipality.

A recreational centre, which was established through an initiative by the oppositional group, represents the location most suited to serve as a social meeting point for all inhabitants of the municipality. It can be used free of charge. The premises were made available by the municipality, but it is up to the population to maintain its operation.

The elected municipal officials do not actively support municipal life. It is exclusively the commitment of individual active citizens of the municipality that determines the development and organization of ideas that would help the social cohesion within the municipality. In this way, activities are financed by the municipal citizens' own funds, funding provided by the regional development agency and municipal funds. Municipal citizens who initiate ideas generally prefer to approach the regional development agency directly and, as far as possible, avoid turning to the municipality.

Apart from the few active citizens, the population of the community – and the older generation in particular – can hardly be motivated to participate in local events.

EVALUATION AND NEED FOR ACTION

The municipality surveyed only partially acknowledges that creating meeting places serves to strengthen social cohesion, which will eventually be beneficial to a successful development of municipalities in the long term. There is little initiative on the communal level, and meeting places are few and far between. Initiatives are largely due to the village renewal society, which is strongly anchored in the population of the municipality. The mayor cares little about issues of social cohesion. In addition to this passivity, the municipal authorities only (co)finance initiatives launched by others in a limited way. Consequently, the population does not view the municipality as the first contact when it comes to realizing ideas, but rather chooses to approach the agency for regional development or bears the costs on its own.

The political group of the mayor is faced with a vicious circle of its own making: Reservations on the part of the municipality are the reason why the municipal representatives are viewed negatively by the population, which, in turn, results in the municipal leaders being involved in the cultural and social initiatives even less. For the long-term welfare of the municipality, it is necessary to curb this progressive alienation of the population from the municipal leadership and to reverse the process. For this purpose, activity on the part of the municipal representatives should be increased. However, the municipality will only become active when it becomes possible to make the mayor aware of the importance of social cohesion for obtaining other municipal objectives, including financial targets. In the municipality surveyed, it is necessary not only for the vicious circle described above to be recognized, but also for the authorities to be made aware that this relationship represents a problem.

Once the educational work bears fruit, which corresponds to establishing the importance of meeting places with the political leadership, further meeting places should be created and active measures should be designed to motivate the passive groups in the population (especially the older inhabitants of the municipality) to participate in municipal life in a lively way.

4.3.1.2 Democratic and pluralist decision-making processes

SITUATION

According to the mayor, meetings with the interest groups in the municipality are held on a regular basis. It needs to be added, though, that the individual groups differ according to the strength of influence they exercise on the political process in the municipality. In this municipality, the decisions proper are made in an authoritative manner and with the general public being excluded. Although on all issues differing opinions are also heard, they are not considered in the decision-making process. Discussions primarily serve to keep up the appearance of democratic leadership and to prevent the strong centralism from being exposed too openly.

Where something is agreed jointly, with the grass roots being seriously involved in the process, it predominantly consists of initiatives launched by the population or by the opposition, which is close to the population (e.g. village renewal society). It is mostly cultural activities, which do not appear to counter the primary interests of the political majority in the municipality and are therefore approved, and in some cases also supported, by the leaders.

EVALUATION AND NEED FOR ACTION

The political life in the municipality surveyed is dominated by centralist decision-making processes. Only in a few cases are interest groups consulted on specific issues, and their influence on the actual decision can be viewed as rather limited. Pluralism of decision-making does not exist.

The mayor does not see why he should share with others the power that he has obtained through democratic elections, after all. If the measure of democratic or pluralist decision-making processes is to be established in the municipality, the decision-makers first of all need to be made aware of the importance of this measure for the development of the municipality in the medium to long term. Building on this awareness, various measures intended to strengthen pluralism can be institutionalized in the municipality. These include, for instance, round tables held at regular intervals, official office hours of the mayor and a clearly perceived consideration of the population in the development of a municipal strategy (which does not exist at present).

4.3.1.3 Integrating the individual measures into a comprehensive development concept of the municipality

SITUATION

Basically, municipalities should have a strategic development plan. However, the law only determines in very general terms what this plan must look like. It is therefore not likely that a municipality that cannot produce such a plan will be sanctioned for this omission. Fundamentally, drawing up a consistent development plan is motivated by the requirement that such a plan needs to be included with applications to the regional development institution and that a higher quality of development plans increases the probability of obtaining funding. The plan needs to be aligned with the development plans of the superordinate territorial entities.

No such strategic development plan exists in the municipality surveyed; at best, there is the election programme of the party in power to which ideas put forward by committed citizens are added occasionally. There is chaos regarding the development of the municipality in the medium to long term. There are neither visions for the future nor clearly identifiable development priorities. The municipality is fond of procrastinating when it comes to the necessary tackling of problem areas that have been known for a long time. One case in point is the extension of the sewer system, which has been demanded for 15 years, but has not yet been started. This increases the dissatisfaction among the population of the municipality.

EVALUATION AND NEED FOR ACTION

In many areas, the municipality is afflicted with problems that could or should have been managed long ago. Accumulated tasks have not been completed, not only because of the administration's tendency to procrastinate regarding unpleasant matters, but also because a strategic development concept is missing. Firstly, this is the reason why there is no systematic overview of the trouble spots in the municipality. Secondly, there is no system of prioritization that could determine where the municipality would need to direct measures most urgently.

Developing a medium- to long-term plan appears indispensable in order to improve the current situation and to ensure positive municipal development. Certainly, first of all, the municipal authorities need to be made aware of the purpose of such a plan. The development plan itself can subsequently be drawn up on the basis of a SWOT analysis. All interest groups in the municipality need to be involved in the development of the plan.

4.3.1.4 Consulting services provided for businesses willing to locate in the municipality

SITUATION

At the regional level, consulting services provided to companies are viewed as an important responsibility of municipal politicians, in particular the mayor.

In the municipality surveyed itself, this view is not shared. The mayor is willing to pass initial information on to businesses willing to locate in the municipality when the respective entrepreneurs actively ask for it. Offering unsolicited help or presenting himself actively as a service-oriented consulting body for businesses willing to locate or for potential company founders does not appear feasible to the mayor. There is, however, a "guide through the authorities" available to businesses willing to locate, which helps overcome bureaucratic hurdles.

Generally, the communication between the municipality and the local entrepreneurs is characterized by a lack of interest on the part of the municipal leadership (and consequently also on the part of the entrepreneurs).

EVALUATION AND NEED FOR ACTION

The mayor of the municipality surveyed displays little interest in the entrepreneurial activities in his municipality. He does not maintain closer ties with the local businesses; where new businesses are concerned, these are rather assigned the role of petitioners. The help granted by the municipality is limited to the willingness to provide information. By offering the brochure on dealings with the authorities, the municipality already signals indirectly that companies should first of all obtain information on the relevant procedures themselves before they turn to the authorities.

The passivity the mayor displays *vis-à-vis* the local business community is a problem. The comparatively autonomous municipalities compete for businesses willing to locate in the area as their functions as employers and taxpayers contribute to generating welfare in the municipality on a major scale. It is to be expected that the relatively mobile companies will locate in those municipalities that are characterized by an accommodating atmosphere. Among others, it is also the first impression that the mayor and the authorities (as first contacts) generate with the entrepreneur that will influence the evaluation of the eligible locations. In this respect, the municipality surveyed loses attractiveness compared with another, somewhat more active municipality.

It is evident that more has to be done in the area of business information. In particular, the mayor, as the person who should take care of the business matters in a municipality, would have to play a much more active part. If resources and competences of the municipality are not sufficient to facilitate effective consulting to businesses willing to locate in the municipality, an alternative option designed to improve the status quo of the municipality surveyed with regard to consulting services could consist in jointly establishing a specialist consulting institution in the microregion.

4.3.1.5 Resolving conflicting goals of municipal development through involvement of all interest groups

SITUATION

It has already been mentioned that the municipality does not engage in any formal strategic planning. Moreover, it lacks a political culture that would consider it a given that the population is involved when decisions about the further development of the municipality are made. Residents of the municipality who bring important matters to the attention of the municipal council are sometimes faced with delaying tactics on the part of the administration for so long that they are eventually worn down and give up. In the course of time, the population has participated less and less in public meetings.

EVALUATION AND NEED FOR ACTION

Basically, it will only be possible to start implementing the measure when the municipality decides to draw up a medium- to long-term development plan. In the absence of a development strategy, there is neither a possibility of nor a necessity for participation.

It appears questionable whether the population would play a part in a future process of strategy development. Should a strategy be developed under the current political conditions after all, it is likely that the plan will reflect the opinions and priorities of only a few influential municipal citizens. This is suggested by previous experience, which shows that the mayor is inclined to make decisions in an autocratic manner. It is to be doubted that a plan that is drawn up under such conditions would remain valid in the medium to long term. Firstly, it would lack the backing of the municipality's population, which would make it more difficult to implement many measures. Secondly, the next political change would probably entail a fundamental modification of the strategic plan. This way, a very important function of a municipality's development strategy would not be fulfilled, i.e. providing a point of orientation for the actors in the municipality that remains reliable in the medium to long term.

Should the current or a future leadership of the municipality decide to plan the municipal development strategically and actually want to integrate views and needs of the population into the planning process, it may be assumed that such an effort would initially generate little interest. As the culture of political participation, which had been awakened after the turnaround of the system, has already been eroded substantially, this would prevent the desired broad participation of citizens. Before a planning and design process is initiated, at any rate, measures that are capable of restoring the confidence of the residents of the municipality in municipal politics should be taken.

4.3.1.6 Actively securing land for construction

SITUATION

The municipality surveyed does not secure land for construction purposes. In the first years of the transformation from a planned to a market economy, properties situated on municipal territory were returned to private ownership. At that time, the municipality completely neglected to secure properties at favourable prices. This is why the municipality owns little land. Today's land prices are out of the reach of the financially weak municipality.

The leaders of the municipality rather avoid the issue of securing property for construction. Properties become relevant, if at all, when infrastructure is extended. The municipality's construction policy is the subject of harsh criticism. The construction plan is said to be unreliable as it is frequently modified. Private individuals or businesses are not offered any help from the municipality when they initiate construction projects. Unfavourable construction decisions add to the negative image of municipal representatives: for instance, a residential area is situated directly alongside the industrial zone owned by the municipality.

EVALUATION AND NEED FOR ACTION

The municipality surveyed is seriously affected by the mistakes that had been committed by the municipal politicians during the period of transformation. Even though the flawed decisions of the past cannot be rectified, the municipality still has sufficient potential to improve the construction policy, if not in the short term, at least in a sustainable form.

Basically, the municipality can appeal to the community spirit of the population in order to purchase properties at a fair price. However, this is most effective where the properties are to be used for an infrastructure project (e.g. road, school) and only where the municipal population displays a strong community spirit and/or confidence in the political leadership. This is not true for the municipality surveyed. Consequently, substantial previous steps need to be taken in other areas, which at first glance appear of little relevance to the issue at hand, so that it becomes possible to secure property for construction based on a principle of "decency and morals", e.g. strengthening social cohesion, involving the population in the political decision-making process of the municipality. Moreover, there would be the possibility of securing strategically important areas by means of a prudent policy of zoning and option agreements.

Critics note that the municipality pursues an unstructured construction policy and frequently modifies the construction plan. This amounts to virtually no planning certainty for the relevant actors in the municipality (e.g. potential developers, companies). The associated unreliability in construction matters does not result from the mistakes made in the past, but rather from faulty strategic planning undertaken by the municipality. The absence of a clear-cut development perspective including priorities and strategies to obtain the specified objectives is the reason why the approach of the municipality is perceived as a zigzag course that cannot be understood by third parties. It is advisable to work out a development strategy that is accepted and consequently backed by the overwhelming majority in order to make sure that the municipal approach is stabilized. Owing to the previously outlined circumstances, which characterize the relationship between politicians and the population in the municipality surveyed, such a plan can only be developed in the medium term.

4.3.1.7 *Joint financing of inter-communal projects*

SITUATION

The municipality surveyed only occasionally cooperates with other municipalities. Regarding tourism, the neighbouring municipalities have at least cooperated to such an extent that, where cycle paths were established, it was made sure that these paths were linked to the paths of the respective neighbouring municipality. However, financing was undertaken strictly independently. Regarding infrastructure, the municipality surveyed is striving for a cooperation with the neighbouring municipality. A shared sewage plant is to be established. However, negotiations are difficult. For the time being, the issue of joint financing is not resolved.

At the level of societies and associations, inter-communal cooperations exist in matters of environmental protection. As a first step, it was possible to realize a conservation area for amphibians across municipalities. Further joint projects are being considered.

EVALUATION AND NEED FOR ACTION

So far, the municipality surveyed has limited its cooperation with other municipalities to coordinating activities regarding (tourist) infrastructure. A closer cooperation, which would be associated with joint financing, is being prepared for the purpose of establishing a sewage plant. The implementation of the measure is hence under way.

The municipality has already taken the first steps in the right direction. Against the backdrop of the limited municipal resources, inter-communal cooperation should be promoted much more intensively. The potential for cooperation is far from exhausted, for instance, with regard to infrastructure, shared industrial zones and joint marketing. Cooperating in these fields would create synergy and consequently facilitate saving resources, while increasing income for each of the municipalities involved. Such cooperations also offer the advantage that they may lead to obtaining financial support specially intended for microregions or inter-communal cooperations.

4.3.1.8 *Inter-communal coordination of efforts to attract new companies*

SITUATION

The municipality surveyed does not cooperate with other municipalities in order to attract businesses to the area. This is due to two reasons: firstly, there is little understanding for the advantages associated with cooperation.

Secondly, attracting new businesses is associated with tax income, additional jobs and prestige – a municipality wants to secure all that for itself at all costs. Sharing is equated with personal loss.

At the regional level, the strong competition between the individual municipalities is emphasized. Coordination of efforts to attract new companies only happens under force, for instance, if a company exhausts the capacities of a given municipality (property, workforce).

EVALUATION AND NEED FOR ACTION

The municipality surveyed does not address this measure, and considerable psychological barriers counteract its implementation. In general, inter-communal competition is keen; doing business is implicitly understood as a zero-sum game in which one's own profit equals the other party's loss. The flawed idea prevails that a cooperation for the purpose of attracting new businesses would reduce the tax earnings of the individual municipality, as these earnings would have to be divided among the partners to the cooperation. The mayor (like the mayors of the neighbouring municipalities) does not realize that an effective cooperation among municipalities would generate more tax earnings, on the one hand, and reduce investment expenses, on the other hand (for instance, owing to advantages of size).

It is necessary to initiate a process that reverses the view of the municipal representatives. Information events that explain the advantages of inter-communal cooperation in attracting new businesses to the location need to be established. An appropriate first step could be specific projects that would financially support municipalities that cooperate in attracting companies to the location and in encouraging the establishment of new businesses. This would make cooperation in this development area crucial to municipalities more popular. It needs to be borne in mind that cooperations with neighbouring municipalities offer the possibility of bundling resources and also represent an attractive strategy for differentiating themselves from other cooperative initiatives.

4.3.1.9 Communication policy and creating a supraregional image

SITUATION

The municipality surveyed has never been known for certain products. It is one of those municipalities that are hardly noted outside their region. Owing to its immediate closeness to a nature conservation site, there is potential for tourism. In this field, first cautious attempts at drawing attention to the municipality are being made. Independently of the municipal policy, the village renewal society has initiated a number of activities that have been favourably received in the region. In cooperation with concerns of environmental protection (e.g. conservation site for amphibia), contests for ideas were organized. At the regional level, these activities led to the municipality being mentioned several times on the radio and in the press.

EVALUATION AND NEED FOR ACTION

As mentioned repeatedly, the municipal representatives practise a clearly passive form of information policy. The municipality does not set any measures that would aim at actively communicating its advantages for tourism. The mistaken view prevails that the existence of beautiful scenery is sufficient to attract tourists. It appears that the few bright spots in public relations have all been initiated by activities on the part of the opposition or of private individuals.

The competition between municipalities in tourism is won by the municipality, which is best at creating recognition value. Effective marketing is an indispensable instrument for this purpose. The municipality is advised to attract more attention by means of participation in fairs (nationally and internationally), advertisements in regional publications and on the internet, and advertising brochures published in several languages that can be placed in regional tourism agencies. Should the municipality lack the resources or the know-how necessary to implement an intensive marketing strategy, it can try to win an external partner for public relations tasks (e.g. a charitable society or a regional development office), or to enter into a marketing cooperation with neighbouring municipalities.

Additionally, it is necessary for the municipality surveyed to have a clear positioning so that a specific image can be created. Tourism in the municipality needs to differentiate itself from tourism in other municipalities. This can be effected by means of specific offers, which can be emphasized within the marketing strategy. In view of the numerous initiatives in the area of environmental protection, one option lies in the municipality surveyed positioning itself as an area of ecological tourism with unspoiled nature. In this context, it is crucial that the "image" is not postulated artificially, but appears authentic and is actually "lived" by the residents of the municipality.

4.3.1.10 *Promoting new businesses in industries not yet well established*

SITUATION

The municipality surveyed does not offer any support to businesses beyond providing first information on the spot. The idea of specifically promoting the establishment of new companies in industries, which have not previously been established in the area, does not occur to the municipal leadership. If at all, such programmes are viewed as the responsibility of the state, and the municipality is not regarded as competent in these matters. Moreover, the municipality surveyed strongly focuses on tourism, which causes the mayor and the opposition to believe that there is no need for manufacturing companies. The village renewal society, which shows strong ecological commitment, generally takes a critical view of any measures intended to attract companies, as companies are viewed as potentially damaging to the environment and could disrupt the beautiful scenery of the municipality with its orientation towards tourism.

EVALUATION AND NEED FOR ACTION

The actors in the municipality surveyed lack a general understanding of the problems and needs of companies. Moreover, the importance of companies or the establishment of new businesses for the development of the municipality is underestimated to a large extent. The fact that strict orientation towards tourism can lead to an unbalanced business structure is largely ignored. Municipalities whose business community is similar to monocultures are not in a position to spread risks and, therefore, are more vulnerable to crises.

The intended specialization would tie the welfare of the municipality surveyed not only to the prosperity of the tourism industry in general, but also to the popularity of a specific kind of tourism in particular, namely holidays in the countryside or in the nature conservation area. This would be hindered by seasonal fluctuations, which are typical of tourist regions. Consequently, it is urgently necessary for the views on business policy to change. An educational measure would lie in organizing subsidized workshops, which would serve to explain the negative consequences of an undiversified business structure of municipalities.

The tendency to view the arrival of new businesses with scepticism rooted in considerations of ecology or tourism could also be used positively. It could encourage increased efforts to attract or promote the start-up of companies in innovative (service) industries, which exercise less strain on the environment than traditional manufacturing companies. Subsequently, the unspoiled nature associated with the municipality could be used as an unusual incentive for attracting small enterprises tired of city life. However, a correspondingly modern infrastructure (e.g. broadband internet) would have to be offered to such businesses. If such investments cannot be covered by the budget of the municipality surveyed, the solution could lie in an inter-communal industrial zone – which currently would be difficult to realize in the case of the municipality discussed owing to the dominance of the view on entrepreneurial activity described.

4.3.1.11 Competitive products by virtue of local origin

SITUATION

At the regional level, there are already ongoing projects that aim at establishing regional food products. Moreover, there are attempts to establish quality certificates. These certificates would be granted to selected products and services that satisfy specified criteria. This initiative was also inspired by the understanding that regional specialities are becoming more important, especially in tourism.

EVALUATION AND NEED FOR ACTION

The municipal representatives, most notably the mayor, do not strive to develop specific services or products in the municipality. Representatives rely on the existing natural resource "scenery" and hope for earnings from tourism. This doubtless offers some opportunities, but active marketing measures are also necessary in order to exploit the potential for tourism to a satisfactory extent.

Regarding a product specific to the region, which could be built into a brand known beyond the region, the high-quality raw material wood appears suitable for further consideration. Unfortunately, no efforts are made in this respect, although there are some feasible alternatives in the medium term. Firstly, a high-quality wood cluster could be initiated, which would also entail attracting a number of wood-processing companies. Secondly, the wood cluster could be combined into a unique regional brand together with the municipality with its strong focus on environmental protection. High-quality wood products (e.g. furniture, toys) manufactured in an environmentally benign way could be produced. Specific certificates could further emphasize the wood quality.

Even if the decision-makers in the municipality had the imagination for such an initiative, it could not be managed by the municipality alone. Rather, it would be necessary to pool the resources of various municipalities. If a microregion were formed, this would offer the additional advantage of being able to apply for funding jointly.

4.3.1.12 Freeing town centres by relocating businesses that generate high emissions

SITUATION

Environmental pollution was an immense problem in Czechoslovakia, which had been characterized by heavy industry. Now there is effective environmental legislation that results in companies whose emissions exceed a certain threshold no longer being tolerated in municipal centres. Consequently, it can clearly be observed that companies tend to locate on the fringes of municipalities.

Currently, there are no manufacturing companies with harmful environmental impacts in the area of the municipality surveyed. Most environmental damage in the area is produced by the residents themselves who burn their household waste in their stoves. The industrial zone is located at the fringe of the municipality. A manufacturer of synthetic materials, which used to produce high emissions, has located there. This was a problem as a residential area is located opposite the manufacturing site and it was exposed to malodour. The company has introduced innovative technology, which has led to a significant reduction in environmental pollution.

EVALUATION AND NEED FOR ACTION

There is no need to apply the measure in the municipality surveyed, as it has already been implemented. Companies located in the municipal centre do not have a negative environmental impact, and companies that damage the environment locate in the industrial zone outside the municipal area. However, in future construction projects, the municipality should refrain from defining residential areas in the immediate vicinity of the industrial zone.

As for reducing the emissions of the municipality, the focus must be on changing the behaviour of the population itself. The practice of burning household waste in its entirety in the domestic stove is to be stopped. In this context, an educational campaign could serve to reduce the behaviour of the municipal residents that damages the environment.

4.3.2 The municipality located in the south of the Czech Republic

The relatively densely populated municipality in southern Moravia is located in a valley close to the Austrian border. The undulating viticultural region was declared a nature conservation area owing to the exceptional diversity of the flora in its surroundings. Both its natural beauty and the historic sights that still remain form a good basis for local tourism. The municipality's history began with the establishment of a parish in the middle of the thirteenth century. A noble dynasty was located in the region, to which a castle bears witness today. There are early records of Jewish municipal life, which prospered in the era of the Habsburg monarchy in particular. While at one stage accounting for half of the population, few Jews survived the period of national socialism. During the Second World War, severe bombing heavily damaged the municipal infrastructure as a whole and the Jewish quarter in particular. Finally, the evictions of the German population after 1945 changed the intercultural municipal life of old for ever.

4.3.2.1 Strengthening social cohesion by creating meeting places

SITUATION

The mayor of the municipality surveyed considers public events very significant, which is reflected in a remarkable number of events: socio-cultural activities include monthly markets, a celebration in traditional costume and a fun fair, which forms the highlight of the municipal year. Numerous other activities are held around the fun fair, which takes place in summer: a traditional "international" football game (the local team plays against the team of its foreign partnering municipality), various exhibitions and concerts, as well as competitions of the fire brigade. However, the municipality primarily focuses on sports. There is a comprehensive range of sports clubs in diverse disciplines. In addition, the municipality boasts a freshly renovated "house of culture", which is popular among the residents.

The municipality supports these measures at different levels. Sport promotion involves the municipality providing municipal property and financial support of major investments (e.g. construction of training premises). The numerous cultural events are actively advertised in the form of a quarterly cultural calendar published by the municipality.

EVALUATION AND NEED FOR ACTION

Social life in the municipality is flourishing, which can be credited, among other things, to the strong commitment of the municipal leadership, most notably the mayor. In this context, it is relevant that the municipality not only provides substantial support when called upon, but also interprets its role actively, for instance, by printing an event calendar or by renovating the "house of culture". The continuity of events (e.g. monthly markets, annual fairs) is also important, as it ensures that the population gets together at regular intervals. This promotes (and strengthens) integration among the population and, consequently, the development of strong social cohesion in the municipality.

4.3.2.2 Democratic and pluralist decision-making processes

SITUATION

The mayor of the municipality surveyed does not consider it important which group makes a suggestion for the development of the municipality. As a guiding principle, the needs of the actors in the municipality are always evaluated. Where suggested measures appear meaningful and feasible, they are considered in the document of planned activities of the municipality. It is, however, the municipal leadership that decides what is meaningful and feasible and what is not. The population and the local companies view the municipal government as an uncomplicated and accommodating partner in negotiations, especially with regard to club matters.

The municipality has long maintained the principle that every good idea is to be realized regardless of its origin. The mayor emphasizes that a joint approach in the form of cooperations yields better results than a strongly competitive mentality. This view has also been practised on the level of local politics: following municipal council meetings, all members used to go to the inn together and discuss problems informally. However, after the latest elections, the atmosphere between the (re-elected) municipal government and the opposition has deteriorated considerably. Now the members of the opposition occupy a different table at the inn. It is viewed as a burden on the municipality that the opposition has recently begun to display unusual aggressiveness and – in the mayor's perception – only criticizes for the sake of criticizing, because this could delay the implementation of measures.

EVALUATION AND NEED FOR ACTION

Up to now, democratic decision-making processes have been practised in the municipality. However, the oppositional forces have changed their manner following the latest elections. The behaviour displayed by the opposition may put a strain on the political cooperation that had previously been maintained across different political groups. Nevertheless, it appears exaggerated to accuse the opposition of subjective opposition policy – also because the opposition rightly points out deficits that can be identified in some areas of the municipality.

Although personally disappointed by the new political culture, the mayor should continue practising his pluralist approach to decision-making. The views of the opposition should not be negated out of defiance, but rather actively considered in decision-making. The mayor could lighten the dulled atmosphere by being forthcoming on certain issues. As such behaviour could be interpreted politically as weakness of the mayor or as victory of the opposition, however, it does not seem very likely that the municipal leaders will opt for such measures.

4.3.2.3 Integrating the individual measures into a comprehensive development concept of the municipality

SITUATION

Two strategic documents provide the direction for the overall development of the municipality surveyed. One is the manifesto, which is drawn up every four years – in accordance with the election periods – and is taken seriously. The second document is the municipality's budget forecast, which is prepared from scratch every ten years, but can be amended with new suggestions every year.

However, these development plans for the medium to long term do not appear to guarantee an approach of the municipal government free of friction. The opposition, in particular, but also individuals in favour of the mayor, frequently criticize the municipality's policy of spatial planning. In this context, contradictory measures of municipal development have been set repeatedly.

EVALUATION AND NEED FOR ACTION

The municipal representatives deal with strategic plans guiding the municipal development in the medium to long term. This is relevant insofar as it offers some planning certainty to the actors in the municipality surveyed. However, no consistent strategy exists for a crucial aspect of municipal development, i.e. construction and location, with inevitable consequences.

In general, the measure outlined appears to have been implemented in the municipality. The importance of medium- to long-term planning is recognized. However, this favourable first impression is considerably dulled by the deficits existing in the field of construction policy.

4.3.2.4 Consulting services provided for businesses willing to locate in the municipality

SITUATION

If companies willing to locate in the area have questions, they can turn to the municipality, which will be glad to help. However, there is no active communication policy targeted at attracting new companies to locate. This is also because the municipality offers quite attractive conditions for companies: the geographic location is strategically favourable (vicinity to the border of a EU15 country), and the municipality is relatively well linked to the motorway and boasts several industrial zones that have already developed, with prices for the business premises still being kept low. Owing to this abundance of advantages, the municipality need not actively woo companies – they come of their own accord.

EVALUATION AND NEED FOR ACTION

The municipality surveyed accommodates companies by means of creating favourable conditions for businesses. Consulting services, assistance in dealings with the authorities, are only provided where companies solicit them. Active communication policy in business matters is neglected, as there is no pressure for change in this respect.

This behaviour is to be considered a problem for two reasons. Firstly, the current conditions may change in the future, for instance, when other municipalities catch up and actively start competing for new businesses to locate in their areas. In such a case, the municipality surveyed will find it difficult to hold its own against other municipalities in the region, as it does not have any instruments for active communication with interested companies.

Secondly, its negligent approach regarding company matters prevents the municipality from making the most of its favourable location and its high investments (e.g. developed industrial zones). As it does not address all companies potentially willing to locate in its area, but only notices those that approach the municipality of their own accord, the municipality sells itself short. Acting more professionally and more actively would facilitate not only capturing financial advantages, but also selecting companies that meet certain criteria (e.g. with a view to a balanced mix of industries and company sizes, environmentally benign production methods, sunrise instead of obsolete industries).

4.3.2.5 *Resolving conflicting goals of municipal development through involvement of all interest groups*

SITUATION

Although the mayor makes an effort to emphasize how much he values the cooperation of all interest groups in the municipality, in reality, there are shortcomings that can also be traced back to a lack of coordination among the objectives pursued by different groups. The most significant problem area in the municipality is the dearth of housing property and construction plots, which exists alongside an excess supply of business premises.

The individual interest groups exert varying influence on the decisions of the municipality. In general, it can be noted that the older generation is favoured over the younger one and that the business community is at an advantage compared to the general population. A more detailed analysis of the business community reveals that foreign companies are favoured over local enterprises. For instance, when competing for a location in the industrial zone, a local company made a much more favourable offer than a foreign company, which managed to prevail in the end.

EVALUATION AND NEED FOR ACTION

The municipal government has repeatedly earned its mandate through elections and is popular with the residents, as it generously finances many sports and cultural activities. Individual measures are supported when they are considered meaningful. This generates little pressure on the municipal representatives to allow participation in matters of medium- to long-term municipal development. Consequently, the municipal government can act in a way it considers appropriate.

In the absence of closeness to certain interest groups, most notably the young generation, the decisions taken lack a holistic perspective. For this reason, development measures are taken that can lead to lasting damage for the entire municipality: without housing property (affordable to young people), the municipal population will age increasingly, and the companies will leave the area in spite of all the advantages offered, owing to a shortage of available employees.

For this reason, the municipal representatives are urgently advised to extend their communication activities to all residents in the municipality and, in particular, to integrate into the municipal development those population groups that have been neglected so far. A first step could be conducting an anonymous survey of needs, complaints and suggestions. Furthermore, all population groups could be involved if they were sent the long-term development plan and were asked to comment on it.

4.3.2.6 Actively securing land for construction

SITUATION

Construction policy has been neglected for a long time in the municipality surveyed. The development of housing and construction in the municipality is characterized by contradictions and faulty planning. This particularly applies to the construction of housing, which is illustrated by several examples. At the fringes of the municipality, three industrial zones were created and developed, which makes spatial growth of the municipality considerably more difficult. Consequently, the construction projects focus on the municipal centre, which is continuously becoming more dense.

Several years ago, construction plots were designated and developed at high cost. However, these plots are located in immediate proximity to water bodies, which gives rise to the danger of flooding. Consequently, the demand for these plots has not lived up to the expectations of the municipal government by far. Construction and location initiatives are not coordinated with other municipal matters. For instance, the municipal pond was cleaned at high cost and, six months later, a chemical company located there.

Owing to a lack of residential properties and appropriate housing plots, more and more young individuals leave the municipality for cities. The municipality surveyed is in danger of becoming over-aged.

EVALUATION AND NEED FOR ACTION

Although the municipality proceeds well in cultural matters, its approach to construction issues needs to be improved. In construction projects, the municipality failed to align the objectives of the business community with those of the population. The availability of numerous business plots serves to attract businesses to locate in the area. However, this works at the cost of the young population, which is hardly offered land for housing purposes.

The construction policy generally suggests that planning is effected top down without the involvement of the population and that these plans are not checked for any contradictions that may exist with regard to other objectives of the municipality surveyed. Securing construction plots with a long-term perspective is only practised to a limited extent.

If the municipality wants to avert the current danger of a rapidly ageing population, the construction policy should be changed significantly. Firstly, the population (in particular, the young) should be involved in the development of the zoning plan, at least in the form of a needs analysis conducted among the municipality's residents. Secondly, the municipality should consider purchasing plots situated on municipal territory, while at the same time introducing models of purchasing options in order to secure sites for construction in the long term. Thirdly, in view of the limitations to spatial growth caused by the municipality itself (the three industrial zones), the municipality should look for solutions to this precarious situation. Fourthly, as the issue of construction is characterized by a large number of contradictions and chaos, the construction policy should be included in an integrated municipal development plan. The individual municipal objectives need to be aligned with the construction projects and checked for possible conflicts between the individual areas of municipal development. This will ensure harmonious development of the municipality surveyed.

Two options would serve to resolve the housing problem: firstly, one of the industrial zones could be abolished and converted into a residential zone, which would involve the companies presently located there moving to one of the other two industrial zones. This would at least ensure the spatial expansion of the municipality surveyed in one direction. Before such a step is taken, the population should definitely be involved in ascertaining which industrial zone could most likely be considered. As the companies would have to be moved at the cost of the municipality, which would have to entice the businesses to relocate by means of special offers or concessions (e.g. tax relief), it is questionable whether the municipality could afford such a strategy. A second option would lie in "gently" abolishing one of the industrial zones over a longer period of time. This strategy would not entail forcing any company to move away, which would eliminate the high costs accruing to the municipality. The municipality would observe the development of the respective companies and hope for abolishment or voluntary relocation; at the same time, it would prevent new companies locating in the respective industrial zone. However, this measure has the disadvantages that its success is dependent on uncertain factors (i.e. the continuing existence of the respective companies) and that it would only become effective in the medium to long term. This could possibly be too late as housing is scarce already today.

4.3.2.7 Joint financing of inter-communal projects

SITUATION

The communication climate between the municipalities of the region is good. Several times a year, the mayors convene in meetings especially held for this purpose. Several years ago, these meetings inspired the formation of a microregion, which comprises eight municipalities (among them the municipality surveyed). Although the microregion already exists, the potential of this organizational unit has not been utilized so far. Cooperation between the municipalities is limited to cultural activities, on the one hand, and infrastructure projects, on the other hand. School transport is organized jointly, cycle paths are established across different municipalities and the road network linking the municipality surveyed to the neighbouring municipalities is being improved step by step. Regarding a sewage plant, there would be considerable potential for cooperation, as some municipalities in the microregion do not have a sewage plant, while the municipality surveyed has acquired a plant that is far too large, as it was designed more with a view to its implementation in cities of medium size. So far, all negotiations in this area have failed.

In the mayor's view, insufficient agreement about the common objectives for the microregion is one of the reasons why the establishment of the microregion has not inspired any further inter-communal projects despite a positive business climate among the municipalities' representatives. A regional association was formed, but there were no (shared) ideas about what the association should entail. Another reason lies in the mentality of many mayors, especially those of smaller municipalities, that cooperation equals exploiting the smaller members.

EVALUATION AND NEED FOR ACTION

It can be noted positively that the working climate among the municipalities in the region of the municipality surveyed is constructive and oriented towards communication and coordination. Despite this favourable climate, however, it has to be argued that the many possibilities associated with inter-communal cooperation have not yet been explored to a large extent: there is no cooperation regarding company matters and potential infrastructure projects (the sewage plant) are not realized.

The mayor of the municipality surveyed knows about the relevance of cooperation. It appears that it is rather the misguided fears of the smaller neighbouring municipalities that lead to inter-communal cooperation proceeding only slowly. Information campaigns on site could serve to change these municipalities' attitude towards inter-communal cooperation.

4.3.2.8 Inter-communal coordination of efforts to attract new companies

SITUATION

When new companies wish to locate in the region of the municipality surveyed, the municipalities only coordinate their approach if a company wishes to locate on the fringe of one municipality and can be expected to generate emissions that will also affect the neighbouring municipality(-ies). There has already been one precedent in this respect in the municipality surveyed. The neighbouring municipalities eventually succeeded in keeping the municipality surveyed from approving a new company locating on the fringe of its territory. Apart from such cases, the municipalities do not work together on locating companies in the region. Owing to its present favourable financial condition and in view of the difficulties that result from inter-communal cooperation in other areas, the municipality surveyed shows little motivation to change anything about the status quo.

The measure outlined has not been implemented in the municipality surveyed; moreover, the respective municipalities do not plan to cooperate regarding companies locating in the area. The municipalities maintain a basis for discussion, which could serve as a foundation for establishing such a cooperation regarding companies locating in the region. The municipality surveyed, which is headed by a mayor keen on cooperating, could initiate such a cooperation. However, as there is little economic pressure on the municipality, there is no interest in such a policy of attracting new companies.

The municipal leaders do not lack understanding of the advantages associated with coordinating company location decisions at the inter-communal level, but rather far-sighted planning. Knowing that the financial situation is reasonable, they are negligent in managing the budget and forgo investing in structures that could safeguard lasting positive development of the municipality. An inter-communal industrial zone or a joint body in charge of information and coordination of company-locating decisions would constitute such investments. The municipality surveyed should be motivated to engage in such efforts by means of education campaigns.

4.3.2.9 Communication policy and creating a supraregional image

SITUATION

All persons interviewed (including the opposition) consider the communication policy a major strength of the municipality surveyed. The municipality is excellent at marketing the large number of cultural activities in the press and on TV. Moreover, the municipality attracted attention beyond the regional boundaries when it was awarded a major amount from an EU fund. These PR successes can be credited to the mayor, who maintains good contacts with politicians in higher national and European positions – which constitutes an additional advantage.

EVALUATION AND NEED FOR ACTION

The measure has already been implemented in the municipality surveyed. Media attention is generated frequently, and excellent contacts in the highest political echelons are maintained.

If there is need for action at all, it relates to utilizing the widespread recognition of the municipality. The municipality can be assumed to benefit from the level of recognition, but does not appear to show any interest in channelling it in the form of a clearly defined image. It does not seem to be recognized (or is simply underestimated) that creating such a clear reputation – for instance, as "municipality of culture" or "entrepreneurial municipality" – would facilitate utilizing the level of recognition much more efficiently. It is, therefore, recommended that the municipality's communication policy, which is doubtless positive, be optimized insofar as the public image is standardized to a certain extent. This would entail issues, which appear simple at first glance, such as developing mottos, slogans or logos, but which could increase the recognition of the municipality considerably – provided they are used consistently.

4.3.2.10 Promoting new businesses in industries not yet well established

SITUATION

The municipality surveyed does not proceed in a systematic manner where the local business structure is concerned. This is the reason why some measures do not appear intelligible rationally: for one thing, established companies are neglected in favour of foreign companies wishing to locate in the area. Moreover, attracting new companies does not involve considerations of the structure of companies already located in the municipality. Consequently, most companies situated in the municipality have similar production profiles and demand similarly educated employees, who are becoming more and more difficult to recruit.

The municipality believes that it fulfils its responsibility sufficiently by providing industrial zones and keeping the level of fees levied low. Politicians and entrepreneurs alike consider any measures that would go beyond that unnecessary or undesirable. On the one hand, this reflects a strong liberal economic attitude on the part of the companies and, on the other hand, it is simply not considered possible that politics can actively induce citizens to engage in entrepreneurial activity. Individuals either form companies based on intrinsic motivation and if needs be despite unfavourable conditions – or they do not.

EVALUATION AND NEED FOR ACTION

The municipality surveyed does not implement this measure. It is hindered by a strong mental barrier: the failure to believe that entrepreneurial behaviour can be initiated by the decision-makers. Consequently, the economic policy pursued by the municipality aims at what can be influenced at any rate, i.e. attracting already existing companies to the area by means of providing infrastructure and levying low fees.

The basic purpose of the measure consists in diversifying the company structure of a given municipality. A municipality with a heterogeneous company structure is better equipped to absorb external shocks (e.g. strong fluctuations in the demand for certain goods) than a municipality whose company structure resembles a monoculture. As the municipality surveyed hosts a large number of similar companies, it lacks the capacities necessary to mitigate the consequences of a slump in demand by means of spreading risk.

The municipality is therefore urgently advised to increase its regulatory influence in this regard and to specifically select companies that can contribute to augmenting the variance of the business structure within its boundaries – all the more so if it is considered that the municipality is in a strong economic position. It can be argued that such an approach could be optimized in the context of inter-communal coordination of company-location decisions. However, this would first necessitate overcoming the barriers to cooperation that exist among the municipalities.

As the municipality surveyed lacks both the know-how and the understanding for measures intended to promote company start-ups – for instance, in the form of incubators – information campaigns and workshops would represent appropriate tools that serve to reduce these deficits.

4.3.2.11 Competitive products by virtue of local origin

SITUATION

The municipality surveyed is located in a region that has traditionally been agricultural. In former times, it was the centre of an agricultural processing company known throughout the country. However, following the turnaround of 1989, the respective company was taken over cheaply by a competitor and subsequently liquidated. Since that time, the municipality has not been in possession of a company or product known throughout the country. No change is expected in this regard for the upcoming years. The mayor of the municipality surveyed makes the point that – if at all – the entire region is known for its positive climate and its beautiful scenery.

EVALUATION AND NEED FOR ACTION

At the product level, at present, there are few possibilities for implementing the measure in the municipality surveyed. The municipality lacks relevant products that could be marketed by associating them with the region. The development potential of the municipality lies largely in the service sector. The beautiful scenery in conjunction with the numerous cultural activities could be integrated into a unique tourism offering. The municipality would be well advised to use these strengths to guide its economic development.

4.3.2.12 Freeing town centres by relocating businesses that generate high emissions

SITUATION

The municipal centre of the municipality surveyed hosts several companies that have located there for a long time. However, their emissions appear to remain limited. There is no intention to induce these companies to move to one of the three industrial zones. New companies automatically locate in the industrial zones situated at the fringe of the municipality.

EVALUATION AND NEED FOR ACTION

Even though emissions do not constitute a reason why the companies situated in the municipal centre should be moved away, the municipality surveyed should consider this step at some stage. Firstly, the companies are offered better conditions for expansion in the industrial zone. Secondly, this would mean that the industrial zone could be utilized more effectively. Thirdly, the housing problem should also be considered in this context: if the companies move from the municipal centre to the zone specifically designated for businesses, the plots thus becoming available could be used for housing projects and the scarcity of available housing could be somewhat mitigated.

The measure is consequently applied only to a certain extent as new companies are automatically assigned to the fringe of the municipality.

4.3.3 The municipality located in the centre of the Czech Republic

The municipality, which is well connected to transport routes, is located beside a low mountain range in the centre of the Czech Republic. In addition to the forests and waters of a nature conservation area, several historic buildings and monuments are situated in the municipality itself and in its surroundings, which contributes to the present municipal development displaying a strong orientation towards tourism. The parish church and fortress, after which the municipality was also named, both date back to the thirteenth century. Mining was the determining theme of the municipality's history in the middle ages. However, it came to an end in the course of the Thirty Years War, which marked the beginning of a decline in municipal life. It is worth mentioning that in the municipality one of the first Lutheran religious associations in Bohemia was established by virtue of the Patent of Toleration granted by Emperor Joseph II. After the Second World War, the municipality was renamed against the will of its population in order to emphasize its Czech identity more strongly. However, after the turnaround towards democracy, its old name was re-established at the urging of its residents.

4.3.3.1 Strengthening social cohesion by creating meeting places

SITUATION

The municipality does not possess a centre generally frequented by all residents for the purpose of communal exchange. For such purposes, the municipality offers clubs and societies the use of its assembly hall and has recently also made the wedding room available to local clubs. This also houses cultural events such as photo exhibitions. The local cinema is also used multifunctionally for amateur theatre performances or by the kindergarten.

Club activities are inconspicuous. There is a voluntary fire brigade, women's associations, a gymnastics club and a music association. The music association, whose members meet regularly, as is emphasized, mainly consists of old-age pensioners. A cultural association, which has taken its name from a well-known Czech painter from the region, is of high importance. The associations and clubs each have their own clientele, and there are hardly any activities across different associations. Public events initiated by associations or societies (e.g. art exhibitions) are usually only frequented by the respective association's members themselves. The population shows hardly any interest in attending events. Such events, which are largely cultural by nature, are predominantly frequented by tourists.

The few initiatives for events that exist are launched by the individual associations. The municipal politicians support these suggestions as far as their limited resources permit. There is a certain reservation regarding the active promotion of initiatives from the public.

EVALUATION AND NEED FOR ACTION

The political representatives of the municipality display a clearly passive attitude towards initiating social encounter. The mayor limits his role to making meeting rooms available. Initiatives on the part of the population are welcomed and supported. It is also acknowledged that support granted by the municipality often leads to subsequent independent proposals on the part of the municipal residents. However, this does not lead to the conclusion that the municipality should venture to make the first step more often. Also the representatives of the oppositional group in the municipal council interviewed assumes it is a given that municipalities are hardly in a position to encourage shared social activities.

The regional development agencies are not expected to provide a solution to this matter. On the contrary: The interview partners view the measure with scepticism and occasionally with ignorance. Against the backdrop of scarce resources, the municipalities would have to set financial priorities. It is uniformly argued that strengthening social cohesion or creating meeting places only makes an indirect, if any, contribution to the regional development of the municipality.

The municipality surveyed is not seen as lacking social meeting places. However, this can be explained by the absence of initiatives and events that would be capable of filling these places regularly. Initiating such events would first of all necessitate that the actors responsible for the development of the municipality change their way of thinking. They must be made aware that closely knit social networks can serve as incubators for initiatives conducive to the development of the municipality. Initiatives developed in this way are particularly important as they are backed by broad acceptance by the municipal residents, which makes it more probable that these bottom-up measures can be realized successfully. However, this requires close social networks, which can primarily be created through joint activities of the municipal population that are held frequently.

4.3.3.2 Democratic and pluralist decision-making processes

SITUATION

Municipal politicians are divided into two camps. These correspond to the two major parties present in the municipality. Permanent bickering is part of the political routine, and cooperation across parties hardly appears imaginable.

The oppositional force complains that some municipal politicians hardly show any interest in the daily routine of the municipal council. The public position primarily serves the purpose of satisfying personal vanities. Motions that are put up for vote are hardly read. Therefore, the mayor has a special role in the decision-making process. The way in which he presents and comments on motions before the respective voting can influence the resulting vote.

In the municipality, everyone can express ideas, which are subsequently also acknowledged by the municipality. However, the mayor makes it clear that the limited financial resources only permit the consideration of a small number of ideas – although help is naturally provided as far as possible. He goes on to point out that mostly the initiator himself needs to see to it that the motion is processed further, as the municipal staff is not sufficient to take over such tasks.

There is an internet forum where municipal issues can be discussed. However, this is viewed as an irrelevant playground for always the same notorious grumblers. The forum does not play a part in the decision-making process of the municipality.

EVALUATION AND NEED FOR ACTION

As some municipal councillors show low commitment, the mayor carries important weight in votes. The way, or whether, he presents a motion can decide the voting result. This concentration of power in the hands of one single person is as detrimental to democratic and pluralist decision-making as the permanent animosity that prevails between the two dominant parties.

It is a problem that ideas suggested by the population are viewed, at least indirectly, as a strain on the municipal routine rather than an opportunity for a positive municipal development. Burdening the initiator of an idea with the additional obligation of handling the processing of his idea as if this were natural does not lead to an atmosphere conducive to encouraging activities in the municipality. On the one hand, this precludes making the most of the potential of ideas present in the population and, on the other hand, it severely restricts pluralist participation in decision-making and municipal development.

The political division of the municipality blocks the road to regional development based on broad consensus. Actively promoting public discussions of municipal issues – on site or on the web – would offer one possibility of making decision-making processes more democratic. However, this requires that the political representatives fundamentally change their view of development proposals put forward by the population. At any rate, the potential of ideas present in the population should not be considered a burden. Rather, the municipal representatives should actively communicate that every idea is welcome and taken seriously.

4.3.3.3 Integrating the individual measures into a comprehensive development concept of the municipality

SITUATION

Like every municipality located in the region, the municipality surveyed possesses a development plan. This action plan, which includes an investment plan, is approved by the municipal representatives. The document is guided by the specific needs of the municipality, and is aligned with regional development concepts. The municipal development is based on this document. The current development priorities of the municipality surveyed concern the sewage disposal system, roads and housing (in this order).

There is a general tendency towards long-term development planning in municipalities. The rigour of such plans is criticized. It is also noted that such development plans lack continuity as each political change at the municipal level is associated with the creation of a new development concept.

EVALUATION AND NEED FOR ACTION

The municipality already possesses a development plan. It implements its measures in accordance with this plan. Additionally, other development concepts exist. These concepts pose a problem – at least in the municipality surveyed – as they change fundamentally whenever political change occurs and consequently provide little planning certainty. In order to maintain the political continuity that is highly relevant for population and entrepreneurs alike, a plan based on broad consensus is called for. Such concepts backed by the most influential parties can also remain unaltered when political changes occur. Owing to the polarity in party politics that exists in the municipality, it appears very difficult to arrive at such a development concept.

4.3.3.4 Consulting services provided for businesses willing to locate in the municipality

SITUATION

The municipality surveyed is rather small and has limited competences. For instance, the planning authority, which represents the first contact for entrepreneurs who intend to initiate a construction project, acts outside the scope of the municipality. This leaves the municipality little room for providing consulting services. In general, the relevance of providing assistance to companies wishing to locate in the municipality is acknowledged. However, the mayor takes a rather passive stance. Companies wishing to locate in the municipality are granted assistance as far as possible when they specifically ask for it. However, a local entrepreneur so far has failed to experience any appropriate assistance from the municipality. However, he is of the opinion that such consulting services are not within the scope of responsibility of municipalities.

Many members of the municipality share the view of this entrepreneur. The general opinion holds that consulting services to companies are or should be provided by regional investment or development agencies as well as the local branch of the chamber of commerce. Moreover, these institutions point out that this is standard practice in all of the Czech Republic.

EVALUATION AND NEED FOR ACTION

The municipality hardly provides any consulting or assistance to companies wishing to locate in its territory. However, this is not a local phenomenon. In the Czech Republic, such services are offered by specialist institutions. At least there is a readiness to provide assistance as municipalities are aware that new companies locating in their areas are necessary for positive municipal development. Still, low expectations regarding the municipality as the driving force in location matters make it unlikely that companies with important concerns turn to the municipality directly. In this context, the municipality could distinguish itself by communicating its general readiness to provide assistance and thereby gain attractiveness, albeit within modest limits, to companies willing to locate. In view of the limited resources of the municipality surveyed, advertisements placed in local papers or on relevant web platforms as well as personal information talks would appear most appropriate.

4.3.3.5 Resolving conflicting goals of municipal development through involvement of all interest groups

SITUATION

The municipality does not rely on a standard method for settling conflicts of interest. Decisions are taken on a case-by-case basis and with a certain inclination towards pragmatism. The possibility of different interest groups working out development objectives of the municipality together is understood as a noble or even idealist objective that cannot be achieved – in the mayor's opinion. Generally, certain fatalism prevails in the municipality: the two adverse camps are described as lacking the capacity for dialogue, and the limited financial means make it impossible to develop a budget that accommodates the different priorities of different interest groups.

Besides, the mayor shows little understanding of the importance of broad dialogue between the municipality and its citizens. He dodges questions about the internet forum, where current municipal issues can be discussed, as this represents a project initiated by the former mayoress (from the opposition party). In general, the population is given little motivation to actively participate in political processes, which is explained by the suppression exercised for decades under the real socialist regime.

EVALUATION AND NEED FOR ACTION

The responses of the interview partners clearly indicate the deficits of the municipality when it comes to municipal development based on consensus. Questioned about the measure, they respond with ignorance or liken the measure to social utopia. The political division of the municipality may provide an explanation for this ignorance. Moreover, it is emphasized that the population does not display interest in broad political participation. Accordingly, little consideration is paid to the dialogue with the citizens. However, this serves to perpetuate the passivity the population displays in political matters.

There are ways to make the relevance of jointly negotiated objectives for municipal development transparent to the population and to increase political participation in general. In view of the bickering of the two major parties, it appears that such measures could only be realized if a higher institutional authority were involved.

4.3.3.6 Actively securing land for construction

SITUATION

The municipality actively secures housing plots and offers these at comparatively low prices. An undeveloped area away from the municipal centre has been designated for the construction of housing. However, the population does not show any interest in this area. For one thing, the meadow is situated beside a large agricultural company, which leads to fears of odour nuisance. Moreover, the exposure of the potential construction area to all directions does not offer any protection from wind.

Several years ago, an industrial zone was designated for locating companies. However, so far, it has not been possible to convince a sufficient number of entrepreneurs to locate in the industrial zone. This can be explained by the geographic location of the zone away from the municipality and far off the main road – in contrast to the industrial zone in a central location maintained by a neighbouring municipality.

EVALUATION AND NEED FOR ACTION

The municipality is aware of the relevance of actively securing construction plots for ensuring positive municipal development. This practice is considered one of the basic responsibilities of a municipality and measures have been taken in this area. However, the municipality has proceeded awkwardly when realizing the necessary measures. This applies especially to the residential zone designated away from the municipal centre. The disapproval the population displays towards the land offered by the municipality suggests that those responsible failed to ascertain the needs of potential residents. Either the population was not asked about the residential land it desires, or the planners went over people's heads when they took the decision. Both instances reflect that the political representatives of the municipality lack the readiness to work together with the residents to create solutions satisfactory to everybody. Prior to the next measure, which is taken in order to secure residential plots, it is necessary to display openness towards the suggestions of those involved.

4.3.3.7 Joint financing of inter-communal projects

SITUATION

Two years ago, a cooperative society was formed. Within the scope of this society, the municipality surveyed works together with neighbouring municipalities, societies and the local small and medium enterprises. The cooperative society aims to care for the joint welfare of the municipalities. A plan of action was drawn up. The renovation and the extension of the municipal paths constitute its priorities. Moreover, cooperation is enhanced in the fields of sport, culture, tourism and preservation orders. Inter-communal cycling paths were established.

In addition to this cooperative society, municipalities have worked together in certain areas already for quite some time. As well as the general advantages resulting from constructive cooperation, the relevance of associations for becoming eligible for support from the state or the EU is highlighted.

Cooperation exists or can exist predominantly regarding general infrastructure (e.g. network of gas, electricity or water) or public services (e.g. clearing of snow). By contrast, industrial and residential zones are considered prestige projects. Every municipality wants to possess such zones on its own. This also applies to the municipality surveyed.

Intended cooperations with other municipalities failed in two areas. Proposals to share vehicles and machines for the purpose of clearing snow could not be realized; the same goes for the establishment of a joint sewage plant. Consequently, the municipality surveyed possesses a sewage plant of which it is the only user. In order to reduce costs via sharing the facility, there are efforts to establish a cooperation with a neighbouring municipality.

Owing to historical reasons, the atmosphere between the municipality surveyed and an important neighbouring municipality is not conducive to cooperation. Tensions and envy prevail between the municipalities.

EVALUATION AND NEED FOR ACTION

The municipality surveyed cooperates with other municipalities and is striving for more cooperation. This applies to the majority of Czech municipalities. Room for improvement is identified with regard to the fields in which cooperation is practised. Cooperation should be extended to include issues that are associated with much prestige for the municipalities. This applies especially to industrial zones. If every municipality possesses its own industrial zone, there is a danger that the municipalities may enter into direct competition for companies willing to locate in their region. Frequently, the losers are the competing municipalities themselves. An inter-communal industrial zone prevents this negative competition and facilitates positive municipal development to its participants – which, in turn, is associated with an increase in prestige.

4.3.3.8 Inter-communal coordination of efforts to attract new companies

SITUATION

The municipality surveyed does not engage in inter-communal coordination of efforts to attract new companies to the area. The likelihood of such a cooperation becoming reality in the future is considered low. This has also been illustrated by the failure of the municipalities to cooperate on the issue of establishing joint industrial zones.

The regional institutions providing consulting services and assistance emphasize that the municipalities are of little relevance in the context of foundations of new companies. Establishing new companies is considered a spontaneous act independent of context, which can consequently not be influenced. At best, municipalities are granted a role in connection with providing industrial zones and incubators. The mechanisms of the market are used as an argument against the option of coordination. Rather than a joint approach, direct competition between the municipalities that try to attract companies willing to locate is considered desirable.

Where coordination occurs, it is practised by authorities at a higher level. Regions with high unemployment rates are supported by means of promotional programmes at the national level. If at all, the municipalities coordinate efforts only in the wake of a major new company locating in the area. For instance, if this should lead to increased commuter activity, they jointly work on improving the conditions for commuters (e.g. by improving the road infrastructure).

Both the municipality and the regional institutions do not consider a joint approach in the context of attracting new companies an option. The regional level promotes the role of the municipality as an individual agent on the market, while the municipal level is apprehensive of losing prestige under such a joint approach. Generally, cooperating in order to attract companies is hardly considered. In order to implement such measures, it would firstly be necessary to communicate the positive effect of inter-communal cooperation in attracting new companies in order to alleviate the present mental barriers. This could be effected by means of presenting "prototype municipalities" where such a measure has led to positive further development for all parties involved.

4.3.3.9 Communication policy and creating a supraregional image

SITUATION

The regional Chamber of Commerce credits the municipality with a large potential for tourism. However, this is not utilized, as there is a dearth of appropriate services for tourists (e.g. restaurants, cultural offerings). Consequently, tourists do not have a reason to remain longer in the municipality. As regards industry, the region has successfully initiated a mechanical engineering cluster. By contrast, it was not possible to launch a wood cluster (the area is densely wooded) because all actors involved failed to reach an agreement and also because yields in this field of business are low.

The regional development agency is in charge of marketing the areas of tourism (cycle paths, hiking paths, horse-riding paths) and industrial zones. Participation in national and international trade fairs is the predominant means of communication used. The municipality displays little ambition to market itself, and the regional Chamber of Commerce perceives a general weakness in its ability to do so. For instance, the mayor does not appear to have any knowledge of the regional development initiatives, which also aim at creating a specific image. Rather, the municipality introduces initiatives that could further such an image in the cultural sector. In this context, the association, which was named after a well-known painter, is particularly highlighted, as this association maintains close ties with the highest national cultural institutions. Additionally, a small cultural festival has been held every summer for seven years.

EVALUATION AND NEED FOR ACTION

The image of a municipality of tourism and culture has already developed on its own, in the absence of noticeable contributions to communication on the part of municipal politicians. However, the municipality fails to capitalize on these possibilities. Besides, the mayor's ignorance of the marketing efforts undertaken by the regional development agency appears to be indicative of insufficient communication between the municipality and regional institutions. At any rate, integrated and professional communication in conjunction with an increased offering of tourism services would serve to achieve significant progress in developing the industrial location towards a municipality of tourism known beyond the region.

4.3.3.10 *Promoting new businesses in industries not yet well established*

SITUATION

The municipality surveyed is aware of the relevance of companies for its regional development. However, no distinction is made between establishing new, possibly innovative companies and attracting already existing companies. In both cases, the assistance provided takes the same form: as far as they are available, premises are provided at cheap interest or industrial plots are offered at a very favourable purchase price. This strategy facilitated the construction of a medical centre in 1993 (the municipality bore three-quarters of the cost), and only recently a hairdresser was housed on municipal property. The representative of the opposition interviewed views this measure in particular with scepticism, because there is no demand for another hairdresser in the municipality. This form of support is said to generate no benefit to the municipality, but to distort its competitive balance – in the form of discriminatory subsidization.

The regional investment agency emphasizes that most municipalities engage in this form of support, which consists in making premises available. If young entrepreneurs are supported, it is those that practise a trade. Apparently, the so-called technological-scientific or innovative start-ups do not exist – however, at present an incubator oriented towards innovation is being worked on at the regional level.

EVALUATION AND NEED FOR ACTION

The municipality does not offer specific assistance to young or innovative companies. Like others, such companies are supported merely by means of favourable rental fees for business premises. However, most municipalities do the same, so that this practice does not constitute an advantage for the municipality surveyed as a business location, but rather an approach that is taken for granted by entrepreneurs. If at all, efforts towards granting specific support, which also includes a focus on innovation, to start-up companies are made at the regional level. Consequently, need for action regarding this measure arises not least because the municipality lacks tourism services. However, it needs to be pointed out that the hands of the municipality surveyed are severely tied owing to its dreary financial situation. The

municipality surveyed would therefore be well advised to cooperate with other municipalities in these areas and, by means of pooling the few municipal resources, to facilitate programmes or industrial zones that would be especially attractive to (innovative) start-ups in a rural area (e.g. broadband internet).

4.3.3.11   *Competitive products by virtue of local origin*

SITUATION

At one time the region in which the municipality surveyed is located stood for high quality in the areas of food production (potatoes, sausages, dairy products) and manufacturing industry (in particular glassware). Some manufacturers were known throughout the country, and glassware from the region especially was able to fetch prices above the market average. However, the food industry is characterized by a development towards standardization in the form of cheap products, as is stated with resignation. No profit can be made any longer from products with superior quality (at superior prices). The production of glassware specific to the region is taking a similar course. The products made by many small glass manufacturers have simply become unfashionable over time. At any rate, the newly established mechanical engineering cluster is expected to provide some potential for compensating for this focus on dated lines of manufacturing.

The regional development agency, which is also responsible for the municipality surveyed, is currently trying to build a regional brand under which quality products typical of the region are to be marketed. Three years ago, a regional trade fair was held where such products were presented. Individuals who hold important social roles in the region were invited in order to act as multipliers and communicate their newly acquired knowledge about regional products. However, this measure, which led to a certain success, was primarily focused on supporting regional products within the region.

In the context of building a regional brand, it is also worth mentioning that, in 2002, a large administrative reform was introduced, which also led to previously separate regions becoming combined. Consequently, the region of the municipality surveyed has existed as a "hybrid region" for only six years. It is difficult to build a regional product identity in such a short period of time. So far, the images of the formerly independent member regions have been utilized.

The municipality surveyed itself used to be famous for high-quality leather products. The bankruptcy of the large tannery has left a gap that has not yet been filled by other manufacturing companies known beyond the region.

EVALUATION AND NEED FOR ACTION

At the regional level, there are efforts to establish regional quality products, for instance, by developing a joint brand. These are attempts to compensate for the losses that are bound to result from the decline of former regional flagship industries. These efforts need to be maintained and to be increased. The example of Austria clearly illustrates that regional quality products, such as food products, can successfully hold their own against cheap products on the national market.

At the level of the municipality surveyed, a former flagship company went bankrupt. Against the backdrop of what has previously been reported about the municipality, its political setting and its resources, there is little hope that any time soon a new flagship company will be able to fill the gap that has been opened by the bankruptcy of the tannery. One solution to the dire straits would be to develop the municipality with a view to making the most of the potential for tourism and in transforming the municipality itself into a tourist brand that is recognized beyond the region.

4.3.3.12 Freeing town centres by relocating businesses that generate high emissions

SITUATION

In the municipality, there used to be problems with emissions from companies that had been located in the municipal centre or in close vicinity to housing estates. The tannery, which no longer exists, was the largest producer of emissions. The other larger companies have switched to environmentally benign burning technologies. This led to a significant reduction in environmental pollution. In the municipality, new companies would generally only be allowed to locate in the industrial zone. All municipalities in the region show this tendency.

The regional institutions assert that financial incentives are available to support the measure of relocating companies with high emissions to the fringe of a municipality or to the industrial zone. However, despite the subsidy, such relocation is taxing on every company concerned. As municipalities mostly only host a small number of companies, one can hardly imagine that these companies would be forced to relocate. In extreme cases, the Ministry of the Environment could intervene and shut down the operation. This case would not appear likely in view of the limited number of companies existing in the municipality surveyed, especially as these operate in an environmentally benign way.

Managing "brownfield" investments could pose a potential problem. For instance, where an entrepreneur revives a vacant factory building situated in the municipal centre, the municipality will hardly be in a position to ask the entrepreneur to build a new plant away from the centre instead. This could lead to a trade-off between the financial objectives of the municipality and the quality of life of its residents. In the municipality surveyed, such a trade-off would occur if the tannery were reactivated.

EVALUATION AND NEED FOR ACTION

In the entire region, there is a tendency towards relocating environmentally harmful companies away from municipal centres or inducing them to switch to environmentally benign production methods. Efforts are made to direct new companies to industrial zones. The municipality surveyed was able to resolve its problems with emissions without resorting to relocations. Owing to the small number of companies, which also act in an environmentally benign way, for the time being, there is no urgent need for action in the municipality surveyed.

4.3.4 The municipality located in northern Slovakia

The municipality situated in the north of the country, close to the western Tatra, is renowned not only for its wooden houses constructed in the traditional manner, but also for its largely unspoiled nature. Owing to its favourable geographic location, it constitutes an ideal starting point for hiking and rafting tours as well as skiing excursions to its surroundings. Remarkable historic buildings, an open-air museum and a spa also enrich the large range of attractions for summer and winter tourism. Over the years, tourism has developed into an important source of income for the local residents.

4.3.4.1 Strengthening social cohesion by creating meeting places

SITUATION

Clubs and societies are not very active in the municipality. The most important societies include the women's singing association and the darts club. Moreover, there are a pensioners' club and several sports clubs. The municipality supports the clubs and societies by providing rooms it owns. For instance, the singing association uses the meeting room of the municipal office. The mayor emphasizes the important role of individual municipal citizens who undertake the organization of these societies or public events. The presence or absence of such committed individuals is an important determinant of the number of clubs and events that exist in the municipality. In this context, the parish priest has an important role; the parish functions as an important meeting point for young people.

In the municipality, a multifunctional sports hall was built, which is made available to the municipal citizens. The municipality bears the operating cost. Once a year, this hall houses the municipal ball, the pensioners' convention and a Mother's Day celebration. Local companies provide financial assistance, which serves to ensure that such celebrations can be held. In return, the municipality shows its appreciation towards the sponsors in certain respects (e.g. in the context of specific approval procedures). The sports hall is far from being used to capacity. In this context, the mayor complains that only rarely does somebody turn up and organize something in the hall. Apart from the hall and the rooms of the municipality, which the clubs and associations are allowed to use, the possibilities for coming together as a community are few and far between. The municipal centre is not free of heavy traffic, and inns or bars are scarce. For this reason, the mayor is planning to convert an old building owned by the parish priest into an inn.

When the municipality surveyed wishes to make premises available for communal activities, it is faced with a major problem: most properties are not owned by the municipality, but are jointly owned. Consequently, the municipality is not entitled to dispose of these properties. This is all the more unfortunate for the municipality, as financial grants from the region or the EU can only be applied for when the property involved is owned by the municipality. Consequently, the possibilities of making rooms available are tremendously limited. For this reason, it has not been possible so far to install a residence for senior citizens, which is needed urgently and could also serve as a meeting place for old-age pensioners. As a consequence, social cohesion among the older municipal citizens is described as weak.

EVALUATION AND NEED FOR ACTION

The municipal politicians are aware of the relevance of social cohesion for successful communal development. For this purpose, measures are taken (e.g. the construction of the sports hall) or supported (providing rooms for the activities of clubs and societies). In this context, certain deficits in the social cohesion within the municipality become manifest. Two barriers obstruct an improvement of this situation. Firstly, there are the constellations of property ownership in the municipality, with few properties being owned by the municipality alone. This is critical insofar as the financially weak municipality can only resort to a limited extent to the most important tool for strengthening social cohesion (i.e. providing favourable premises). Secondly, there is the population's passivity when it comes to actively managing the activities of local clubs, societies and events.

The problems in connection with land available for construction will be further discussed at length below. The passivity of the population appears to result from the passivity on the part of the municipal politicians. These hold the view that it is up to the citizens to make suggestions for living together in their society and to carry out these suggestions. In their opinion, the role of the municipality is limited to one of mere support. Although this is basically correct, the municipality appears to restrict its activity to waiting until initiatives are launched, which happens very infrequently (for example, the under-used sports hall) – as is pointed out critically. The municipal representatives do not seem to be aware that, in fact, there are ways of specifically promoting the level of activity of the local residents. In view of the limited financial possibilities and the problems regarding ownership of property, the municipality should focus its local policy on precisely this area of "specific promotion of activity", for instance via competitions for creative solutions to certain problems in the municipality.

4.3.4.2 Democratic and pluralist decision-making processes

SITUATION

In contrast to other municipalities, the municipality surveyed is not divided into opposing political camps. Granted, according to a representative of the opposition, there are opposing views on certain issues. At any rate, all suggestions are generally treated fairly in the municipal office. The mayor considers it a must that all meaningful suggestions that are feasible in both financial and practical terms are implemented. He does not differentiate according to who has put forward the suggestions. At the same time, he points out that not all suggestions that are basically feasible can be realized at once. Communicating this to those that have raised a suggestion in a way which makes sure that they are not offended and subsequently refuse to contribute any further ideas requires a large amount of tact and delicacy. The mayor attempts to encourage the population to show continuing commitment by personally thanking those in the municipal paper who have made a contribution for the municipality.

Formally, the pluralism of decision-making processes in municipalities is ensured by means of obligations institutionalized under the law: firstly, in the form of office hours of the municipal delegates (to be held once a month). Secondly, in the form of meetings with the mayor where a certain issue can be discussed. Thirdly, by way of a mandatory medium-term plan for the economic and social development of the municipality, which has to be drawn up in cooperation with the citizens. Fourthly, by means of a long-term construction plan, which also has to be developed jointly with the population. This form of cooperation between the elected representatives and the population is lived in the municipality surveyed. Each family living in the municipality was sent the current construction plan together with an invitation to make comments. The resulting 37 comments were integrated into the final construction plan, as far as was possible and meaningful. It is emphasized that this is part of the standard decision-making procedure in the municipality. Despite the noticeable efforts at the administrative level, the commitment displayed by the population is described as requiring urgent improvement. Residents are said to discuss points of criticism and possibilities of improvement in informal settings, but to be noticeably reserved when it comes to expressing criticism or comments in the municipal office.

The appropriate regional development agency promotes pluralist processes of decision-making by means of financial support to so-called action groups. In these action groups, entrepreneurs, municipalities and other interest groups work together on development strategies for the respective municipality.

EVALUATION AND NEED FOR ACTION

The comparatively harmonious political atmosphere in the municipality surveyed encourages decision-making processes, in which all municipal citizens participate, or may do so. The measure of publicly thanking those that contribute ideas, on the one hand, reflects the intention to present desired "role models" to the population. On the other hand, it represents an (affordable) reward in the form of local prestige. The population also participates in the medium- to long-term planning of the municipal development, for instance, the construction plan.

It appears that the municipality has implemented democratic and pluralist decision-making processes. It is noticeable that the responsible politicians strive to involve the citizens in their decisions. However, the residents themselves appear to be partially immune to these measures. For instance, suggestions are not raised in the course of the public meetings. One explanation may be that the official setting has a daunting effect on the population, especially where rather rough ideas, which have yet to be fine-tuned, are to be presented. Introducing a public internet forum that guarantees anonymity could help solve this issue. However, this would necessitate the municipality facilitating internet access for everybody, for instance, by installing a computer room.

The way in which participation by municipal citizens is promoted needs to be improved as well. As far as possible, contributors of ideas are treated respectfully and efforts are made to realize the suggestions put forward by them. However, this constitutes entirely responsive behaviour on the part of the municipality. In view of the passivity of the population, which municipal representatives complain about, it is necessary for the municipality itself to approach potential contributors of ideas and actively invite suggestions for improving the communal situation. The residents could be motivated more strongly to become involved by such a strategy rather than by merely being treated respectfully when approaching the municipal office or by having their names mentioned in the municipal bulletin. The municipality must act and not just react to initiatives.

4.3.4.3 Integrating the individual measures into a comprehensive development concept of the municipality

SITUATION

The municipality surveyed possesses two documents that have recently been approved: the construction plan and a plan for the economic and social development of the municipality. Both can be considered medium- to long-term development plans. The construction plan covers a period of 20 to 40 years and includes the development of tourist attractions and of the road network as well as the housing plan. The municipality developed this plan voluntarily, as it ranks below the threshold of 2,000 inhabitants that defines the minimum mark from which a municipality is obliged by law to draw up a construction plan. This voluntary effort has been made, as such a strategic paper makes it more probable that financial applications to the state or the EU will be approved.

The same goes for the plan for economic and social development. This plan, which has been developed for a period of four to five years, to a large extent serves the aim of obtaining public funding. Anything that will be associated with financial expenses in the next four to five years is recorded as a pro forma entry in the plan – even if it does not command any economic or social importance. The paper defines a framework and a perspective for the development of the municipality and considers not only material aspects, but also cultural and social issues.

There is no consensus about the use of these superordinate planning instruments in the municipality surveyed. The mayor primarily considers them a means to the end of obtaining grants – the planning certainty represents a welcome side-effect. Others point out that these plans are very relevant to each citizen's views regarding the possible further development in the municipality.

EVALUATION AND NEED FOR ACTION

The municipality possesses a medium- to long-term framework for development, which takes the form of a construction plan and a plan for economic and social development. Regardless of the actual motivation for developing such plans, it is noted that the measure of integrating individual projects in a larger development perspective has already been implemented in the municipality surveyed.

4.3.4.4 Consulting services provided for businesses willing to locate in the municipality

SITUATION

Generally, companies interested in locating in the municipality can turn to the mayor or the municipal office to enquire about possibilities for construction or potential tax relief – both fall within the scope of authority of Slovak municipalities. The potential entrepreneur is also entitled to inspect the construction plan as well as the plan for the economic and social development of the municipality. However, in most of the municipalities, such consulting is not offered in a professional manner, as they are too small to be able to assign and finance a separate specialist for certain matters. For this reason, in Slovakia, there is the tendency for several municipalities to install a superordinate municipal office for specific issues – among others, questions relating to company-locating decisions. This office provides information competently.

In addition, in the municipality surveyed, the consulting services mentioned are provided with rather limited professionalism. There is no individual who specifically addresses issues of company locations. This is due not only to the small size of the municipality, but also especially to the fact that the municipality is hardly in a position to broker or sell industrial plots to companies willing to locate in the area. Should it become possible to solve this problem and should the municipality consequently become more attractive to companies, the mayor wishes to focus especially on providing information, for instance, by upgrading the municipality's website.

EVALUATION AND NEED FOR ACTION

There is no strong demand for professional consulting services offered by the municipality as long as the question of rights of ownership to property has not been resolved. However, this question could be settled in the next few years. Therefore, the municipality would be well advised to start making preparations for the time following the state of joint ownership. The idea of intensifying the information offered via the municipality's own website appears useful. Owing to the limited resources of the municipality, it also appears advisable for the municipality to follow the Slovak trend and establish a superordinate municipal office for specific purposes together with other municipalities in order to ensure the quality of consulting services provided to companies willing to locate in the area.

4.3.4.5 Resolving conflicting goals of municipal development through involvement of all interest groups

SITUATION

During the latest term of office, a construction project was planned in the municipality surveyed in such a way that only the municipal council, a few entrepreneurs and individual citizens with special contact to the municipal office were involved in the development. When those affected by the measure who had not been involved in the planning stage learned about the planned measures, they overthrew the project – not least because they had felt left out during the planning stage. The new mayor currently in office has learned from this experience and strives to inform the municipal population in advance of any projects that affect the long-term development of the municipality and seeks to ask the residents' opinions on a planned project – for instance, in the case of the construction plan or the plan for economic and social development. However, where matters have an effect in the short term – for instance, in the fields of sports or culture – decisions are made centrally at the top.

Owing to the municipality's particular situation characterized by unresolved ownership rights, this integrative approach pursued in connection with larger projects appears to constitute the only way of preventing complete stagnation in the municipality. If the individual citizen feels that the municipality considers him in important decisions, he will feel more attached to the municipality. If he feels attached to the municipality, he will be more willing to be accommodating for the welfare of the municipality – for instance, by selling property to the municipality at the market price instead of charging extortionate prices.

EVALUATION AND NEED FOR ACTION

All municipalities must consider the needs and objections of the entire population when drawing up the construction plan and the plan for economic and social development. However, in practice, there are ways and means of circumventing this requirement. Still, the municipality surveyed assigns high importance to integrating all groups of the population in important projects. This tendency appears to be inspired by negative experiences in the past and the problem of joint ownership of land. In this sense, the measure has been implemented.

In this context, the question arises whether the municipality will continue to involve all parties in decision-making once the problem of land ownership has been resolved. Should the pressure to consider everybody be drastically reduced, the municipality may possibly fall back into a state of village oligarchy. In view of the high relevance of broad backing of development measures in rural municipalities, this should be prevented at any rate, for instance, by institutionalizing the medium- to long-term planning instruments even more strongly at the municipal level.

4.3.4.6 *Actively securing land for construction*

SITUATION

Regarding land for construction, the municipality surveyed has to address a complex problem. As this constitutes the core problem of the municipality, it is discussed at more detail at this point.

Part of the municipal territory is protected under a preservation order and, consequently, this land must not be built on. A considerable portion of the remaining municipal land is jointly owned by all inhabitants of the municipality. This constellation of ownership results from the process of transformation in the course of which state property was passed on to the population in the form of certificates (reprivatization). Each jointly owned property is managed by a separate company.

A regulation, which in hindsight must be viewed as most unfortunate, stipulates that the sale of a plot can only be effected if it is approved by all co-owners. In order to purchase a small plot in the municipality surveyed, it can be necessary to secure the approval of as many as 500 co-owners. One missing signature will be enough to prevent the purchase.

The purchasing process, which is exceptionally taxing and time-consuming, is made more difficult as several co-owners of municipal land are unknown and others no longer reside in the municipality or in Slovakia. It becomes especially complicated if one of the co-owners dies and the legacy procedures, which also serve to determine the new co-owner of the property, take several years.

Against the backdrop of joint land ownership, which is cited as the main cause of virtually all difficulties in the municipality, the municipality surveyed has striven to buy land for years. The former mayor managed to purchase property for the construction of family houses after a long struggle. The respective land was offered to prospects virtually at cost. In order to forestall property speculations and waste of the scarce resource, guarantees were agreed, which obliged the buyers to start building their houses within a specified period of time – otherwise, the property would return to municipal ownership.

The current mayor shows high commitment as regards securing and obtaining land for construction. In negotiations with co-owners of property, he always strives to draw attention to the communal relevance of a necessary property for the municipal residents – for instance, where a property is needed in order to facilitate road construction. In most cases, this enables the mayor to purchase plots at a fair price. Every plot that is extracted from joint ownership is celebrated as huge success.

The municipal representatives limit their activity to securing land for the construction of housing, in the same manner that the construction plan of the municipality surveyed basically only addresses the construction of residential buildings. The needs of companies are hardly acknowledged. This is remarkable insofar as it is precisely the fringes of the municipality where most jointly owned plots are located. And these peripheral areas have already traditionally been company sites in the municipality.

EVALUATION AND NEED FOR ACTION

The municipality actively secures land designated for construction. Despite the exceptionally difficult situation (joint ownership), some successes have already been achieved. Land for construction is secured in a specific manner: the municipality takes on the bureaucratic runaround when jointly owned property is developed and offers the land it has obtained to prospects for the purpose of construction. At the same time, regulations are in place that safeguard the municipality against inappropriate utilization of land zoned for construction.

No strategies are used that would include options for private land so that the municipality would have secured the right of first refusal *vis-à-vis* other prospects. Should the relations of ownership be settled finally at some stage (Slovakia was planning this measure for the entire territory by 2010), it would definitely appear worth considering such instruments of securing land for construction.

By treating land designated for housing as an absolute priority when obtaining and securing land for construction, the municipality attempts to counteract the successive migration predominantly of the young residents to urban areas or abroad. The companies active in the municipality are ignored in the process. The companies locate right in the centre of the jointly owned property, which severely limits their spatial expansion. In order to prevent the small number of businesses that reside in the municipality from relocating to a neighbouring municipality as they encounter no perspectives for development, the construction plan should be altered in favour of the companies. The municipality should be made aware that young individuals not only leave because of inappropriate housing possibilities, but also because they fail to find appropriate jobs. Moreover, it is precisely the small and medium enterprises that create new jobs in rural areas.

4.3.4.7 Joint financing of inter-communal projects

SITUATION

In certain areas in Slovakia, it is becoming increasingly common for municipalities to form so-called microregions. Such formations are primarily sought for the purpose of tourism, but also for developing infrastructure or for the purpose of nature protection. If a large investor approaches a municipality, it is conceivable that several municipalities may join forces to establish a joint industry park that encompasses several municipal territories.

For several years, the municipality surveyed has considered forming a microregion together with three neighbouring municipalities. This cooperation was to be realized under consideration of a recreational area in the municipalities. Eight years ago, an association comprising the respective municipalities was registered. However, it has not been active for a long time now. The plans for establishing a microregion were soon shelved at the time: strong individualism on the part of the residents and the municipal councillors led to the understanding that cooperation is something that secures a benefit for the partner – to one's own disadvantage.

Cooperating would also represent an option in connection with ironworks that were closed down and are owned by the municipality surveyed, but situated on the territory of a neighbouring municipality. The mayor can imagine a cooperation in the form of a foundation or an association that would aim to convert the ironworks into a museum in a combined effort.

EVALUATION AND NEED FOR ACTION

The potential for cooperation present in the municipality has stalled, although inter-communal cooperation appears necessary in many areas. The largest barrier to cross-communal projects is psychological: scepticism towards cooperations prevails. It can be assumed that this reserved position also reflects the result of 40 years of communal economic mismanagement.

It appears necessary to initiate a far-reaching change in the way of thinking both in the municipality surveyed and in the neighbouring municipalities. Superordinate instances (region, state, EU) need to increase their efforts to realize programmes that focus particularly on generating and raising the awareness of the advantages of cooperative behaviour for all those involved. Workshops could serve to make the advantages of inter-communal projects transparent to the population and to the decision-makers in the municipalities. Advertising competitions for the best inter-communal projects could work to inspire municipalities to break through the barriers to inter-communal cooperations themselves.

4.3.4.8 *Inter-communal coordination of efforts to attract new companies*

SITUATION

This measure is not applied in the municipality surveyed. In general, it appears that such a measure cannot be imagined, at least in connection with small and medium enterprises, given that companies are considered very relevant for the tax earnings of a municipality. If at all, coordination is practised where large companies wish to locate in an area or where companies already active in a municipality plan to expand and would consequently go beyond the capacities of their local municipality.

At the regional level, it is felt that coordinating the location of new companies would be more beneficial to the overall development of a region than the competitive way of thinking that prevails today. And, in view of the strong competition, coordination efforts on the part of the higher authorities would also be advisable. However, owing to the principle of subsidiarity, which is of high importance in the Slovak municipalities, the state or region is not entitled to issue instructions, but may at best give recommendations. In view of the economic situation of the Slovakian municipalities in general, and the precarious situation of the municipality surveyed in particular, such recommendations would probably not be successful anyway.

EVALUATION AND NEED FOR ACTION

The municipality surveyed does not cooperate with other municipalities in order to attract companies to locate in the area. Cooperations of small and medium enterprises are unusual for Slovak municipalities. In this aspect, which is critical to the development of rural areas, the municipalities work against each other and do not act jointly.

Given the strong individualism and the considerable tendency to think in competitive terms – which results from the large autonomy of Slovak municipalities – a bottom-up approach to realizing inter-communal coordination of efforts to attract companies to locate in an area is definitely not to be expected. In order to ensure balanced development of rural areas, it appears appropriate that higher authorities intervene in this area. However, this cannot be realized via coercion (principle of subsidiarity). Nevertheless, attractive grants for enticing companies to locate, which are only awarded to microregions, would constitute a possible instrument appropriate for improving the business situation in many rural municipalities in the short term, and for evoking a change of view on the local level in the medium to long term (i.e. cooperation can generate advantages for all parties involved).

4.3.4.9 Communication policy and creating a supraregional image

SITUATION

As far as possible, communication policy takes place at the municipal level, with measures oriented towards tourism predominating. The municipality communicates via its own paper, the regional press and its own website; it prints information brochures in several languages and participates in national and international trade fairs, as far as possible. Every four to five years, the municipality issues a major publication, which contains information, attractions and news in several languages. The mayor considers the measures relatively successful, and points to the entries of foreigners on the municipal website, which bears witness to the international popularity of the municipality.

At the regional level, it is possible to publish articles in a national municipal paper, which is issued by the Slovak association of Cities and Municipalities. In return for a small fee, municipalities can outsource the advertising activities to the respective regional development agency.

Generally, advertising expenses are borne by the municipality surveyed in their entirety. The local companies are not prepared to advertise in association with the location. The service companies, which are mostly very small, cannot afford such advertising activities. Years ago, the municipality had a regional tourism agency, which promoted its popularity. The agency was financed by commissions from the local tourism industry. However, the increase in guests was accompanied by an increase in black-market activities; wage dumping ensued, and offers were made at inferior prices behind the agency's back. Eventually, the tourism agency could not be financed any longer and had to close down.

EVALUATION AND NEED FOR ACTION

It is noticeable that the municipality surveyed strives to market its advantages for tourism – with economical means. Hence, it engages in communication policy. This constitutes a first necessary step towards a regional image. In order to build an image that goes beyond the region, it takes more than merely advertising. It requires interesting offerings that underlie the advertisements. In this regard, the municipality displays considerable deficits. There is hardly an offering of tourism services. Tourists do come time and again, but there are hardly any possibilities for enticing them to remain longer in the municipality. Accommodation is only available to a limited extent, and gastronomic venues are rare. It is doubtful whether the modest offerings in the municipality leave a good impression with the guests. However, this would be very relevant for the visitors recommending the location to others. Owing to the limited tourism services on offer, the municipality can hardly benefit financially from the tourists.

Before efforts are made to develop an image as a tourist destination known beyond the region, at least a minimum level of tourist infrastructure should be established – otherwise, the efforts will come to nothing. If the resources required for such an undertaking are too limited, the municipality should strive to bring about a tourist microregion in a joint effort with the neighbouring municipalities. It is easier to seek investors or to apply for financial support if several municipalities join forces. Moreover, this also makes creating an image as a tourist region both more efficient and more effective.

4.3.4.10 Promoting new businesses in industries not yet well established

SITUATION

As already mentioned, the municipality surveyed does not possess the resources necessary to support companies financially. At best, vacant premises owned by the municipality are provided or assistance is offered in connection with legal issues or permits. The mayor does not see that or how he could promote start-ups. In general, there is relief if new companies locate in the municipality at all. Against this backdrop, no attention is paid to the individual industries to which the start-ups belong. The main point is that new entrepreneurial activities that create jobs take place.

Experience shows that promotion of innovative companies is limited to urban areas. These possess the financial resources necessary to establish business incubators, for instance, in cooperation with a local university. In several Slovak cities, such projects are promoted by the Ministry of Economics. An individual municipality can definitely not afford such incubators. All actors are aware of this and, consequently, view promoting or developing companies in industries that have previously not been established or in innovative industries as a task that could only be taken on by an association higher up the ranks (i.e. at the regional or the national level).

EVALUATION AND NEED FOR ACTION

The municipality, which is economically weak and at present not attractive to companies, does not see any options for particularly promoting new businesses, let alone businesses that could contribute to diversifying the company structure in the municipality surveyed. The municipality consequently depends on the market success of few businesses. Slumps in sales or one single important company leaving the municipality would turn the economic situation, which is already unstable, into a considerable crisis for the municipality.

This scenario needs to be forestalled. The right answer to limited funds often lies in pooling the resources of several actors. Hard as it may be to induce several municipalities to work together on company issues (in contrast to cooperating regarding e.g. tourism, infrastructure), it constitutes the best option for safeguarding the municipality from potential financial ruin. If four or more municipalities worked together, they could still not provide sufficient resources to establish an incubator. However, the following options would be feasible if realized in a joint effort: firstly, a joint industrial zone with effective transport connections, the customary utilities as well as internet. Secondly, a separate body that actively pursues exclusively the goal of attracting small and medium enterprises to the cooperating municipalities and that is in charge of managing financial grants (region, federal province, EU). So that such a measure can be realized, the municipal politicians involved need to change their way of thinking profoundly.

4.3.4.11 Competitive products by virtue of local origin

SITUATION

In Slovakia, efforts are made at the regional level to increase the promotion of local brands – be it products or services. In the municipality surveyed, such specific products or services do not exist. As regards products, the potential for such specific goods is very low, given that few companies are active in the municipality. Only trifles, such as artful wood carvings, could be marketed. At best, these could be sold as souvenirs to the few tourists visiting the municipality. Tourism services offer the highest potential, as the municipality is situated in an attractive nature reserve.

EVALUATION AND NEED FOR ACTION

At present, manufacturing products specific to the region does not represent an option, owing to the currently low number of companies and the complex structure of land ownership. The municipality surveyed would not be competitive compared to other municipalities. Moreover, the municipality does not have a tradition as a manufacturer of certain products. Consequently, it is impossible to reactivate a past image and to add to it by means of new advertising strategies.

Nature constitutes the most important resource of the municipality. If the municipality wants to become known beyond the region, it needs to be for its touristic value. In order to cultivate this image, though, it is necessary to invest in developing specific attractions and in expanding tourism infrastructure in the medium term. The municipality could turn its major disadvantage – i.e. the small number of businesses – to its advantage. For instance, it could position itself as a municipality of unspoiled nature, undisturbed by company activities.

4.3.4.12 Freeing town centres by relocating businesses that generate high emissions

SITUATION

At the supra-local level, there is agreement on the feasibility of the measure. It is pointed out that, as a rule, new companies are located at the fringe of a municipality (for instance, in an industrial zone). The long-established businesses situated in the municipal centre are not forced to relocate, provided their emissions do not exceed specified thresholds. Municipalities that need to fight for every additional entrepreneur would not permit this for rational reasons. Instead, businesses are offered new peripheral locations that boast considerably better conditions – such as concessions of tax relief and low cost of land.

Companies active in the municipality surveyed have traditionally located at its periphery. In the centre itself, there are no companies that could pollute the environment or reduce the quality of life for the residents.

EVALUATION AND NEED FOR ACTION

Slovak municipalities appear to have recognized the problems that can emanate from companies located in their centres. As a rule, new companies are located at the periphery and, if possible, old companies situated in the village centre are offered better conditions and induced to relocate to the outskirts. In the municipality surveyed, this measure does not entail any direct need for action, because there are only a few companies, which have always existed outside the village centre, where the industrial zone has now officially been designated.

4.3.5 The municipality located in western Slovakia

The municipality is located alongside a large river in the centre of western Slovakia. The flat countryside offers few attractions that could be utilized for tourism. However, the municipality boasts several buildings of historic interest, among them a castle ruin and a château. First mentioned in official records at the end of the twelfth century, the municipality suffered under the Hussites and the Turks. Beginning in the middle ages, a rich tradition of craftsmanship developed. Subsequently, the increasing influence of the Jewish community also helped to promote the development of the municipality, as it facilitated expanding supraregional trade relations.

4.3.5.1 Strengthening social cohesion by creating meeting places

SITUATION

Clubs and societies are active in the municipality surveyed. Their activities are promoted by the socially active mayor and by the Catholic Church, which enjoys strong support in the municipality. The mayor – a former active sportsman himself – predominantly strives to establish facilities for different sports disciplines (e.g. tennis, soccer, field hockey) and generally welcomes project proposals put forward by the residents. The Church supports the activities of the young in the form of the local Young Christians Association. This association and the very active pensioners' association are among the largest and most important associations in the village.

There are fewer cultural activities in the municipality compared to sports. Such cultural activities are mostly initiated by individual members of clubs or societies. Time and again, individual outdoor events are organized. For instance, there is the traditional concert on the day of Epiphany, which is held in the church, or a competition for cooking goulash, but, apart from the traditional concert, cultural events held in the municipality at regular intervals are scarce.

The municipality supports the social activities financially (backed by strong support from sponsors), and it also provides municipal premises and in some cases (for instance, in the case of the pensioners' association) also bears the operating costs for the premises. As regards the premises available for social activities, no central "house of culture" exists in the municipality. This explains why many municipal events are (or rather have to be) held outdoors and consequently are exposed to the weather. Recently, the Catholic cultural centre, another meeting place, was demolished to give way to a nursing home. The municipal representatives consider establishing a new cultural centre a top priority.

EVALUATION AND NEED FOR ACTION

Social life appears to be strong in the municipality surveyed – thanks to the active involvement of municipal leaders, the Church and the local clubs and associations. Still, the municipality surveyed needs to catch up when it comes to implementing the suggested measure, which would strengthen cohesion among the municipal residents even more. There is no shared meeting place that would enable the municipal residents to exchange views beyond the boundaries of individual clubs or societies and to develop projects jointly in the long term. Hence, there is need for action regarding the establishment of a central municipal meeting point. The municipal leaders have realized this, and the construction of a cultural centre is currently being planned.

4.3.5.2 Democratic and pluralist decision-making processes

SITUATION

In past years, the political atmosphere in the municipality surveyed was fraught with mutual tensions. These resulted, among others, from the former mayor's practice of treating certain interest groups differently. The said mayor was voted out of office, and the new mayor is not a member of any political party. Since that time, communication within the municipality has improved noticeably. There is a general rule that every citizen can file motions (for instance, for the approval of funds from the municipal budget for the purpose of realizing projects) by the end of November every year. The municipal council openly discusses all motions, and residents who do not hold a political function are not only tolerated at sessions of the municipal council, but also encouraged to attend.

The mayor almost always asks the opinions of the municipal councillors where motions are concerned, although he is entitled to make a decision about them by himself. All parties praise this behaviour. Before important strategic documents are drawn up, an intensive process of discussion, which integrates all groups of the municipal population, is always initiated in the municipality. In individual cases, the population is invited to comment on a certain municipal project via surveys (the corresponding questionnaires are made available and also collected at the local grocery stores).

EVALUATION AND NEED FOR ACTION

The fact that the mayor is not affiliated with any party already signals to the residents of the municipality surveyed that, as a rule, in the municipality decisions are made without considerations of party politics. Equally, the participatory approach of the mayor creates an amicable and constructive political atmosphere in the municipal council. The residents know that they can approach the mayor with problems and initiatives. Major proposals, which affect the future of the municipality, are decided in the course of a broad discussion process, which includes the population. Hence, it appears that the measure has already been implemented.

4.3.5.3 Integrating the individual measures into a comprehensive development concept of the municipality

SITUATION

A detailed plan for economic and social development specifies the development measures of the municipality. This document also lists the development priorities and the order in which individual measures are to be implemented. The existence of this plan is partly motivated by the intention to obtain grants (many promoting institutions request that applications be accompanied by a municipal development plan); partly, the plan for economic and social development is actually considered to be a "vision" for municipal development put down in writing.

In addition to the development plan, there is a zoning plan, which includes the medium-term construction projects of the municipality. Both documents result from a lengthy discussion process, which involves the entire municipal population.

EVALUATION AND NEED FOR ACTION

The integration of individual measures into a comprehensive development concept has already been implemented in the municipality surveyed. It is noted positively that the development concept was drawn up in cooperation with the municipal residents. This ensures that the planned measures correspond to the effective demand of the mainstream of the population (rather than to the desires of privileged interest groups) and also that the residents can identify with the measures taken by the municipality. This, in turn, ensures support from the population, which makes it more probable that the medium- to long-term development plans will be realized.

4.3.5.4 Consulting services provided for businesses willing to locate in the municipality

SITUATION

If entrepreneurs (willing to locate in the municipality) ask the municipality for assistance in official matters, there is a general willingness to help. The mayor is open towards company concerns and makes an effort to involve the local companies more in local politics. For instance, this is evidenced by the introduction of a New Year Convention between the mayor and local entrepreneurs, which mostly has symbolic significance. The fact that at the first New Year Convention most entrepreneurs were amazed that they were not asked to sponsor certain municipal activities goes to show that the mayor's approach to companies is in sharp contrast to the communication policy of old.

Although there is a general readiness to offer consulting services, the mayor of the municipality surveyed does not expect potential entrepreneurs to turn to the municipality where official matters are concerned. He is of the opinion that the decision on the foundation of a new company is taken exclusively against the backdrop of already extant knowledge about financing or official procedures. Citizens who are not informed about the processes involved in incorporating businesses would consequently not start their own companies.

EVALUATION AND NEED FOR ACTION

The municipality surveyed is basically prepared to offer consulting services to potential entrepreneurs. However, the opinion prevails that, owing to the specific nature of entrepreneurs, such services would rarely be sought. Hence, consulting services to potential entrepreneurs are not considered very relevant. As a consequence, active forms of support for start-ups are non-existent in the municipality surveyed.

The municipality is not aware that the start-ups that have already been realized need not represent the entire entrepreneurial potential of the municipality. Active support of start-ups (e.g. information events, creating a positive atmosphere, highlighting services of consulting and assistance) could enable the municipality to reduce potential psychological barriers to entrepreneurial activity (e.g. general indecisiveness, vagueness of information about the process of founding a business, access to financial resources). This could lead to lasting improvement in the rate of enterprise creation and, consequently, also in the economic structure of the municipality.

4.3.5.5 Resolving conflicting goals of municipal development through involvement of all interest groups

SITUATION

As outlined already, the municipality surveyed strives to involve the local population in planning and deciding about major projects as well as in the municipality's strategic perspective for the medium to long term. As pluralism is lived in the municipality, no conflicting developments are noted.

EVALUATION AND NEED FOR ACTION

The measure that stipulates that involving all interest groups serves to avoid conflicting goals in the development of the municipality appears to have already been implemented in the municipality surveyed. The successful approach needs to be continued in the future.

4.3.5.6 Actively securing land for construction

SITUATION

The municipality surveyed faces two fundamental problems where its construction plans are concerned. Firstly, owing to its small size, it only possesses limited financial resources. Secondly, it does not own any (vacant) land. These conditions make actively securing land for construction especially difficult. It is not sufficient to change the zoning of municipal property situated at the periphery of the municipality – rather, the municipality is compelled to purchase land with the help of loans and earmarked grants. In this context, it is faced with fragmented ownership constellations, with some owners being unknown, and with financial claims of landowners that are generally (too) high.

As the municipality already had to turn down companies willing to locate within its territory owing to a lack of available land, the problem of securing industrial land has high priority. There are intensive efforts to purchase plots situated at the periphery in order to designate an industrial zone at the location. Only recently, the municipality has managed to take an important step towards ameliorating the dearth of housing space, as it had a residential building comprising 24 apartments built on its reserve asset of land – the playground beside the school building.

EVALUATION AND NEED FOR ACTION

The current leaders of the municipality bear a large burden, which results from acts of omission committed during past terms of office, which neglected to secure land designated for construction. The municipality is now faced with aggravated land problems, the fast settlement of which will determine the entire medium- to long-term development of the municipality surveyed, because, without land available for construction, companies cannot be attracted and, without residential land, the young will move to the city situated in close vicinity.

There is no way to solve the current problem other than what the municipality is already doing: by means of buying land in a taxing and time-consuming process and financed via bank loans. The mayor can attempt to appeal to the community spirit of landowners, when the property sought after is meant to house a construction project in favour of the municipal community (e.g. a road bypass). In some cases, such appeals could lead to a reduction in prices.

At any rate, the current municipal representatives must avert such an acute scarcity of land available for construction for the future. This can be accomplished in the course of the current purchasing programme if the municipality attempts to enter into option or pre-empting agreements with landowners who are at present not prepared to sell their land.

4.3.5.7 *Joint financing of inter-communal projects*

SITUATION

The municipality surveyed forms part of a microregion, which consists of one city and several municipalities from its surroundings. All parties describe the microregion as moderately successful at best. It was possible to develop a joint system of sorting waste and to establish cycle paths for tourism purposes, which cover a total distance of 80 kilometres across several municipalities, but other measures conceived, which should have been resolved at the microregional level (and which would have had to be resolved for reasons of efficiency), never went beyond the planning stage. As mentioned by one entrepreneur located in the municipality surveyed, this results in the municipalities still not possessing basic infrastructure facilities that are assumed to be the minimum standard for rural municipalities in Western Europe, such as a sewer network and treatment plant.

The poor results achieved for the microregion have been caused by egotistical behaviour of individual municipal representatives. Driven by the intention to maximize their own short-term profits within the microregional context, they reduce their own contributions and are hardly prepared to compromise. This behaviour is evident in the example of a very significant funding application: the microregion applied for funds for the purpose of establishing a sewer network, which was planned to cover the entire microregion, and the application was credited with a high likelihood of success. However, instead of pooling their joint forces and focusing them on optimum lobbying, for instance, individual municipalities started squabbling for the chickens before they had been hatched, e.g. by specifying which local companies should be commissioned to construct which sections of the sewer network. Eventually, a different microregion was awarded the grant.

The failure outlined above also represents a turning point in the activity of the microregion, as it has not been possible to realize any important projects at this level since that time. Only recently, two projects for cooperation initiated by the municipality surveyed have failed: firstly, the proposal calling for shared use of the large capacities of the school located in the municipality surveyed (the schools of the neighbouring municipalities are underutilized to a large extent), and, secondly, the shared financing and use of an information system acquired by the municipality surveyed.

EVALUATION AND NEED FOR ACTION

The municipality surveyed strives to carry out infrastructure projects jointly within the framework of the microregion, but frequently meets with opposition. This is one of the reasons why the structural development of the municipality is rather slow: it is not possible to realize cost reductions based on economies of scale, so that funds that would be necessary for other areas of municipal development are depleted owing to inefficiency. Funds that are exclusively granted to microregions cannot be accessed.

The municipality surveyed needs to question whether maintaining its membership in the microregion is at all useful. Owing to the relative large number of members (12 municipalities) and the resulting coordination problems, this inter-communal network appears to have failed. The municipality consequently needs to weigh up whether it would be more advisable to develop an alternative structure for inter-communal cooperation together with selected neighbouring municipalities with complementary development objectives. This alternative form of cooperation could become active in those fields where the microregion fails to reach an agreement about joint initiatives.

4.3.5.8 Inter-communal coordination of efforts to attract new companies

SITUATION

The representatives of the municipality surveyed basically consider it useful to cooperate at the inter-communal level for the purpose of attracting new companies, although they view it as unlikely that within the microregion a cooperation could be initiated for this purpose. Firstly, such a project would require an initiator who would get this form of cooperation going. The mayors of the neighbouring municipalities are reported to be too busy tackling their own problems to make efforts towards realizing matters of inter-communal relevance. Secondly, the municipalities still compete strongly against each other when it comes to attracting new companies to locate in the area, which would prevent far-reaching cooperation in this respect. Thirdly, discrepancies of opinion between the individual mayors have already caused projects with less potential for conflict to fail in the context of the microregion.

EVALUATION AND NEED FOR ACTION

The municipality surveyed does not apply the measure of coordinating efforts to attract new companies at the inter-communal level. One reason is the actors' lack of understanding of the relevance of cooperation when it comes to attracting businesses. This seems to apply less to the political representatives of the municipality surveyed, but all the more to the potential cooperating partners (i.e. the neighbouring municipalities).

In addition to general barriers to cooperation – such as the high importance of autonomy for the individual municipalities and the generally keen competition between the municipalities – one distinction is frequently made, which poses a particular problem. This refers to the distinction between problems particular to one municipality and problems shared by all municipalities. It is reflected in statements to the effect that no time is left for cooperation as one's own difficulties are already enough to deal with. This dichotomous differentiation is counter-productive as it disguises that many of the allegedly internal problems could also (or possibly exclusively) be solved in cooperation with other municipalities. This also applies to issues of attracting new companies or supporting start-ups by providing consulting services or infrastructure, which can usually only be financed if municipal resources are pooled.

In view of the poor understanding of the advantages of, and the necessity for, inter-communal cooperation, it is necessary to conduct workshops that illustrate the significance of cooperation between municipalities – for instance, on the basis of case studies.

4.3.5.9 Communication policy and creating a supraregional image

SITUATION

The primary medium of communication used by the municipality surveyed is the municipal newspaper, which is published quarterly and covers a wide range of topics, from announcements of upcoming events to reports on municipal life and political comments. The municipality is hardly mentioned in the regional media (newspaper and TV) because the mayor is not prepared to support the commercial publication policy of the regional paper and TV station (purchased media coverage). This reserved attitude towards media policy also results from the fact that the mayor currently in office is not prone to self-promotion. For instance, at his own request, the municipal paper does not publish any photos of him. Factual coverage is given priority over personal announcements from the mayor's office.

As well as the municipal paper, there is a brochure about the municipality, but this is considered obsolete. Moreover, in the context of the microregion, the members advertised jointly at tourism fairs, but this form of communication policy is no longer used.

EVALUATION AND NEED FOR ACTION

It appears that communication policy has been largely neglected, or can at best be termed average, in the municipality surveyed. The mayor does not appear to attach much importance to increasing the media presence of the municipality, or at least does not consider this a priority of municipal development. As the level of awareness of a municipality can exercise decisive influence on the development of different business sectors (e.g. tourism, regional products), the municipality surveyed should consider measures destined to raise its level of awareness.

Especially in view of the potential for tourist and culinary offers (and of combinations of the two), it would, for instance, be appropriate for the municipality surveyed to be continuously present at specific tourism and product fairs. However, this will only make sense if the municipality is actually in a position to offer local attractions or products. As financial resources are scarce, trade fairs should be attended in cooperation with other interested municipalities.

4.3.5.10 Promoting new businesses in industries not yet well established

SITUATION

Years ago, the municipality surveyed participated in planning an incubator in the city situated in its vicinity, which goes to show that the municipality does have an awareness of the importance that start-up companies have for municipalities. However, the incubator project was never put into practice, and since that time no new initiatives have been launched in order to promote the development of new businesses. The municipality itself lacks the resources (especially premises) necessary to establish an incubator of its own. However, among others, the municipality is planning to create premises for young entrepreneurs in the course of constructing the new cultural centre.

In general, it can be noted that the entrepreneurial potential in the municipality surveyed is high: many entrepreneurs whose companies are located in the city nearby reside in the municipality.

EVALUATION AND NEED FOR ACTION

The municipality surveyed appears to be aware of the high relevance that start-up companies have for the economic structure of a municipality. However, so far, start-ups have been promoted only within narrow limits, but the municipality at least wants to provide office space to young entrepreneurs, as far as this is possible. The municipality generally lacks the resources that would be needed to take more far-reaching measures that would ensure that the office space would actually be used. An inter-communal cooperation – such as a shared incubator – would represent one approach towards solving this problem. As cooperation does not appear to work in the microregion (any longer), it appears to be worth considering whether inter-communal cooperation should rather be sought outside the structure of the microregion. It could prove fruitful to cooperate with selected municipalities in the region, which are fully aware of the relevance of start-ups for the lasting development of the local economic structure.

4.3.5.11 Competitive products by virtue of local origin

SITUATION

Before the turnaround of 1989, the municipality surveyed was known nationwide for its high-quality bakery products. Following the turnaround, the bakery was privatized, the product name was changed and quality was reduced. The mayor has the nostalgic wish to revive the bakery tradition. The auspices are fundamentally good, as tourists and travellers passing through frequently still ask for the bakery products, which are no longer offered, and the infrastructure necessary for production (especially the oven) is still functioning. All interviewees concur in the opinion that it would be possible to ask a higher price for the bakery products.

Beer is a second agricultural product in the municipality surveyed that is credited with potential profitability. Hops are cultivated in the municipality, and the mayor is toying with the idea of having a brewery complete with integrated restaurant and a brewery museum constructed nearby.

EVALUATION AND NEED FOR ACTION

The municipality enjoys a reputation as a producer of bakery products, which it has built over decades of high-quality production. In conjunction with the means of production that are still in place, this represents an almost ideal starting point for (re)establishing a locally integrated product line. If successful, the food production could be complemented with the produce of the brewery (simultaneously pursuing both perspectives would in all likelihood overtax the capacities of the municipal leaders). The municipality could position itself as producer of traditionally high-quality agricultural products. In a further step, appropriate tourist attractions could be added, e.g. guided tours through the bakery including tastings, bread-baking museum, restaurants offering regional specialities, courses for baking bread.

However, such plans can only be realized once the problem of land ownership in the municipality has been resolved. Based on the knowledge that a positive image loses effectiveness if it is not reconfirmed continually, the municipal leaders should insist on a fast resolution of the difficulties surrounding land ownership and should subsequently make establishing the local label of bakery products the next priority, before the potential competitive advantage of the municipality surveyed is largely eroded and the formerly good reputation can only be revived in consumers' minds with extreme marketing efforts (that could no longer be financed).

4.3.5.12. Freeing town centres by relocating businesses that generate high emissions

SITUATION

Most enterprises in the municipality surveyed are located more at its fringe. When new companies want to locate in the area, which happens fairly seldom owing to the precarious situation concerning availability of land, efforts are made to induce them to locate in the periphery. Where local companies situated in the municipal centre provide disturbances, the municipality does not ask them to relocate, as they are too important for the tax earnings of the municipality. At best, these companies need to reckon with the anger of the population they affect and with requirements imposed by the municipality, such as limitations of the time of day when work is allowed.

However, the main source of noise pollution in the village centre is not the local companies, but the heavy traffic passing through the centre. The municipality is planning the construction of a bypass road, which would significantly contribute towards reducing the flow of traffic in the village centre.

EVALUATION AND NEED FOR ACTION

The municipality surveyed addresses the problem of emissions to the extent that it tries to make new companies locate at the fringe of the municipality.

Little is done to induce already existing companies to relocate, as the municipality is noticeably more dependent on the tax earnings generated from these companies than the companies are dependent on a location in the municipality surveyed. Moreover, the municipality is not in a position to offer financial incentives to move companies to land that has not yet been built on, because it lacks the means necessary for such measures, or needs to use the available means for implementing more important measures.

4.3.6 *The municipality located in western Hungary*

The municipality is situated in a low mountain range in the Balaton uplands. Archaeological finds provide evidence that Neolithic settlements existed in the region as early as the fifth century BC. The region houses one of the oldest dioceses in Hungary, which was established in 1009 when the kingdom came into existence. In the seventeenth century, Germans were made to settle in the municipal territory, which had been depopulated in the course of the Turkish Wars. These German settlers were later also referred to as "*Donauschwaben*" (Swabians from the Danube). After the Second World War, these families were largely expelled or else were assimilated, whereas Hungarian families were encouraged to settle in the region. The social and cultural life in the municipality still reflects this German-Hungarian history of the region. Traditionally, economic activity in the municipality has focused on smaller manufacturing businesses and especially on agriculture. However, in recent years, more and more pastures have remained unused.

4.3.6.1 *Strengthening social cohesion by creating meeting places*

SITUATION

The "house of culture" from the 1960s – formerly one of the largest in the region – still serves as an important social meeting point for all ages. Larger events, be it theatre performances or ballroom dances, are held there. In addition, music and folk dance groups regularly use the building for their activities. In this way, they also contribute to promoting the cultural identity among the local population, while keeping the historical-cultural heritage alive (e.g. traditions of the German community).

A sports club for the municipality is currently being created. In the "house of culture", table tennis has been played for several years already, and on the adjoining sports ground the friends of the beautiful game come together. It is important to the mayor that the planned sports club also includes a separate chess group. Fishing is also very popular with the residents of the municipality, which is evidenced, among others, in a competition held regularly at the municipality's own fishing pond.

One attraction, which particularly appeals to the young residents of the municipality, is the public internet access provided in the "house of culture", which was established with the aid of external funding four years ago. As the majority of residents do not have access to the internet, this platform of virtual communication has become more and more important.

During the 1970s, many joined youth clubs that, ideologically speaking, were close to the ruling Socialist Party. Since the system changed, these organizations have disappeared, and the municipality has attempted to create new spaces specifically for the young.

Between the church and the "house of culture", there is a small village square, which was affected by the recent renovation of the church. The municipality is currently working on making the square more attractive as a social meeting place again, e.g. by installing benches. Moreover, it has traditionally also been in the inns located in the municipality where residents come together after church on Sundays and discuss the incidents of the previous week.

EVALUATION AND NEED FOR ACTION

The municipality is trying to provide an attractive infrastructure for social activities of any kind to its population, as far as its limited resources permit. Public facilities, such as the "house of culture", frequently date back to the era of communism and, consequently, are in need of renovation. Yet, by virtue of the variety of events offered, the municipality manages to induce different groups of the population to participate in the events held there. This encouragement is matched by the initiatives launched by the residents, for instance, when it comes to keeping the cultural heritage alive in the form of activities of clubs and societies.

At the regional level, especially, the offer of sports and leisure time facilities could be further improved by means of inter-communal financing, construction and use. In this context, the municipal representatives are frequently reluctant to cooperate. Until the turnaround of 1989, inter-communal cooperation was hardly practised, as the central government in Budapest opposed endogenous regional development of any kind.

4.3.6.2 Democratic and pluralist decision-making processes

SITUATION

Where the positive development of the municipality is concerned, the municipal leaders consider suggestions put forward by different interest groups. Ideas for planning and implementing measures are contributed by municipal councillors, entrepreneurs and the population, but also by regional consultants. For instance, the new design of a village square was driven mainly by the older residents who wanted to reinforce historical elements typical of the region, such as paving the roads with basalt or planting green areas with boxwood, which used to be typical of the municipality in the old days. Many residents also considered a hairdressing salon – established in the style of the 1970s – inconsistent with the characteristics of the municipality and opted for its modernization. The municipal leaders themselves made renovating the church the top priority on their agenda. When such development measures are planned, this is communicated to the population early on. In doing so, the municipal representatives also seek to have individual discussions with citizens.

In the context of economic policy, the residents especially want new companies to locate, or for an industrial park to be established so that new jobs are created on site. The mayor hopes for valuable impulses from the LEADER programme, because it emphasizes both inter-communal cooperation and increased participation by different interest groups.

EVALUATION AND NEED FOR ACTION

If the leader of the opposition in the municipal council praises his competitor as a capable mayor, this is a very positive indicator of the political atmosphere in the municipality. On this basis of mutual appreciation, projects can be planned and realized across different political groups, which constitutes an element of consensus democracy as important as tough discussions of intended measures. The parties represented in the municipal council aim to pursue a policy that is guided by rational arguments and to develop concepts for the future in view of the situation in the region, which after all must be characterized as difficult, in both social and economic terms. When the repairing of municipal roads was discussed, the oppositional group managed to convince the ruling party to wait until the funds necessary for repairing the underlying sewer and water networks were available, to avoid road works being carried at two different times.

Although the residents of the municipality surveyed proactively bring their issues to the political process and instigate projects, civil movements can also turn out to be a hindrance to economic policy oriented towards the labour market. For instance, in the municipality surveyed, a civil movement prevented a local rubber manufacturer from expanding his operation, which would have created additional jobs. Officially, the objections raised referred to an expected increase in emissions. In reality, ill-conceived communication on the part of the company – which had insisted on using the sports ground for expanding its operation and on being granted tax exemptions for the next ten operating years – caused resentment in the population so that the positions of all those involved became entrenched. Eventually, the conflict ended in the municipality losing approximately 80 jobs and substantial tax earnings, because the company moved to a neighbouring municipality and since then has mainly worked with the labour force available there. The case illustrates the difficulties municipal leaders face when they need to enforce an employment policy aiming for growth even in the presence of opposition from larger groups in the population. At any rate, it is helpful that municipal representatives communicate possible advantages and drawbacks of new companies locating in their territory early on and in a transparent form.

4.3.6.3 Integrating the individual measures into a comprehensive development concept of the municipality

SITUATION

For reasons of costs and effectiveness, the municipal leaders are convinced that meaningful comprehensive development concepts beneficial for the development of individual municipalities should be created at the local-area level. This is borne out by the intention to establish a LEADER region together with 40 other municipalities, and also by a regional association recently established for the purpose of school reforms. The predominant aim of this latter cooperation lies in improving the quality of teaching in secondary schools in rural areas by establishing school centres across municipalities. The municipality surveyed has decided to act as location for such a school centre. It offers the neighbouring municipalities sufficient human resources and space capacities to facilitate high-quality education of their students. Installing a school bus system complete with supervising personnel is planned as a flanking measure.

EVALUATION AND NEED FOR ACTION

The municipality surveyed draws a consistent conclusion from the low number of residents and its weak financial position. These necessitate increasingly focusing the development policy in rural areas on the level of local areas. In future, savings in administrative costs will also probably become an issue, for instance, by means of combining municipal offices and other authorities. However, such reforms can also amount to a loss in living quality for the local residents, as is illustrated by the example of school centres. This will apply especially in cases where the regionalization of infrastructure is not accompanied by improved quality of services offered.

Nevertheless, the individual municipality also needs a development plan in the sense of a catalogue of future measures that coordinates different policies. In this respect, the municipality surveyed also lags behind. In the municipalities of the region, it has become customary to draw up development concepts only after financial subsidies have been put up to tender. In the past, this frequently led to deadlines for submitting projects not being met. In addition, the municipality surveyed is only slowly beginning to develop prudent and integrated concepts that focus on school infrastructure and road construction.

4.3.6.4 Consulting services provided for businesses willing to locate in the municipality

SITUATION

The mayor of the municipality surveyed is a politician who thinks like an entrepreneur, which is also confirmed by the representatives of different interest groups in the municipality. He personally takes charge of assisting companies willing to locate in the municipality. This assistance predominantly consists in identifying an appropriate and affordable piece of land and in speeding up approval procedures at the municipal level. For instance, only recently an investor has been able to acquire 20 hectares of fallow pasture from the municipality at a favourable price. As well as breeding Hungarian grey cattle, a livestock typical of the Hungarian lowland and threatened to become extinct, this entrepreneur wants to open a restaurant in the municipality. The mayor has invited the entrepreneur to various information events (e.g. in the context of the LEADER initiative) in order to explore possibilities for promoting the business idea together with him.

The municipal leaders also signal assistance to companies willing to locate by being prepared to lower the corporate tax rate. If a major company displayed an interest in locating in the municipality, the municipality would even be willing to grant complete exemption from taxes for a specified period of time. However, the municipality does not have the financial capacity to grant direct subsidies of any kind. Entrepreneurs located in the municipality subsequently benefit by being treated preferentially when public contracts are awarded. This has happened only recently when the local church was renovated. Moreover, the municipality makes concessions to companies as it prolongs deadlines and allows instalment agreements for the payment of municipal taxes.

EVALUATION AND NEED FOR ACTION

Thanks to an especially active and entrepreneurial mayor, the municipality surveyed proactively approaches interested entrepreneurs and attempts to provide them with very comprehensive consulting and assistance in all matters related to locating in its territory. The rural municipalities located in the region surveyed generally offer assistance in finding an appropriate location and speedy approval procedures to entrepreneurs willing to locate there.

Creating jobs is so crucial for the municipalities concerned, however, that municipal governments are even inclined to provide land virtually free of charge and to bear expenses incurred in the construction of business operations.

These measures need to be discussed within a broader economic context. Against the backdrop of sustainable municipal development within a region, such instruments are only sub-optimal for the purpose of promoting entrepreneurial activity. Such subsidies can lead to cut-throat competition between locations situated in the region and to a limitation of the future municipal development, if financially weak rural municipalities, in particular, concede their possessions to companies at discount prices. In the rural region surveyed, small and medium enterprises find it difficult to generate sufficient demand for consumer and industrial products. Moreover, frequently the well-educated specialists that the companies would like to recruit locally are missing.

There is a further aspect to this measure, which has not been sufficiently considered by the municipality surveyed. It refers to the municipality supporting regional cooperations among companies so that new economic activity and jobs can be generated. Even though they did not receive noticeable support from the municipal representatives, seven wood-processing companies operating in the region still managed to enter into a cooperation with a regional power plant. Under this cooperation agreement, they deliver their wood waste to the power plant, which uses it as raw material for producing renewable energy. In future, municipal representatives should act as catalysts in forming and stabilizing such regional business networks.

4.3.6.5 Resolving conflicting goals of municipal development through involvement of all interest groups

SITUATION

The municipal representatives remember the problems of unresolved conflicts of interest vividly when it comes to creating new jobs. The example of the rubber manufacturer has already been explained above. Owing to the residents' resistance to the intended company expansion, the company withdrew from the municipality. Both the municipal representatives and the company itself had failed to communicate to the population early on that the company complies with all environmental regulations and that its expansion would not entail health hazards. Besides, the municipality does not draw urgent attention to the economic necessity of expansion, which is required to maintain and create local jobs. On the other hand, neither the municipality nor the company sincerely discussed the location decision with the residents, which would have signalled flexibility to those concerned. A transport company's attempt to locate in the municipality took a similarly negative course. It had intended to establish its logistics centre in the municipality, but, in this case, the outcome of a survey among the citizens caused the project to fail.

While nowadays the cooperation between the Hungarian and the German communities hardly poses any problems any more – especially because these two groups have largely become assimilated – it no longer works between the generations in the municipality. In politics, education, the activities of clubs and societies, and also in the business community, the older generation has neglected to motivate and involve in decision-making its potential successors, i.e. those municipal residents aged between 18 and 30 today. For this reason, for some time, a group of committed citizens has formed around one municipal councillor. It aims to win back the young population for municipal life. For instance, after years of inactivity, school dances are held again now, the proceeds of which are contributed to educational institutions. Similarly, an interest group of (prospective) parents has formed in order to maintain the local kindergarten.

EVALUATION AND NEED FOR ACTION

In the future, the municipality will certainly have to deal with conflicting interests regarding new companies locating in its territory, because it appears urgently necessary to establish a municipal industrial park. Therefore, it is even more important that all those responsible draw the correct conclusions from the errors committed in the past.

Resolving conflicting objectives in the municipality surveyed is generally also made more difficult as, so far, the residents have mostly formed only temporary and loosely organized interest groups. Issues of village renewal provide one case in point. More stable organizational structures would facilitate better involvement of interest groups in municipal planning and would make the discussion process easier. The municipal representatives report their experience that the residents do formulate proposals relevant for the municipality when they communicate directly with municipal councillors, but that the so-called interest groups show little willingness to develop and realize solutions jointly.

The passivity that can be observed where problem-solving initiatives are concerned also has its roots in the real socialist system, under which it was not necessary, or even forbidden, for the residents to take care of municipal matters themselves. Moreover, all age groups display a certain resignation, caused by unemployment and consistently low living standards. For instance, fines imposed by the municipality are frequently ignored for a long time or not paid at all.

The current municipal leaders want to confront this passivity displayed by some groups in the population more vehemently. For instance, if a citizen repeatedly does not comply with the regulation obliging him to care for and maintain meadows or roads, he will be threatened with a fine in the future. It remains to be seen whether this measure will lead to a sustainable learning effect in those concerned. In this context, municipal representatives like to reminisce nostalgically and point to the "Swabian" tradition of the municipality, which is said to have been characterized by an inclination to work hard and by public order. The discussion of the measure also illustrates the current problems in the context of personal interaction and appreciation for public property in a municipality, which is in the process of transformation.

4.3.6.6 Actively securing land for construction

SITUATION

The zoning plan of the municipality provides the basis for planning and implementing this measure. It is the declared objective of the municipality surveyed for the next few years to purchase and convert properties situated at the outskirts of the municipal territory in order to be able to offer these plots to prospects as affordable land for building and housing. The mayor wants to have 60 new plots developed in this way, to increase their attractiveness by means of expanding infrastructure (e.g. roads), and eventually to put them up for sale at a price of approximately two million forints. Recently, the prices of plots located in the inner and the outer municipal territories have been regulated in order to forestall distortions of competition and property speculation.

The prices of comparable plots situated in the neighbouring municipalities range between four and seven million forints. In view of the considerable development costs, the mayor considers the targeted construction plots a very good offer destined to attract young families in particular to the municipality. According to the municipal leaders, the extant infrastructure represents a further competitive advantage. For instance, the municipality possesses a sewer system, gas piping and telephone lines as well as relatively good traffic connections owing to its own train station and its vicinity to a main road. An area close to the freight terminal, which belongs to a former bauxite quarry, has been designated as an industrial zone. The municipality has already extended its corresponding access road.

While the financing necessary to secure land for construction purposes was discussed within the municipality, a conflict of interest arose between the municipal leaders and those responsible for the school, as the latter would rather have seen an increase in financial support for their institutions instead. The municipal representatives are of the opinion that developing the land would serve to induce young families with children to move to the municipality, which, in turn, would be beneficial for both kindergarten and school.

EVALUATION AND NEED FOR ACTION

In the region, plots of land for housing and construction are offered by municipalities at prices far below their current market value in order to attract new companies and also private individuals. This leads to rising competition between locations of the municipalities in the region, which is increasingly pushing potentials for inter-communal cooperation into the background.

Complex legislation, the consequences of the restitution by the state as well as property speculations, hinders the securing of land for construction purposes. Plots potentially suitable for construction and housing have come into the hands of private owners who only keep them as assets and do not care about their maintenance. Consequently, uncontrolled growth and dilapidated buildings have become a burden on public life in the municipality. The municipality is trying at all cost to return these properties into the hands of the municipality and has decreed a right of first refusal for real estate. However, this appears to contradict national and European legislation, which is why the validity of this decree is now doubted.

In the municipality surveyed, there is no evidence of the price-enhancing effect of real estate purchased by citizens from the EU15 countries that has been observed in other regions of Hungary. Foreigners did buy land and real estate a few years ago, but the majority are currently trying to sell again, as they have found the location to be too far away after all for a stay that amounts to an average duration of approximately three weeks per year.

4.3.6.7 Joint financing of inter-communal projects

SITUATION

At present, it can be observed that local areas are increasingly being formed in the area surveyed, with the respective municipalities focusing on economic issues. As well as the manufacturing trade, municipalities emphasize agricultural production, be it viticulture or farming and breeding of livestock.

In one inter-communal project in tourism, a network of cycle paths is established, which links five municipalities in the local area. The project is supported financially, so that it is possible to rent out 12 bikes in return for a small fee. But the cycling tourist is to be offered even more convenience: on completion of the cycling tour, he is to be able to leave the bike in the respective destination from where an operating company will return it to the municipality of departure.

In the administrative field, for reasons of cost, the municipality surveyed maintains a rural district together with a neighbouring municipality with which it has traditionally had close ties. Moreover, the mayor can also envisage mergers of municipal governments in the local area in the near future. The measure also includes establishing and extending a regional association of schools among initially three, and later six, participating municipalities, which aims at improving the quality of teaching. Every year, the number of children attending the schools located in the local area declines by six to eight children. The smallest class in the municipality surveyed consists of ten children, the most recent graduate class comprised sixteen students. In the same year in which this survey was conducted, the upper secondary levels of the municipalities were to be combined, and the lower secondary levels were scheduled to be consolidated a few years later. The inter-communal cooperation also includes the kindergarten, the "house of culture" and the library.

Inter-communal projects of a different kind exist between the municipality surveyed and its partnering municipality in Germany. The latter's dance group and choir perform in Hungary every year, and financial support from the German municipality helped to renovate a country inn. In this context, the German minority residing in the municipality surveyed played a crucial part, as its representatives appealed to the German Ministry of the Interior directly to obtain the financial support.

EVALUATION AND NEED FOR ACTION

Even 20 years after the turnaround of 1989, the conditions for inter-communal cooperation are still difficult owing to the heritage of the system of real socialism. At that time, the central government opposed inter-communal cooperation, because it suspected such cooperations were a guise for dissidents colluding at the grass-roots level. Besides, the municipalities have to grapple with the heritage of poor infrastructure in traffic and communication, which makes the municipalities look like largely isolated systems. In order to improve transportation routes, large investments in acquisitions of land, renovations and construction, for which the municipalities do not dispose of sufficient funds, need to be made. Those responsible at the municipal level have already recognized the necessity of inter-communal cooperation and ambitiously pursue cooperation projects. However, when it comes to attracting companies to municipalities, the region is characterized by competitive thinking.

Village tourism in the municipality is as yet largely underdeveloped and could benefit from enhanced regional cooperation and the resulting know-how transfer. For instance, the municipality surveyed lacks accommodation facilities, which should at any rate be pooled with a view to establishing a tourist destination. Beyond the borders of the municipality, it can be observed that, in other municipalities, traditional houses have been renovated and serve as accommodation for tourists. Frequently, older residents live in only some quarters of their spacious houses, as the other family members have long moved out. If some areas of these houses were adapted for tourists, the respective owners and the municipality would find a new source of income.

4.3.6.8 Inter-communal coordination of efforts to attract new companies

SITUATION

As a rule, the municipalities concerned coordinate their efforts when new companies wish to locate in the area. However, at present, the entrepreneurial community shows hardly any demand for relocating or starting new businesses. Among other issue, the mayor sees the need for inter-communal coordination of this measure in establishing an appropriate infrastructure for the companies active in the local area. To give an example, a former service road was renovated together with a neighbouring municipality, and at the same time land in its surroundings was secured for construction purposes. The mayor also has high hopes for the planned extension of the trunk road into a motorway. This would add to the attractiveness of the municipality as a location for both Hungarian and foreign companies. However, this decision is ultimately up to the respective ministries in Budapest.

EVALUATION AND NEED FOR ACTION

The negative experiences that the municipality surveyed has had with attracting new companies to its location show that increased inter-communal cooperation could help to defuse conflicts between the interest groups early on. For instance, establishing a joint industrial zone would facilitate local jobs and also tax earnings for all municipalities involved. Those responsible in the region surveyed are only gradually beginning to prefer cooperation over competition in this regard. This becomes evident in the inter-communal planning of an industrial zone that is to be connected to an expressway. Such an industrial zone would also facilitate expansion of already existing compa- nies, which could otherwise threaten to relocate to neighbouring munici- palities. Although the initiative for establishing inter-communal industrial zones is primarily driven by the municipal governments, the ultimate decision rests with the Ministry of Economic Affairs in Budapest. It needs to be pointed out that smaller municipalities, in particular, are hardly familiar with these decision-making procedures.

4.3.6.9 Communication policy and creating a supraregional image

SITUATION

The municipality surveyed aims to communicate its development programmes and long-term objectives in regional papers. The mayor considers it highly important that the residents of neighbouring municipalities are also informed about the business, cultural, social and sports activities that take place in his municipality. A free telephone directory for the local area is to be published shortly. It will include the "yellow pages" for local companies and a supple- ment that lists cultural activities and important dates for the individual municipalities. The municipalities have generally begun to coordinate the timing of their individual events in order to avoid competing against each other for an audience.

   The municipalities are currently also trying to position themselves as a "health region" by increasingly advertising cycling as a sports and leisure- time activity in the regional media (the sport has not exactly been popular during the last 40 years). Extensive information on the regional cycle paths is to be available on the internet in the future. The same applies to the planned route under the theme "glass art in the region". These planning activities have also inspired the idea of interlinking the municipal websites more closely so that the individual municipality can generate a stronger marketing impact.

The municipality surveyed takes a wider view and establishes both regional and international networks, which is conducive to building a strong image. Following the turnaround of 1989, the multi-ethnic tradition of the area was reactivated and contacts to Germany were intensified. This has contributed to the municipality surveyed becoming known beyond the region for its cultural exchange across borders. In future, it could also generate an important multiplier effect in tourism. Those expelled from the area and their offspring are increasingly becoming interested in their Hungarian roots and want to visit the region. The municipality can offer these visitors a generally harmonious image of a local community that has come to terms with a problematic chapter in Hungarian history. This attitude is reflected in the statements made by various representatives of the municipality. In addition, supposedly small attractions can add to the positive image of the municipality. When a municipal councillor mentions in passing that a composer who is popular far beyond Hungary has spent his summer vacation in the municipality several times, this can attract international tourists. However, such potential for tourism can only be utilized if the municipality improves its infrastructure, also through individual initiatives of its residents. It is not sufficient to renovate the municipal museum; rather, houses throughout the municipality should be refurbished and, in particular, accommodation for tourists should be created. The municipality is heading in a good direction, especially owing to its activities within a LEADER region. However, in the absence of financial support, the present image of the municipality, which is limited to marginalized agriculture or a regional fishing contest, can be substantially improved.

4.3.6.10 Promoting new businesses in industries not yet well established

The municipal representatives feel that their hands are virtually tied as regards this measure. The region lacks consulting centres for start-up entrepreneurs, and the authority to grant necessary loans (e.g. for new technologies) is beyond their sphere of influence. Consequently, the promotion of start-up companies at the municipal level is fundamentally limited to developing land for construction, expanding local transportation infrastructure, investing in primary school education and providing the entrepreneurs with "moral support", as the mayor aptly puts it. In the industries catering to tourism and leisure-time activities, there is visible progress in the generation of new entrepreneurial activity. In these fields, increased inter-communal cooperation has led to the potentials of the individual municipalities being utilized more effectively.

EVALUATION AND NEED FOR ACTION

Despite the structural problems that exist in the rural area of the region surveyed, the municipal representatives make an effort to actively support entrepreneurs. The newly elected mayor, himself an entrepreneur, wants to draw on the municipality's tradition of promoting innovations. After all, the municipality surveyed was the first in the area to boast a telephone, a cinema or a swimming pool. However, in the discussion of these measures, it becomes particularly transparent how a rural municipality feels the negative consequences of the process of economic transformation. Starting up new companies is only successful if the entrepreneurs have a positive general attitude and the courage to take risks in order to be prepared for the future.

By contrast, one entrepreneur from the region expresses a rather pessimistic view when he doubts whether at present anybody in Hungary knows what the future will look like. Nevertheless, reference to successful measures of economic policy implemented at the municipal level in Austria and in Slovenia reveals that municipal representatives and entrepreneurs attempt to become active on their own account and strive for know-how transfer across national borders. The pessimistic view results from the inefficiency of communication channels between the individual levels of regional policy in the area surveyed. These channels are still organized according to a top-down approach. Consequently, the rural municipalities should be involved much more strongly in planning processes of regional policy in the future, so that a bottom-up approach is initiated and these municipalities can communicate and contribute their concerns, as well as their knowledge, more effectively.

4.3.6.11 *Competitive products by virtue of local origin*

SITUATION

The municipality surveyed is known beyond the region particularly for its ceramic products. However, national demand tends to decrease owing to the low level of income. Still, the mayor focuses on traditional products of rural craftsmanship, such as hand-woven baskets, or and agriculture for the future, such as breeding Hungarian grey cattle. Traditionally, the wood-processing industry has played an important part in the municipality's economic life. However, the wood industry is also currently under pressure owing to low demand and strong competition from Slovakia and Romania. Hardly any product manufactured in the municipality is explicitly marketed under the regional image. However, the economic and political actors in the municipality welcome this idea and can envisage regional labels, in particular for arts and crafts and for agricultural food products.

EVALUATION AND NEED FOR ACTION

When it comes to marketing its products effectively, the municipality surveyed certainly has not yet achieved its full potential. The products of regional origin, such as ceramics or honey, should be increasingly advertised as such and marketed internationally. Foreign tourists, in particular, display a comparatively high willingness to pay for traditional products of regional origin. The local residents, by contrast, need to redevelop their sense of quality, which need not necessarily be accompanied by an increased willingness to pay. Yet, consumer awareness appears to be developing in the region surveyed, in particular with regard to food products. The strong presence of international retail chains on the market is leading to consumers increasingly questioning the transparency of production of the food these retailers offer. This, in turn, creates a market niche for the food and agricultural industries, which focus on regional origin and can also communicate and prove this in an authentic way.

In their marketing strategy, the entrepreneurs active in the municipality should utilize the traditionally good relations of the municipality with Germany as a door opener for entering new markets. A further advantage can be gained from cooperating with neighbouring municipalities with a view to establishing a region strong in tourism and peaceful relaxation. Establishing a LEADER region has already constituted the first step in this direction. In this context, the municipality also benefits from attractions located in its vicinity, such as viticulture. At any rate, the municipality surveyed itself is attractive to national and foreign tourists who are interested in history and seek to experience nature.

However, regionality in marketing can only lead to lasting economic success if the product quality is also improved and ensured. This necessitates investments in means of production and in human resources, which definitely constitutes a critical issue for the economic future of the region surveyed. Reinvesting proceeds from tourism should, therefore, constitute a definite priority.

4.3.6.12 Freeing town centres by relocating businesses that generate high emissions

SITUATION

At present, there are virtually no high-emission companies in the village centres of the municipality surveyed. At any rate, the municipal representatives and the entrepreneurs appear to be aware that this measure is necessary. Companies that cause emissions and noise, such as a wood-processing firm, are located at the fringe of the municipality. It is also intended that the intercommunal industrial zone, which is currently in the planning stage, will be situated in an area that has traditionally not been densely populated, but has always been used by industrial and mining firms. Besides, the zoning plan rules out residential and industrial zones being mixed.

EVALUATION AND NEED FOR ACTION

Although at first glance the application of the measure does not appear problematic in the municipality surveyed, it is worth recalling the conflict surrounding the expansion of the rubber-manufacturing company. Some residential groups considered themselves affected by its emissions, or feared that these would increase, which contributed to the opposition against the company's expansion and ultimately to its relocation. On the other hand, the entrepreneur and the municipality were of the opinion that the level of emissions was well within the respective norms. The representatives of the citizens were accused of having used the emissions as a pretext in order to prevent the company from expanding to the neighbouring sports ground. This conflict shows that implementation of this measure not only concerns protection of the environment and of the quality of life, but also interest group politics.

4.3.7   *The municipality located in southern Hungary*

The municipality is situated in the lowlands in the south of Hungary. Its territory was first documented officially in the fifteenth century, but conquered by Ottoman troops 100 years later and subsequently burned to the ground in the course of the Turkish Wars. Many locations in the region only came back to life when Slovakian farmers of Protestant creed were specifically made to settle there. Their influence is still reflected in the social and cultural life of the region today. The agricultural sector, in particular, is of high economic importance in the municipality. Owing to the attraction of a natural reserve located in the vicinity, ecotourism is becoming increasingly important as well.

4.3.7.1 *Strengthening social cohesion by creating meeting places*

SITUATION

The "house of culture" constitutes the central social meeting place in the municipality. It houses a library and, as it offers public internet access, it also serves as "infopoint" for the local residents. This attracts young people, but also interested entrepreneurs and persons looking for employment, who want to obtain information from the worldwide web. Citizens' forums and lectures for the local entrepreneurial community are held in the "house of culture". However, the mayor states that so far interest in these events has been rather limited, which may also be due to the small number of residents in the municipality.

The demand for cultural events in the municipality is also influenced by the amount of admission fees to be paid. For instance, the majority of the population would not be willing to pay to go into a concert or a recital.

Consequently, it is mainly local groups (e.g. the school choir) that perform in the "house of culture" without charging admission fees. On traditional holidays (Christmas, Easter or the First of May) and during village fairs, a large number of residents gather regularly in the municipality for different events.

EVALUATION AND NEED FOR ACTION

It is one thing to grant state subsidies for establishing "houses of culture" in order to compensate for the diminishing importance of inns or weekly markets as meeting places in rural municipalities. Motivating different groups of the population to participate in the events held in the "houses of culture" is an entirely different matter. On the one hand, the municipal representatives are called upon to clearly communicate the benefits of citizens' forums or lectures to the population. On the other hand, the quality of these events needs to be ensured. This is closely linked with the infrastructure available on site: comfortably furnished rooms can contribute much to generating a positive atmosphere among those attending and in this way increase the likelihood that visitors return, or recommend the "house of culture" to others.

The operating costs for "houses of culture" constitute a particular burden on the municipal budgets, which show a deficit anyway. Consequently, smaller municipalities are forced to close down their respective "house of culture" after a short period of time, because they prefer using their budgets for maintaining local health care or the local post office. In the foreseeable future, when the young people of the municipality surveyed will be able to access the internet from their homes, even this offer of the "house of culture", which is currently used with frequency, will be devalued.

Both the mayor of the municipality surveyed and the respective regional development agencies are aware that there is a need for action at the political level if meeting places in rural areas are to be established, maintained and improved. At the municipal level, the necessary budgets hardly exist. Therefore, a current regional development project will focus on renovating village squares in the area surveyed so that these become more attractive as social meeting places again. Moreover, the residents should be encouraged to show more initiative for this measure. This presupposes that the population is appropriately motivated to make contributions for the communal good without direct compensation. However, this is an issue that may raise problems especially in countries in transformation like Hungary, as, owing to history, the term "community" carries a negative connotation there.

4.3.7.2 Democratic and pluralist decision-making processes

SITUATION

Apart from the party of the mayor, who already held this position before the democratic turnaround in 1989, there is practically no other political group worth mentioning in the municipal government. Nevertheless, different interest groups can be identified among the residents, which appear in public in a more or less organized form and bring their concerns before the mayor. These include old-age pensioners, handicapped persons, youth clubs, choral associations, sports clubs, the group of the Slovak minority and a heritage society. For instance, the sports club managed to convince the municipal representatives of the necessity to modernize the sports facilities. A choral association was able to win the support of the municipal leaders in finding an appropriate room for rehearsals.

It is also the municipal leaders who have launched initiatives for the interest groups mentioned. This is also the case for the proposal to establish a separate youth centre. When implementing projects for the individual interest groups among the population, the mayor primarily considers the sustainability of a measure. For instance, prior to modernizing the sports facilities, he had the projected utilization of their capacity assessed.

EVALUATION AND NEED FOR ACTION

The fact that no diverse political groups, and no oppositional party, are present in the municipal council has a negative effect on the democratic and pluralist discussion process surrounding decisions of communal policy. Frequently, the municipal council fails to discuss suggested measures critically and to consider alternative concepts. Activities of (informally) organized interest groups within the population can only partly compensate for this deficit in democratic politics. As these interest groups remain excluded from important bodies of communal policy and from decision-making proceedings – unless they form a civic political group that is actually elected for the municipal council – they are basically forced to limit their activities to the political instrument of lobbying.

The context of transformation means that the population still needs to become more strongly aware that it can get proactively involved in political planning processes at the municipal level, and that it may adopt a rational and critical stance *vis-à-vis* the political powers that be. Like in the "old" EU member countries, the phenomenon of the population losing ever more interest in political processes and displaying suspicion of politicians can also be observed. Particularly in the region surveyed, this societal phenomenon could be increased by the relatively high rate of unemployment that has been prevalent for years.

On the other hand, it is up to the municipal representatives themselves to implement instruments of grass-roots democracy in the municipal development and to tolerate and accept criticism voiced by the opposition and by civic groups, but also by members of its own political party. If few residents attend the sessions of the municipal council, this may also be due to the fact that presenting issues does not entitle individuals to remain involved in the political process. Besides, the willingness and the competence to engage in modern municipal politics are closely linked to the personalities and the experience of those in charge, and in particular of the mayor, especially if he has already been politically active before 1989 – as is the case in the municipality surveyed.

4.3.7.3 Integrating the individual measures into a comprehensive development concept of the municipality

SITUATION

The municipality is obliged to draw up a zoning plan, which in political practice is sometimes used flexibly. There is no comprehensive concept for municipal development, i.e. a concept that would link several policies. If at all, the mayor himself sees such an approach in the long-term planning of an industrial zone, which has been going on for three years already.

In Hungary, it is mandatory predominantly at the regional level, and for larger municipalities (from 10,000 inhabitants upwards), to draw up integrated, long-term development plans. In a new law on municipal government, smaller municipalities are now also asked to draw up economic development concepts. However, the municipal representatives doubt the practical sensibility of individual development concepts for smaller municipalities, as they now possess hardly any budget for economic measures and depend on state subsidies or private investment in matters of economic policy.

EVALUATION AND NEED FOR ACTION

In the region, municipal policy tends to focus little on sustainability and on several legislative periods. Mayors frequently decide to implement measures at short notice, with a view to particular interest groups who could influence their being re-elected. Even where individual development concepts of a more comprehensive kind exist at the municipal level, it will ultimately depend on whether those in charge also have internalized them and act accordingly – especially prior to elections.

A representative of the regional development agency responsible for the municipality surveyed also adds that traditionally the rural regions and municipalities in Hungary have hardly engaged in strategic planning. Although during the era of real socialism development plans were drawn up – first for a period of three years, and later for a term of five years – the fundamental objective was to meet certain indicators that were desired by national politics. Only in recent years has a top-down approach been employed in the context of national development planning and efforts have been made to establish the significance of integrated strategic planning at all political levels in Hungary. So far, these efforts have hardly reached the lowest governmental levels, i.e. the municipalities.

In fact, in view of the municipality's low number of residents and its modest financial means, designing comprehensive development concepts at the level of local areas appears to be a sensible approach for the future. However, the following also applies to regional development: budgets are tight as no nationally uniform guidelines for proceedings exist and, consequently, the concepts developed are frequently not put into practice. For the time being, the leaders of the municipality surveyed could look towards best-practice examples from other administrative regions in Hungary, which are already practising integrated municipal planning.

4.3.7.4 Consulting provided for businesses willing to locate in the municipality

SITUATION

The mayor of the municipality surveyed is trying to take a proactive approach towards implementing this measure. He makes an effort to explore personally the possibilities for implementing business ideas with companies willing to locate in his municipality and subsequently to find an appropriate location for the intended operation together with the entrepreneurs. The mayor is in a position to offer favourable land prices and tax relief. If the project turns out to be mutually beneficial, the municipality has been known to complete the conditions for implementation speedily. In such cases, the mayor instructs the municipal administration to carry out the necessary approval procedure, to designate the appropriate piece of land for construction and to draw up a sales contract. The mayor considers such a speedy process of location and approval an advantage that facilitates tying entrepreneurs to the municipality for the longer term.

Still, the consulting offered by the mayor is limited and essentially only concerns the approval procedure within the municipality. If entrepreneurs require assistance in specialist fields, such as issues of health or environmental protection, which also constitute important factors in the location decision, they need to turn directly to the respective regional authority.

EVALUATION AND NEED FOR ACTION

The rights of municipalities to decide about company locations autonomously, and the low number of inhabitants – as in the case of the municipality surveyed – enable the mayors to consider the individual needs of companies willing to locate in their municipalities. However, the quality of consulting offered in matters related to company locations basically depends on two aspects: firstly, it is the personal engagement of the respective mayor, who can possibly make construction permits at all and who is also able to speed up administrative matters substantially, which may well constitute an advantage in the eyes of the individual entrepreneur. On the other hand, relying on expert consulting offered by a mayor or by municipal representatives makes only limited sense, which is why it appears more useful to entrepreneurs to turn to the specialists in the appropriate regional and national authorities directly. It is these authorities that ultimately also grant the respective permits (e.g. health authorities, environmental agency).

In contrast to other municipalities situated in the region, the mayor of the municipality surveyed is well aware of the fundamental importance of this measure. One possible reason why other municipalities in the region show reservation in this regard may lie in the harsh approach that the respective authorities (e.g. health authorities, internal revenue office or labour inspectorate) take when auditing companies. As coordination between the regional and supraregional administrative levels does not work, the municipal representatives fear that they can be made responsible for problems arising in connection with a company's location in their municipality.

Faults identified in the running of operations are resolved in a way that is not sufficiently cooperative, i.e. characterized by a lack of coordination between the companies and the municipality. This can lead to municipal representatives being made directly responsible and prosecuted for any problems that may arise.

4.3.7.5 Resolving conflicting goals of municipal development through involvement of all interest groups

SITUATION

Conflicts among the population are generally not very substantial, and the mayor aims to identify conflicting objectives in strategic development for the municipality early on. As far as possible, an important measure is to consider the needs of several interest groups simultaneously so that unnecessary duplication can be avoided. For instance, the care for the elderly was organized in a way that ensures a maximum range of care, while still allowing for customization to each target group. There is a nursing home, domestic care in the urban area and mobile care for remote farms in the territory of the municipality.

This measure can be implemented more easily, as in the small municipality the residents frequently belong to several interest groups (e.g. old-age pensioners are also members of the cultural heritage society, and young people are also members of the sports club). Hence, from the perspective of the municipality, it is the same persons that become involved in negotiations about different issues of municipal development. Moreover, every three to four months, public sessions of the municipal representatives are held, where projects important for the municipality are presented and discussed.

EVALUATION AND NEED FOR ACTION

The decision-making processes in the municipality lack an important democratic and pluralist element: an opposition (such as a civic group) that is represented in the municipal council. This may lead to the impression that measures are not discussed rationally and extensively. At the informal level, the discussion with the individual interest groups works well, but will always be characterized by asymmetry of power between the discussion partners. The fact that the same persons negotiate different issues can also be viewed negatively, as such a blending of issues dilutes the focus on the individual interest group and, consequently, reduces the general objectivity with which decisions are made.

Consequently, the regional development organizations also aim to promote a strong civil society in the municipalities. For one thing, this takes the form of assistance in establishing interest groups. Moreover, it is the intention to institutionalize the discussion between municipal representatives and the population so that decision-making processes can become more objective and transparent. Frequently, this provides the foundation for identifying possible conflicting objectives.

What the municipality surveyed definitely lacks is fundamental information that has been substantiated scientifically and prepared by experts and on which decisions can be based. Such information would serve to bring to light the different viewpoints of stakeholders in a given project. Where decision-making in a municipality is characterized by lack of objectivity and of possibilities for discussion and moderation, interest groups or individual citizens may prefer to resort to the regional media to voice their criticism. These media are always receptive to unresolved conflicts. However, at this level, it will hardly be possible to discuss a measure rationally any longer.

4.3.7.6 *Actively securing land for construction*

SITUATION

Only recently, the municipality has designated a total of 30 plots for the construction of company premises and housing. Some houses have already been erected, and the plots have been almost completely developed. For this purpose, the water pipework was extended and the respective sites were provided with electricity. There already exists a plan for the extension of the sewer network, and only the connection with the gas piping is still missing. At approx. 250,000 forints (roughly 1,000 euros), such a municipal plot is affordable by local standards. As well as companies, the municipality intends to attract predominantly young people to its territory, although, so far it has had little success.

When providing land for companies, the municipality has had rather negative experiences up to now. For instance, a building located in the centre was made available to smaller service companies in order to contribute to ensuring local supply. However, as the municipality is located near to a city, many of its residents commute to this city and also do most of their shopping there. As a result, after only a few years, the shops in the municipality had to be closed down owing to low demand.

EVALUATION AND NEED FOR ACTION

Again, implementation of this measure is closely connected with the personality of the mayor. More specifically, it depends on whether he thinks like an entrepreneur and actively engages in regional economic policy, as is the case in the municipality surveyed. If a municipality does not act as the buyer of land for construction, mayors in the region surveyed frequently try to maintain close contact with the private owner of a property or an industrial zone so that they can represent municipal interests in a construction project. In such cases, companies moving to the municipality are frequently granted subsidies that take the form of tax relief. The geographic and infrastructural location of a municipality is often sufficiently attractive for investors to locate there at market prices. Nevertheless, only a small number of the rural municipalities situated in the region proactively engages in securing land for construction.

Frequently, it is also foreign private individuals that drive land prices for the construction of housing in Hungary, as they acquire land at prices they consider favourable. This means that young local adults frequently are forced to continue living with their parents as they are not in a position to pay the high prices that construction plots fetch.

4.3.7.7 *Joint financing of inter-communal projects*

SITUATION

In the domain of education, in particular, the municipalities situated in the local area analysed cooperate intensively. For example, the school and kindergarten of the municipality surveyed are also used by the neighbouring municipalities, and the operating costs are borne jointly. Moreover, eight municipalities of this local area cooperate to provide coverage of social security for the local population. New projects in inter-communal cooperation also arise at the administrative level. As the municipal council of the neighbouring municipality will have to be abolished, the municipality surveyed will take on its administrative responsibilities.

However, the willingness to cooperate in economic matters is less pronounced, in particular where issues of location policy and attracting companies are concerned. This is certainly due to the low budget capacity, but also to the municipal representatives thinking in competitive terms to an exaggerated extent. Economic cooperation works best in the domain of tourism, but newly made investments in infrastructure frequently end at the municipal border. For instance, often the cycling paths of the municipalities are not connected or clear signposts are missing. As long as only visions for regional cooperation are discussed, it is evident that the actors are willing to cooperate. However, as soon as concrete projects are to be drawn up and submitted, the contrasts are suddenly emphasized again.

In addition, the regional consultants view inter-communal projects in the region surveyed with criticism. For instance, it does not make economic sense to link 20 municipalities over a long geographic distance to establish a shared sewer network with a central sewage treatment plant. It would be more effi-cient to effect water purification and treatment locally, i.e. at the municipal level, which would also be supported by financial grants. Apparently, the case of shared purification and treatment of water in the local area surveyed represents an example of specific intervention motivated by interest politics, which, at the same time, promotes a cooperation that does not make sense economically.

EVALUATION AND NEED FOR ACTION

Increasing cooperation would also be called for in other matters of infra-structure so that the needs of the regional population can be met. Those residents that still have to drive on unpaved roads and paths do not see why the neighbouring village already has paved roads. Investments frequently end at the border of the municipality because those responsible at the national, regional and municipal levels disregard the needs of the population across borders. Besides, apparently some parts of the population only start caring about their fellow citizens' problems when they themselves have achieved a certain living standard.

Increased regional integration in the region surveyed in the domain of tourism would also be called for. A destination can only be competitive internationally when the local infrastructure is used to devise varied offerings for the tourist. Where new investments in tourism are made, it should even be explicitly stipulated that these be integrated regionally in order to avoid duplication. Also from the marketing angle, inter-communal cooperation appears meaningful as the individual municipality lacks the resources neces-sary for covering advertising in its entirety.

The LEADER programme should generate important impulses for inter-communal projects in the region surveyed. The funding directives make cooperation among regional partners mandatory. The projects, which regional consultants help prepare and guide, could serve to establish far-reaching awareness of the benefits of cooperation among municipal repre-sentatives and the population as a whole. Cooperation across the borders of local areas also needs to be enhanced, but frequently fails owing to the actors' psychological barriers *vis-à-vis* other parts of the country. Those involved need not relinquish the municipal identity in the region surveyed in return for such cooperation.

4.3.7.8 Inter-communal coordination of efforts to attract new companies

SITUATION

In the local area surveyed, it is the exception rather than the rule that municipalities cooperate in order to attract new companies. However, frequently, it is the entrepreneurs that wish to locate in the region who create a competitive setting among the respective municipalities – for instance, when one investor negotiates price and tax reductions with up to 20 municipalities simultaneously and plays them against each other.

The mayor of the municipality surveyed questions the basic soundness of this measure as he thinks that each municipality can only engage in its own location policy individually in order to further its overall economic development. Consequently, the municipal leaders officially pursue a strategy of confidentiality in their project of establishing a new industrial zone so that no information about competitive advantages is revealed to outsiders. All the more so as larger municipalities in the region attract many investments, which leads to jobs and frequently also employees from neighbouring municipalities moving to these larger municipalities.

Currently, negotiations are under way with a major producer of bioethanol who considers locating in the municipality surveyed. As the region surveyed is well provided with natural resources, the economic sector of renewable energies, in particular in connection with bio-mass, is credited with great potential. This could also present a new challenge in inter-communal coordination for the municipal representatives. It has been agreed with the investor that he will take delivery of the locally produced corn. This would also represent a promising opportunity for the agricultural enterprises located in other municipalities of the region, as growing beets, which have traditionally been cultivated in the region, is becoming less and less attractive, also because subsidies have been cut.

EVALUATION AND NEED FOR ACTION

Ideally, the local area should coordinate its efforts to attract companies. The respective municipal representatives should coordinate their positions *vis-à-vis* an investor in advance of a (major) company (such as the producer of bioethanol) locating in the area in order to improve the bargaining position for the municipalities in the region. As unemployment is fairly high in the region surveyed, a joint approach could facilitate the employment of more local workers in the new companies. By the same token, local enterprises could be integrated into the network of suppliers and customers of a larger company. Networks that exist among local companies in the local area could also constitute an advantage for companies moving to the area.

Municipalities that present an impression of a "region in discord" can ultimately prevent an investor from a commitment and cause him to shift his investment to another local area. Especially when the network of regional suppliers to a major company needs to be adapted, the cooperations need to extend to all levels and mutual trust must exist between the partners, as the existence of many small enterprises is at stake.

If the municipal representatives maintain their view that a competitive approach is advantageous in attracting new companies, this damages possible inter-communal cooperation. It also takes third parties to induce a change in the mindsets of those responsible at the municipal level, which is why the regional agencies with their training courses are of high importance in this context. In addition, regional politics can promote inter-communal cooperation, for instance, by stipulating that zoning is to be effected at the level of a local area. Moreover, the municipal leaders should keep trying to consider their local companies, especially where public contracts are awarded.

4.3.7.9 Communication policy and creating a supraregional image

SITUATION

The municipality's website is rather basic and is only available in Hungarian. The municipal leaders are looking for ways to ensure more user-friendly presentation on the internet and to make their website more readily available (e.g. by means of search engines).

Besides, the municipality advertises its attractions and fairs predominantly via local and regional information folders. These frequently also refer to the municipality's history, which is associated with the lives and achievements of two famous Hungarian scientists and educational reformers. A monument and the municipality's school are dedicated to them. The municipality's territory also houses a manufacturer of embroideries, which is known beyond the region, and a leather manufacturer. Every five years, the municipal government presents local arts and crafts in a large exhibition. In addition, regional papers report about the artists and their exhibitions. In reality, most of them have long moved to the large cities. Nevertheless, the municipality honours them if they exhibit their work "at home" on certain occasions.

EVALUATION AND NEED FOR ACTION

The rural municipalities of the Pannonian Plain frequently are not aware which potentials they could emphasize in their communication – for instance, in contrast to cities and mountainous regions. In the case of the municipality surveyed, this applies particularly to the potentials that could be tapped by establishing regional networks and focusing more strongly on ecotourism. Owing to its small size, the municipality can only create an image effectively within a regional network (e.g. signposted theme paths throughout the local area). This would enable the municipality to define attractive offerings for the destination and also to obtain additional marketing resources. For instance, the local area could present itself and its diverse attractions of cultural history and its natural treasures via an interactive map on the internet. In this context, the knowledge of history and natural sciences that the members of diverse associations possess should also be drawn on.

Regional cooperation projects, e.g. projects under the LEADER programme, should be positioned in regional papers with high media impact. Also the (private) regional TV station could be utilized more as a channel of communication for the activities of the local area. This would also communicate to the local residents that in the region in various domains things are happening, which can additionally activate new initiatives.

The municipality should continue to build its image, together with the neighbouring municipalities and supported by the experts in regional development. Under a regional destination brand, the municipality would be in a better position to emphasize its current attractions for tourism, such as its cultural heritage or the traditional craftsmanship. Moreover, the strong identification of the population with the region makes it easier to communicate this image to national and international guests in an authentic way. For this reason, the residents should be explicitly involved in the design of projects that address initiatives for image building. As a first step, however, the municipality's internet presence should be designed attractively and updated regularly.

4.3.7.10 *Promoting new businesses in industries not yet well established*

SITUATION

In the municipality, agriculture (especially cultivation of grain and breeding of livestock) is the most important economic sector by far, with approx. 60 per cent of the economically active residents working in this field. This is followed by the manufacturing sector (e.g. masons, carpenters) and trade (especially food retailing). The construction of a production plant for bioethanol represents a large project in a promising industry, which is currently prepared and almost completely privately financed. This investment is to generate 80 to 100 jobs in the municipality and to secure the future of the regional agricultural enterprises, which are to supply the industrial company with corn as a raw material for producing bio-mass on the basis of long-term contracts.

The large project for the production of bio-mass illustrates the approach the municipality takes when promoting the incorporation of new companies. The mayor holds that the effects of participating in regional start-up centres or incubators for small companies are too limited and instead has focused on attracting one larger company to the municipality for years. The municipal government has tried to convince the investor of the municipality's attractiveness as a location by means of negotiating effectively, offering tax relief and providing the necessary infrastructure (e.g. land, transport connections) fast and flexibly. The mayor hopes that the new company's location will also generate impulses for other industries.

Apart from the project outlined, there is hardly any interest in start-ups of new companies in the municipal territory. However, the municipality declares its general willingness to assist start-up entrepreneurs in finding appropriate land for construction or real estate. In such a case, the mayor would also secure land on the premises of the industrial zone, which is currently in the planning stage. Moreover, he can envisage granting subsidies in the form of tax relief to start-up entrepreneurs.

The municipality closely cooperates with the regional employment office to ensure the training of skilled workers in diverse industries. Financed via a foundation, the municipality employs job seekers for the duration of six months in order to enable them to learn and gather work experience (e.g. computer specialists, gardeners, agricultural specialists). This should subsequently make it easier for them to find a qualified job in the region.

EVALUATION AND NEED FOR ACTION

The municipality is certainly headed in a positive direction when it comes to promoting the incorporation of new companies in promising industries, such as renewable energies, with the means it has at its disposal. It frequently happens in smaller municipalities of the region that companies that have become unprofitable or entire industries are kept alive by means of subsidies, and it is not considered whether these subsidies can have a lasting effect. The municipality's efforts to attract a major investor are to be evaluated all the more positively as, contrary to the official position, the actual government funds for the promotion of renewable energies are still rather limited.

Nevertheless, the municipality surveyed should also extend its assistance to small companies in other industries. Otherwise, it runs the risk of becoming unilaterally dependent on one large investor, to whose individual decisions (e.g. relocation) the majority of businesses in the municipality and in the region could be exposed, which could possibly threaten their existence.

In times of globalization, when regions tend to be competitive only as larger entities, measures designed to promote the incorporation of new companies can only be effective at the inter-communal level, especially where innovative industries are concerned. However, at present, the municipal representatives of the region still display little readiness to cooperate in order to attract new companies. The intended investments in renewable energies could also lead to municipal representatives revising their views and could ultimately generate more economic cooperation in the region.

4.3.7.11 Competitive products by virtue of local origin

SITUATION

An organic plant nursery as well as a meat-processing company located on the municipal territory have become well known nationally and refer to the region in the branding of their products. The slaughterhouse, in particular, offers the Hungarian speciality sausage Kolbász under the "regional origin" label in its outlets in the regional capital and in Budapest.

In general, it can be observed in the region surveyed that products already established on the market tend to be associated with regional names or that regional origin is marketed more strongly later on so that consumers are made aware of the products' regional roots (e.g. also in the cases of schnapps and salami). Food products, in particular, are frequently also labelled as "organic" in an attempt by local producers to justify a higher market price. Frequently, local regional or company consultants encourage entrepreneurs to pursue this marketing strategy. At this point, only the municipality's permission to use its name or the name of the region for the product is missing.

EVALUATION AND NEED FOR ACTION

In contrast to the "old" EU member states, the Hungarian market for high-quality and also possibly high-price products with regional origin or certified organic production has not yet been saturated; in fact, the opposite is true. However, the trend towards organic products also offers opportunities for free riders, as consumers frequently do not really have detailed information about the actual quality standards and their supervision. This has also increased consumer sensitivity towards abuse in food labelling.

As in other countries in transformation, in Hungary, two more effects in consumer buying behaviour of regional products need to be considered: frequently, consumers prefer foreign (i.e. Western) over domestic products, as the former suggest higher quality. This pattern of consumer behaviour certainly stems from negative experience with products during the era of communism, or the period of transformation, as well as from the resulting low public opinion of domestically produced goods. Awareness of the quality of domestic products is only beginning to arise.

On the other hand, it is the level of income that ultimately determines which goods are actually bought in the shop. For this reason, the numerous consumers in the medium- and lower-income segments of the country are rather price-sensitive when purchasing food and, consequently, tend to shop in discount stores – also influenced by appropriate advertising. These stores do not offer the expensive originals (e.g. liqueur or sausages), but stock own-label brands at affordable prices. By contrast, domestic brands known beyond the region, which have managed to establish themselves in the premium retail segment, are bought by foreign tourists and the high-income segment of the Hungarian population.

In promoting this measure, it is necessary to consider that opportunities for sale and generating additional revenue need to correlate positively with the level of income of the target group. In particular, products of regional origin should be sold via several sales channels simultaneously in order to ensure that the dependence of regional manufacturers on international retail chains is not increased further. For example, the prices charged by a farmer for herbal tea sold on his farm are not competitive in comparison with those charged by the discount store located in the municipality. At the same time, the said farmer provides a German wholesaler with his high-quality medicinal herbs and is dictated quality standards and a low selling price.

Owing to this competitive situation, actors of economic and regional policy are called upon to increasingly promote and advertise alternative concepts of producing and marketing rural products. Such concepts include cooperations between agricultural and food producers, agricultural producer groups, farm shops, farmers' markets and similar forms. In order to develop appropriate markets and the intention to pay for regional products, it is necessary for small and medium enterprises, but also Hungarian consumers, to become more aware of the importance of these products (e.g. effect on health, ensuring regional added value, fair price policy, creating a regional identity). In the medium term, actors should aim to maintain the added value in the rural region and, in this way, secure the existence of the regional small and medium enterprises and the jobs associated with them.

4.3.7.12 Freeing town centres by relocating businesses that generate high emissions

SITUATION

In the course of the location project of the manufacturer of bioethanol, the municipality must perform a detailed environmental impact analysis. The location is scheduled to be situated approximately two kilometres outside a village centre, which is also necessary according to stipulations of the fire authorities. It has also been ensured already that the plant will be connected to the regional sewage treatment plant. According to the results of the environmental impact analysis, the new company will produce hardly any hazardous emissions as its main waste again will be bio-mass, which can be reused in production. As regards possible emissions generated by the agricultural operations in the municipality, the corresponding guidelines are derived predominantly from the zoning plan, which defines the pieces of land where the breeding of livestock or the use of fertilizers are permitted.

EVALUATION AND NEED FOR ACTION

As regards implementation of this measure, there are, in fact, grey areas: in the case of doubt, rather than risking the investor cancelling a project, the municipality is rather forthcoming, especially towards strategically important companies that desire certain locations for their production or warehousing facilities. Even where location decisions are made the subject of a referendum, the municipal governments are able to use the constellations of power for creating a fait accompli and to influence the public opinion accordingly.

Eventually, companies that create high emissions are usually located where they attract the least attention and provoke the lowest resistance among the residents, that is to say predominantly in rather small municipalities.

4.3.8   The municipality located in northeastern Hungary

The municipality is situated in the very northeast of Hungary, close to the Ukrainian border. The flat landscape with vast pastures, meadows and marshlands as well as the rather cool average temperature are typical of this part of the Hungarian Plain. Over the centuries, the development of the region was primarily affected by the numerous wars and associated shifts of borders as well as administrative reforms. Since the middle ages, the municipality has held a central role in the region as it collected the toll for the road to the East. The proliferation of the Protestant creed in the sixteenth century has had a lasting effect on the social life in the municipality. Compared to the rest of Hungary, the economic development of the local area is to be considered rather poor. Most residents live on agriculture, which is limited to a few products as the soil is of only mediocre quality. The agricultural enterprises of today are the companion businesses of the production cooperative of old, which had been centrally organized. The potential for tourism in the region has hardly been exploited so far.

4.3.8.1 Strengthening social cohesion by creating meeting places

SITUATION

As in many Hungarian municipalities, the "house of culture" is also an important social meeting place in the municipality surveyed. As well as cultural events, it also houses meetings of representatives of the local area at regular intervals, as well as specialist lectures and conferences. By contrast, the construction of a leisure centre close to the sports ground is still in the planning stage. It is essentially the financing of this ambitious project that causes problems. Situated beside a river and a forest, it is intended to invite both local residents and tourists to engage in various leisure-time activities. The municipality already possesses sports clubs for volleyball and football, and the mayor emphasizes that both young people and old-age pensioners are equally involved in these clubs. A meeting point for senior citizens established by the municipality is very popular among the older residents. Food is served there, and senior citizens also gather for prayer and for sewing circles. Besides the sports clubs, the school has an important role as a social meeting place for the young. The municipality takes this into account as it participates in a regional community of schools, which develops educational concepts for the future. As well as establishing a kindergarten, the community is also planning to erect a central school for the surrounding municipalities in order to counter the fragmentation of pupils among smaller villages and to pool resources. The municipality surveyed also possesses a pavilion, where regional products are offered. The pavilion has become a central meeting point for the residents and also constitutes an important platform for the presentation of local agricultural products.

EVALUATION AND NEED FOR ACTION

When aiming to implement this measure, the municipality is hampered by the fact that there are hardly any civil organizations, such as associations or interest groups, which would launch initiatives or would realize projects in cooperation with the municipality. The young, in particular, are not offered much freedom or outlets for activities. The situation is aggravated further as older youngsters change to schools situated in urban areas and are thus lost to the social life in the municipality. The cultural and leisure-time activities available in urban areas are frequently more attractive to young people than the respective offerings in their local rural municipalities. Nevertheless, the municipal representatives should try to increasingly involve the young in existing organizational structures and decision-making processes as early as possible so that they become attached to their local municipality. The initiative of individual residents should also be called on where the planning of the new leisure centre is concerned so that financial investments can be kept low. Moreover, the municipality should join already existing initiatives for village and town renewal, which are currently focusing on reactivating and establishing public places.

4.3.8.2 Democratic and pluralist decision-making processes

SITUATION

In the municipality, different interest groups discuss decisions, and suggestions raised by local residents are integrated into the process of discussing municipal development. Traditionally, the farmers' associations have provided a good example of self-organization by citizens. They represent the interests shared by the farmers in the small area, so that, for instance, higher sales proceeds can be achieved.

Currently, the regional development agencies and the management of the local area are a force that drives the successful implementation of this measure. They aim to establish regional discussion forums in order to secure the maximum extent of backing for concepts regarding the future of the area surveyed. At the first stage, the consultants transfer know-how on strategic and planning tools not only to the mayor, but also to entrepreneurs and basically to any citizen residing in the small area. The objective is to enable the community to design development concepts independently on this basis in the medium term and to contribute to drawing up applications for funding. More structured processes of development in the local area are also intended to make it easier for the citizens to find cooperation partners for their economic or cultural initiatives.

EVALUATION AND NEED FOR ACTION

The regional consulting agencies have set themselves quite an ambitious agenda for strengthening pluralism and grass-roots democracy in the local area. However, experience from other local areas shows that such changes in the structure of regional politics only have a lasting effect if they are accompanied by changes in the attitudes of the actors involved in them. This implies that the process needs to be guided very carefully, as both the decision-makers and the residents are adopting completely new views and experiences. The approach taken by the consultants, who view themselves as facilitators of self-organization and guides, rather than leaders of the regional forums, is to be judged as fundamentally positive.

However, there are also opposite tendencies in the region surveyed. For instance, the farmers' associations, which are officially independent, nowadays show stronger political inclinations than only a few years ago, and the range of issues they address has become increasingly narrower. The loss in memberships that they are afflicted with indicates that the farmers desire neither the polemics of party politics nor a limitation of their concerns to questions of price. It should also be interpreted as a signal of alarm for the development in the small area that the results of discussions between the municipal representatives and citizens – for instance, on the issue of environmental protection – are regularly diluted later on. In general, the municipal representatives avoid making concrete commitments, which does not exactly strengthen the population's trust in the local government.

4.3.8.3 Integrating the individual measures into a comprehensive development concept of the municipality

SITUATION

The municipal representatives have a development plan for the coming years, which encompasses several areas of politics and also explicitly considers cooperation with neighbouring municipalities. As regards social services, a new ambulance station is intended to shorten the distance to patients. In addition, a day-care facility for the disabled is to be established. The necessary funding has already been approved.

Educational projects form a core element of the development plan in the municipality surveyed. For one thing, the school is to be renovated. Moreover, it was possible to secure a construction permit for a new kindergarten. The restoration of the school is also of strategic importance, as the building is to be extended to a regional school centre in the future. The schools situated in the neighbouring villages were closed down owing to financial problems. Budget cuts enforced by the government in Budapest have forced the municipalities to take this step.

In addition, the management of the local area possesses a multi-level development plan for the area surveyed, which focuses on education and training as well as on improving the social infrastructure. Regarding the latter, there is a cooperation with the municipality surveyed for the purpose of establishing a day-care facility for the disabled. The regional development agencies also try to generate impulses regarding employment policies, for instance, a plan for reintegrating unemployed persons into the occupational world has been developed. Regional representatives of employers and employees are to be involved in its implementation. Employers who hire unemployed persons, on a temporary basis to begin with, receive financial support from the government.

EVALUATION AND NEED FOR ACTION

The measure is implemented in the area surveyed as corresponding development plans exist at both the regional and the local levels. However, a significant obstacle is posed by the failure to work together both on the part of interest groups within the municipality and on the part of different municipalities in the local area. The activities of the regional development agencies outlined above target these two levels in particular.

It needs to be added, however, that the regional offices are understaffed, and their employees have to spend the majority of their time on administrative tasks. Better coordination of responsibilities between the regional development at the levels of the administrative region and the small area, respectively, would serve to increase the effectiveness and efficiency of the consulting services provided. It would also be beneficial to optimize the way in which the financial grants are divided among the individual regional levels so that planned projects can be realized more easily. The regional development agency has put forward the idea of establishing a mayor for the local area so that local administration and the inter-communal coordination of individual activities can be effected more efficiently. This idea can be classified as truly innovative.

The high level of social contributions prescribed by law enhances the trend towards black-market labour. As, in the area surveyed, unemployed persons who draw unemployment benefits and work illegally can obtain a higher income than if they pursued a regular official occupation, it can be doubted whether regional employment initiatives can actually create new jobs in a lasting manner. All the more so as such initiatives are usually implemented for only a short time-span. Moreover, improved supervision of black-market labour and reforms of the social system are sensitive issues of national politics in Hungary, which relegate the local level to the rank of a mere spectator.

4.3.8.4 Consulting services provided for businesses willing to locate in the municipality

SITUATION

At present, very few entrepreneurs display an interest in locating in the area surveyed. The local economic life is dominated by traditional agricultural enterprises, and small trade companies play a fairly insignificant role. Still, the mayor personally deals with the enquiries of each individual entrepreneur as far as possible. The consultations do not focus on issues relevant to the location proceedings, but rather on possible assistance to be granted in the course of ongoing business operations.

As more stringent regulations on the sale of local agricultural products have recently been introduced, the producers are increasingly turning to the municipality for assistance. The mayor prepares information and the necessary documents for those concerned so that they can keep obtaining the permits necessary for operating local retail stalls. A similar situation exists where the new environmental regulations are concerned, which have become more stringent owing to membership in the EU and the associated *acquis communautaire*. For instance, if weeds are not destroyed in time, high fines are charged. The municipality informs the agricultural entrepreneurs in detail about the new regulations and their consequences.

Complementary to measures at the municipal level, there exist regional development institutions that offer entrepreneurs assistance in finding premises or land, and in establishing business contacts. They also provide so-called "innovation audits", which screen a company for potentials for optimization for payment of a small fee. However, one regional manager fears that the entrepreneurs do not sufficiently realize the benefit of this service. As the development agency is currently planning to introduce a retention requirement in the amount of 40 per cent of the consulting price, he fears that there will be a drastic reduction in the number of entrepreneurs that use this service. Financial support granted for investments, e.g. in machinery, hardly results from initiatives launched in the region itself, but comes mostly from national programmes for the promotion of economic progress.

EVALUATION AND NEED FOR ACTION

The main problem hindering the implementation of the measure does not lie in the municipalities failing to provide assistance. Rather, at present there are hardly any entrepreneurs that wish to locate in the area surveyed. The mayor believes the residents' reluctance to think like entrepreneurs is responsible for this. He describes them as too averse to risk. This is certainly not the only reason, because the location also lacks human resources (e.g. regional potential of specialists) and capital. According to the mayor, all levels of regional development as well as the educational system should see to it that the

population becomes more knowledgeable about the incorporation of companies and about entrepreneurship. Moreover, it needs financial incentives to
induce potential entrepreneurs to put their business ideas into practice.
In view of the collateral required and the high interest charged on loans,
potential start-up entrepreneurs who have little equity quickly lose enthusiasm
about becoming self-employed.

In addition, the official procedures for companies willing to locate in an
area are time-consuming and not transparent – for instance, for the purpose
of obtaining a construction permit. The administration is slow, which is also
evident in the fact that frequently officials are not substituted by anybody for
the duration of their holidays. Entrepreneurs and residents already distinguish
very clearly between the individual administrative levels and between private
and public providers of consulting services. For instance, a newly incorporated innovation agency very deliberately differentiates itself in its marketing
from the regional administration, as it is aware that the residents view the
latter rather with scepticism. Some municipalities in the region try to respond
actively to bureaucratic obstacles. For instance, they have hired municipal
officers specifically for the purpose of handling company requests, which
would certainly also constitute a useful service to be provided by the municipality
surveyed.

4.3.8.5 Resolving conflicting goals of municipal development through involvement of all interest groups

SITUATION

Apart from agricultural organizations, the area surveyed largely lacks organized interest groups. Consequently, it is predominantly the mayor and the
municipal council that determine the municipal development. Areas of conflict, which are clearly reflected in the statements made by different municipal
representatives, are not resolved in a process of broad discussion with
the population or with entrepreneurs. Such conflicting issues include village
renewal, the educational system, and labour market and location policies. The
municipal government prescribes the courses of action, but does try to
respond to enquiries from the population.

EVALUATION AND NEED FOR ACTION

All those involved in municipal activities display a certain degree of passivity
when it comes to resolving issues of development. The most promising activities in the context of this measure definitely appear to be efforts made by the
regional development agencies. These strive to promote truly broad and
pluralist processes of decision-making in the region, for instance, by establishing regional forums. What is hardly mentioned in the discussion of this
measure is the role of regional media, be it newspapers, radio, local TV or the

internet. In fact, they should provide platforms for the discussion of regional issues and should not serve as mere advertising media or the communication outlets of party politics. In this context, the municipalities can also provide content and take on an important role in creating a setting for discussions and in managing the implicitly conflicting objectives more openly.

4.3.8.6 Actively securing land for construction

SITUATION

The financial resources are not sufficient to realize this measure in the municipality. While the mayor sees little opportunity for securing land for construction in the near future, he can basically envisage securing rented property. Surprisingly, the municipality, and also the regional agencies, count on entrepreneurs taking the initiative in matters related to location decisions. Providing entrepreneurs with cheap land for construction is considered too risky as the respective company might turn out to be unprofitable after a short period of time. There also exists a small industrial zone in the region surveyed, where entrepreneurs can rent space at favourable terms. So far, however, only two companies have decided to locate there.

EVALUATION AND NEED FOR ACTION

As interest in starting new businesses is generally low in the region, this also hinders the implementation of this measure. In addition, most municipal residents make their living in agriculture and (can) hardly make new investments. The general attitude both of the municipal government and of other institutions of regional development needs to be viewed critically, as they have not yet internalized the relevance of this measure for attracting new entrepreneurs. They do complain that young individuals move to the cities, but fail to draw the corresponding conclusions for municipal policy. For instance, they fail to provide affordable and renovated apartments. The municipal representatives could target the many houses in the region that have been vacated as their residents have moved to the cities. The municipality could take over the role of intermediary between potential prospects and owners so that both groups' interests are protected. What is currently happening regarding the execution of this measure may at best be interpreted as benevolent gestures, but cannot be considered effective assistance to investors and the local population alike.

4.3.8.7 Joint financing of inter-communal projects

SITUATION

Supported by EU financial grants, the municipality surveyed has joined forces with the neighbouring municipalities and formed a local area, which strives to develop the region as a whole. As in other local areas in Hungary, this includes merging the schools, which is also encouraged and supported by the state. The regional school will be located in the municipality surveyed. In return, its residents will be able to resort more to the social and cultural infrastructure available in both of the neighbouring municipalities, which includes a residence for the elderly and a large "house of culture". In addition, sewage treatment will be shared by all three municipalities, and an inter-communal landfill is currently in the planning stage. The municipality surveyed has recently entered into an association with another municipality for the purpose of developing an area of lakes and floodplain forests for tourism and, what is most important, for advertising it jointly. For the time being, plans exist for the ecological restoration of a lake and for establishing a nature reserve.

EVALUATION AND NEED FOR ACTION

A closer analysis of the use and progress of inter-communal cooperation also reveals opposing views existing in the region surveyed. For one thing, this refers to the different mentalities of the individual municipal governments and also among the population, which clearly hinders the cooperation, especially at the initial stage. This implies that the work of the regional consultants needs to focus on channelling discussion processes meaningfully by means of moderation and mediation, and on resolving misunderstandings. The mayors additionally display a form of competitive thinking when it comes to obtaining financial grants for their municipalities, while the European trend is developing towards promoting local areas.

The plans for merging the schools in the local area meet with resistance from the residents of the villages concerned. This is understandable, as at present it remains unclear whether the measure will improve the quality of teaching and whether the longer distances will reduce the quality of life for the families concerned. In addition, regional assemblies that include representatives of all interest groups concerned would be called for so that comprehensive information can be offered and also fears can be alleviated. On the other hand, the new inter-communal cooperation will definitely lead to advantages for the population, as it will be accompanied by an extensive offer of social and cultural institutions. From an economic viewpoint, the increased regional integration is indispensable for the purpose of realizing potentials for growth. As regards tourism, the representatives of the municipality surveyed have already internalized this insight to a large extent.

4.3.8.8 Inter-communal coordination of efforts to attract new companies

SITUATION

Coordinating the location of new businesses represents uncharted waters for the municipal representatives, but also for the regional development institutions, in the region surveyed. Hardly any municipality is currently actively pursuing a policy of attracting new companies that is coordinated with the neighbouring municipalities. Basically, the approach presently pursued focuses on optimizing the individual municipality's competitive position *vis-à-vis* companies willing to locate in the area. A recently established industrial zone in the region surveyed is attracting the majority of (new) company investments. Besides, employees have already started moving to the respective municipality, which negatively affects its neighbouring municipalities.

EVALUATION AND NEED FOR ACTION

Although hardly any companies wish to locate in the region and the competitive pressure on the individual municipality is increasing, when it comes to coordinating efforts to attract companies, the municipalities still adopt a short-term view. In reality, incentives to investors can only be created by means of a regionally coordinated policy of attracting companies, as the infrastructure available in the individual municipalities is poor. Interestingly, cooperation works well in connection with establishing new cycle paths or a nature reserve and where educational reforms are concerned, but not when it comes to attracting new companies. In particular, the cooperation in the domains of education and social services creates an infrastructure that makes the location attractive also to companies and new employees. As regards establishing this general framework for a positive economic development, the region surveyed is already headed in a positive direction.

4.3.8.9 Communication policy and creating a supraregional image

SITUATION

When creating a unique image, the region surveyed can certainly build most on the regional agricultural specialities and on festival tourism. The leaders of the municipality surveyed particularly emphasize a one-week festival held every August, for which a camping site has been made available and which is very popular with tourists. As the existing infrastructure is not sufficient to accommodate the crowds of visitors, the municipal representatives are considering establishing additional accommodation in the region and equipping the existing camping site with showers. The municipality surveyed expressly advertises this festival on its website. Moreover, the municipality surveyed also benefits from hot springs that exist in the administrative region, which are even advertised in the neighbouring countries. Where regional agricultural specialities are concerned, the focus is on mixed farming. One promising domain is a series of events about the topic of plum jam, which includes show cooking and tastings. In addition, a kind of schnapps can be considered a product known beyond the region. It has come to be advertised as a speciality from the region surveyed in Budapest as well as in Brussels. The municipal representatives also consider that arts and crafts will become increasingly important to image building in the future. Therefore, more budget should be allocated to arts and crafts.

Word of mouth is the main instrument for communicating the image of the region. Advertising via electronic media, which could also reach target groups beyond the region, is still in its beginnings. One problem is the lack of funds necessary for developing advertising brochures, placing ads in print media or commissioning advertising spots in electronic media.

EVALUATION AND NEED FOR ACTION

Considering the low level of available resources, the measure is implemented fairly well within the region, and in particular also in the municipality surveyed. The mayor strives to use the available agricultural structures specifically for image building. Nevertheless, the individual municipalities of the region surveyed should emphasize their strong points in the different sectors (e.g. agricultural products, village tourism, festivals) more strongly and communicate these more efficiently via a shared platform that also reaches beyond the region.

At any rate, cultural-historical tourism still offers untapped potentials. There are church ruins dating back to the middle ages, which could be prepared for visitors. A further possibility lies in establishing outdoor museums, which could present the former social structures in the region surveyed in the sense of an installation. In the medium term, the municipality should focus on national tourism. As the attractions offered to tourists are rather limited at present, it does not appear realistic that many foreign tourists can be attracted to the municipality, even if the destination were advertised more actively in the international arena.

4.3.8.10 Promoting new businesses in industries not yet well established

SITUATION

The municipality surveyed does not rely on any organized initiatives to attract companies active in new industries. This also applies to the regional context, as the few industrial zones or low local corporate tax rates alone are not sufficient for a comprehensive innovation policy.

The individual interest groups cite a number of obstacles and difficulties. At the communal level, the obsolete infrastructure (transportation, energy, communication) of the villages reduces the attractiveness of the location for innovative industries. The regional and national levels hardly possess concepts of a promising innovation policy in these rural areas. This relates in particular to the development of human resources, to financial resources and to the promotion of regional innovation networks (institutions of research and development, universities, companies, consultants). The management bodies of the local area are not in a position to provide the financial resources necessary for start-up entrepreneurs; at best, they are capable of offering basic consulting on the incorporation of a new business.

In view of the agricultural structure of the region, the sector of bioenergy especially is considered a possibility for attracting innovative companies. The municipality approaches local partners with the aim of establishing a cooperation of producers of bioenergy and local agricultural suppliers in the region in the medium term.

EVALUATION AND NEED FOR ACTION

The mayor of the municipality surveyed is of the opinion that concessions of tax relief alone will suffice to attract new companies. However, this assumption appears to fall short of an innovative location policy and to be even somewhat counter-productive. Rather, the point is to find investors who display a lasting interest in the location and the sustainable development of the region. For this purpose, only a concerted approach on the part of the municipalities can be effective.

Attracting a major producer of bioenergy could certainly generate important impulses for growth for the region, as it could also lead to the formation of a local network of suppliers. However, the agricultural structures must not become too strongly dependent on one single company, as the future opportunities are difficult to ascertain for this industry owing to the present energy crisis. What appears more advisable is developing a strategy of diversification, i.e. besides one major industrial producer in the region, it is ecological agriculture and small trade enterprises, in particular, that need to be promoted. For the latter, it could predominantly be the emerging domain of tourism that could generate investment impulses.

4.3.8.11 Competitive products by virtue of local origin

SITUATION

Products which are competitive beyond the region are most likely to be provided by agricultural production in the municipality surveyed. The municipal government supports these initiatives by promoting a pavilion where regional products are marketed and which is used jointly by five municipalities. However, the cohesion among the farmers in the individual villages is considered problematic. As a consequence, it is mainly the larger producers, which are more potent financially anyway, that benefit from such marketing initiatives, while smaller farmers fail to agree on the distribution of proceeds and on shared financing concepts.

Besides, when the agricultural sector suffers a disaster – for instance, in the cases of droughts or flood – the assistance offered by the public sector is too limited. In the case of damage, the insurance farmers need to have in order to qualify for compensation payments is high. For instance, in the year before the survey relating to this study was made, the failure of crops amounted to 30 per cent. In order to qualify for an appropriate subsidy from the state, the farmers had to fund a substantial portion themselves.

In general, local producers are becoming increasingly dependent on major retail chains. As the pressure of production is mounting, the yields of crops are becoming worse. Less was invested in further developing regional quality products and marketing them locally. In the future, connecting regional tourist attractions (e.g. nature reserves, arts and crafts) with regional agricultural products (e.g. jam, beef) is planned to enhance the competitiveness of the municipality surveyed.

EVALUATION AND NEED FOR ACTION

At present, the marketing efforts of the farmers in the municipality surveyed are not sufficiently integrated, and the farmers have not yet fully realized the advantages of cooperations for purchasing, selling and marketing. Possibly, this exaggerated form of individualism still derives from the memories associated with cooperative agricultural societies enforced by the state. The municipality, and also regional consultants, should work to convince the farmers of concepts of partnership more strongly.

At any rate, it appears useful to build a regional brand, which can comprise different product groups (e.g. meat, fruit, drinks) in the sense of an umbrella brand. It would facilitate emphasizing the speciality food products of the entire region. Coupling the brand with other tourist initiatives of the region could enhance the advertising effect (e.g. cycling tours including visits to regional farmers and tastings of speciality products).

4.3.8.12 Freeing town centres by relocating businesses that generate high emissions

SITUATION

At present, there is little potential for problems and conflict associated with the implementation of this measure in the municipality surveyed. In the village centres, hardly any harmful substances are generated by local enterprises. As a mine located in the vicinity has been abandoned, the main source of emissions is now the local agricultural businesses. However, the land they cultivate and their processing facilities are predominantly located at the outskirts of the villages. Moreover, nuisance caused by agricultural production and manufacturing basically only occurs for two weeks per year, when the grain is dried.

EVALUATION AND NEED FOR ACTION

Although the municipality does not have any problems associated with company emissions at present, this does not signify that the municipal representatives display pronounced awareness of environmental concerns. For instance, the statements given by representatives of different interest groups do not permit a clear interpretation of how emissions generated by new companies would be handled. Particularly in view of the intention to promote tourism in the region, the decision-makers should be more sensitive in this respect. The municipality should actively participate in developing, and should also promote, environmental standards for different sectors of the economy so that it can position itself as an environmentally benign municipality, particularly in ecological tourism.

4.3.9 *The municipality located in northwest Slovenia*

The municipal territory lies in an idyllic location in the Julian Alps adjacent to a well-known national reserve. The main villages are situated in a narrow mountain valley, which gives way to a large lake at the top. Given that it is situated in a remote area, the municipality is dominated by agriculture. Nevertheless, the valley was also developed for tourism as early as at the beginning of the last century, but so far has not been discovered by mass tourism, even after Slovenia became independent. At any rate, the landscape offers good potential for mountaineering or skiing.

4.3.9.1 *Strengthening social cohesion by creating meeting places*

SITUATION

The inns have traditionally served as central meeting places in the municipality. This is where the residents exchange ideas and experiences. To some extent, they are frequented by organized, well-connected interest groups that show inclinations towards certain political orientations. Adults also come together for sports activities, such as tennis. Yet, the municipality itself does not provide sufficient infrastructure for sports and leisure-time activities.

In addition, the population comes together in the "house of culture", which is opened only irregularly and mostly exclusively for particular events. In particular, the young residents of the municipality have hardly any possibilities for meeting each other socially. A youth club was closed down again after its rules had been broken by some members. Consequently, the young mainly come together in the public space. To counter this tendency, the corresponding regional development agency strives to establish a network among students from the municipality in the context of business projects by organizing business plan competitions. Moreover, the regional development agency provides infrastructure that enables entrepreneurs of the region to exchange experiences.

The identity of the population has been seriously damaged by historical animosities and prejudice between the individual villages and valleys. Separate worlds have developed, which are already evident in the language spoken

by the residents. This represents a difficult starting point for developing measures of municipal policy for the purpose of strengthening social cohesion.

EVALUATION AND NEED FOR ACTION

The municipal representatives presently in office are not in a position to assume the role of integration necessary in this municipality. They are averse to taking risks and, consequently, fail to plan, establish or revitalize social meeting places.

Consequently, networking among the population mostly results from informal initiatives, and it is rather citizens' initiatives and the regional development agency that launch activities that strengthen social cohesion. These actors have realized how important such measures are to sustainable municipal development.

The infrastructure that exists in the villages of the municipality, i.e. "houses of culture" or facilities for functions, could be used specifically for citizens' assemblies. Moreover, "houses of culture" and clubs should be made more attractive for visitors, for instance, by means of cooperating with a local gastronomic operation. In addition, youth clubs should be designed to accommodate the interests of the young so that they feel at ease there and frequent them regularly. The first steps towards establishing a virtual network in the municipality (internet forums) should be extended and advertised more prominently among the population.

4.3.9.2 *Democratic and pluralist decision-making processes*

SITUATION

Ideas and projects, which can be suggested to the mayor by various parties, are presented by him to the municipal council. The municipal administration uses its specialist know-how to refine the suggestions for discussion in the municipal council. However, the mayor, or the coalition headed by him, strongly influences the selection of topics to be discussed. The mayor himself considers feasibility and benefit to the municipality the central criteria for selecting measures in his municipality.

However, the opposition claims that rational debates are rare in the municipal council. Frequently, the coalition parties turn down suggestions raised by the political minority following previous consultations and in the absence of rational discussion. At the same time, in practice, the opposition makes too little use of its right to make suggestions. In addition, the citizens' initiative has only limited possibilities for influencing decision-making processes in communal policy. In fact, it is frequently the manner of the presentation, or the position of the speaker, that will determine whether the mayor will act on measures suggested by the opposition or the population.

In the past, the entrepreneurs have not always been told the truth about business projects, and they feel uncomfortable as the municipal representatives have previously broken promises. Besides, the domain of tourism has priority over other industries in the discussion and also in the implementation of measures of economic policy. The municipality and its mayor see a central leadership role for themselves in planning and implementing business projects.

EVALUATION AND NEED FOR ACTION

The mayor holds a key role in the decision-making processes of the municipality. In fact, the personality structure of those responsible will determine to a large extent how intensively they can, and should, fulfil their administrative functions and the scope associated with them.

Traditionally, communal measures and projects have worked best in this region when the population identifies closely with them and citizens actively participate in planning and implementation. For instance, this could be observed when a school was erected in the region. The residents felt responsible for "their" project. In fact, during the era of real socialism, the residents were used to taking things into their own hands and this showed that a role of leadership is not always necessary in the municipality, and can even hinder the progress of a project. Consequently, today, when planning and implementing projects, the municipality should strive to encourage the municipal residents to take the initiative and should make use of this potential for municipal development. This would facilitate activating endogenous forces in the municipality. Besides, neutral and specially trained actors, such as regional development agencies, would be better suited to carry out tasks of coordination and organization.

The residents in the region still negatively recall the practice of only pretending to follow communal decision-making processes, which had been common in the period prior to the transformation. The lack of transparency in decision-making processes today particularly damages the economic development in the municipality, as the entrepreneurs are not prepared to take the risks associated with uncertainty.

One way of ensuring that decisions become more democratic and transparent to all those involved would be to establish committees that act in an advisory capacity to the municipal council (e.g. for spatial planning, finances or tourism). These committees should not be staffed with party members, but with specialists and interested citizens. This would serve to strengthen the trust that the residents and the business community have in the municipal government.

4.3.9.3 Integrating the individual measures into a comprehensive development concept of the municipality

SITUATION

The municipality does not possess a comprehensive and integrated development concept. Rather, planned projects are consolidated in different concepts according to the guiding issue (e.g. tourism, agriculture, municipal adminis-tration). It appears that the most detailed development plan exists for the domain of tourism. It calls for gradual improvement and extension of the infrastructure of this sector over the next few years. Among other projects, cycle paths are to be extended and a skating rink is to be constructed. It needs to be added that the different development plans are also changed or amended with additional measures at short notice.

Moreover, the municipal representatives coordinate their development plans with colleagues of the region and also with experts in regional develop-ment in a regional development council, or a mayors' council. In this context, the regional development agencies play an important part as intermediaries that moderate discussion processes and aim to ensure that different development plans in the region are compatible with each other.

EVALUATION AND NEED FOR ACTION

Not all groups of actors present in the municipality are involved in discussing the design of development plans. The present municipal government decides too much on its own. It also neglects to involve experts – such as regional consultants – in such development processes. Like other municipalities in the region, the municipality is in a transition phase, in which decision-makers from the older generation in particular need to learn how to deal with external consulting and/or moderation.

In view of the municipality's geography (Triglav national reserve, Julian Alps) and the resulting economic potential, it makes sense for municipal development to focus on measures of tourism. However, this must not result in projects necessary in other domains being neglected. In the municipality, the necessity of connecting different domains receives little attention, although this would make the location as a whole more attractive and would contribute towards increasing the quality of life (e.g. roads, pavements, public transport connections).

The municipal representatives should internalize this integrative aspect more strongly, as well as the lasting and binding nature of development plans. It is equally necessary to evaluate the measures regularly, so that adjustments can be made and learning effects utilized. In this context, the municipality should ask entrepreneurs, residents and tourists for their feedback more. Citizens' assemblies represent one possibility for making the discussion of future projects more democratic.

4.3.9.4 Consulting services provided for businesses willing to locate in the municipality

SITUATION

Spatial planning and basic decisions about company locations constitute an important responsibility of the municipality. However, the appropriate approval procedure is outside its scope of authority.

The municipality actively approaches interested entrepreneurs on its own initiative. However, the actual consulting services relating to permits and financial grants are provided by the regional development agencies. Moreover, the municipality delegates enquiries to other administrative units in the region.

Where assistance to new companies locating in the municipality is concerned, the municipality clearly focuses on the sector of tourism. Small companies in trade or industry are neglected, and their concerns are met with hardly any interest in the municipality. For instance, the municipal government has stalled the construction of an industrial zone for some time, claiming that its location would offer a potential for tourism. However, the further development of necessary capacity for tourism, such as accommodation, which is promoted by the municipality, is faced with a number of difficulties that result from intransparent legislation for construction permits on the territory of the Triglav national reserve. As the municipality does not actively resolve legal uncertainties, potential investors consider the corresponding risks too high.

EVALUATION AND NEED FOR ACTION

The municipality should actively engage in providing consulting to companies willing to locate in its territory and should delegate such consulting less frequently to other instances. Despite its limited authority in these matters, it remains a central point of contact in questions regarding location decisions for entrepreneurs. Therefore, it should be able to offer a basic, and above all competent, initial consultation regarding approval procedures and possibilities of obtaining subsidies. However, this presupposes that those responsible in the municipality (e.g. economic committee and zoning committee) clarify their actual scope of authority with other administrative units in the region and also acquire the necessary knowledge on the laws applicable at present. Moreover, in providing consulting services to companies willing to locate in its territory, the municipality should also increasingly draw on knowledge already available in the region (e.g. by means of establishing a network with neighbouring municipalities).

4.3.9.5 Resolving conflicting goals of municipal development through involvement of all interest groups

SITUATION

The present municipal government strives to integrate the different interest groups into the decision-making process when conflicting objectives exist. As an example of this approach, the mayor cites the decision about constructing a chapel on the municipal territory. The population is divided on this matter, and the municipality decided to hold a public discussion with each party to the conflict.

However, the usual approach taken by the municipal council when conflicts need to be resolved looks different: prior to sessions of the municipal council, different interests are discussed only among the members of the coalition presently in office, and informal agreements are reached. By contrast, no exploratory discussions are held with representatives of the opposition or with citizens' initiatives in the municipal council, which is bound to lead to decision-making processes fraught with conflict.

In contrast to its official claims, the municipality does avoid resolving conflicts. This is illustrated by the example of the interests of the agricultural association, which are diametrically opposed to those of other groups of the population. This conflict is increasingly poisoning the atmosphere for discussion prevailing in the municipality.

EVALUATION AND NEED FOR ACTION

The way in which the conflict surrounding the agricultural association is handled indicates that there are informal alliances, which exercise an influence on municipal policy and are one reason why the municipal politicians act in an intransparent manner. The municipality should be genuinely interested in resolving conflicting objectives in a transparent way and in organizing public discussions not merely for the sake of formality.

Objectives should also be discussed with representatives of the oppositional groups early on so that potential for conflict can be identified and consensual solutions can be explored. What works well in the informal arena of the local inns should also be possible in the official setting of the municipal council. This approach requires courage on the part of the municipal government. At any rate, those responsible do not sufficiently resort to neutral mediation provided by external specialists (e.g. in the regional development agencies) when it comes to resolving conflicts. This is obviously a generational problem in the municipal policy, just like the fact that agreements and solutions are put down in writing too rarely, which makes the steps towards finding a consensus considerably more difficult. If the municipal representatives fail to acknowledge these necessities, the only alternative remaining is what a voice from the entrepreneurial community describes as the necessary process of rejuvenation of those responsible in the municipal government.

4.3.9.6 Actively securing land for construction

SITUATION

At present, the municipality owns only a few plots, although it owns quite a substantial area of land jointly with the agricultural association. However, in order to designate some of these plots for the construction of housing or business premises, it would first have to reach agreements with approximately 125 co-owners. Besides, the designation of many construction plots is inappropriate, as it lacks binding benchmarks that determine the size of the buildings to be erected. Recently, the municipality issued an appeal for the exchange of land. However, this has met with little approval from the population, as the municipality has obviously failed to accommodate the interests of the landowners sufficiently.

EVALUATION AND NEED FOR ACTION

The pressure to privatize and to restitute public property (e.g. to the Church), which was exercised by the state in the course of the transformation process, has aggravated a policy of actively securing land for construction. National legislation was not very foresighted with regard to securing affordable land for the construction of housing and business premises in the municipalities. In order to purchase needed land, municipalities are sometimes forced to buy back their former plots – frequently complete with buildings – from private landowners at high prices. The prices at which citizens were able to buy apartments following independence are in no way proportionate to the costs that the municipalities would have to bear if they bought these back today.

Besides, a uniform strategy for the purpose of actively securing land for construction is hindered by the intransparent zoning legislation, which frequently does not permit unambiguous interpretation. Consequently, the municipality lacks a meaningful zoning plan as well as complete documentation of the present ownership structure in the land title register. These would form the basis on which an active land policy could actually be pursued.

4.3.9.7 Joint financing of inter-communal projects

SITUATION

Once a month, the mayors of the region hold a coordination meeting where possible inter-communal projects are discussed. As well as projects in the domain of tourism (e.g. establishing riding and cycling paths) and a shared employment initiative, the municipalities are planning a central waste collection facility for the region, the financing of which they will share. However, the exact location has not yet been determined. By contrast, plans for the financing of a common industrial zone, which has been advocated by various parties, have not yet made any progress. Every mayor wants to make sure that his municipality will benefit from the tax advantages resulting from the geographic location of the industrial zone.

In inter-communal projects, the regional development agencies play a crucial part in developing and coordinating these projects and in searching for additional financing. For instance, where private entrepreneurs participate in inter-communal projects, the proportion of public funding equals 50 per cent.

EVALUATION AND NEED FOR ACTION

Frequently, the municipalities do not clearly see the potential of cooperation. Instead, parish-pump politics and competitive thinking prevail in
the individual municipalities at the expense of the competitiveness of the
region as a whole. This is illustrated by the fact that several competing
"aquaparks", which basically feature the same attractions, were established in
the region.

The regional development agencies also complain that entrepreneurs are
reluctant to enter into cooperations with others that would go beyond jointly
attending trade fairs and would lead to concrete projects. Much convincing
still needs to be done so that both private and public actors in the region
come to internalize the benefits of cooperative networks. The objective should
lie not only in encouraging cooperation projects by means of external impulses, but also in causing promoters to actively pursue their ideas for cooperations
in the municipalities.

The municipal budgeting process lacks consistency, which constitutes a
further obstacle. If one mayor has accumulated the budget necessary for one
concrete project, his successor may cancel the budget and have it developed
anew, which delays, or even completely prevents, implementing the respective
project.

4.3.9.8 Inter-communal coordination of efforts to attract new companies

SITUATION

The municipalities in the region hardly strive to coordinate their activities in
attracting companies. Unfortunately, frequently, the opposite is true, as illustrated by the example of the almost identical "aquaparks" outlined above.
Consequently, it comes as little surprise that the mayor considers coordination
only necessary, if at all, when major companies are involved, but not in
connection with medium-sized enterprises.

If they occur at all, impulses for coordination are rather launched by
external parties, such as regional development agencies. There exist concepts
for joint initiatives to attract companies, such as a regional slaughterhouse, an
apiary or a regional centre for innovation. However, financing via EU funds
will only be granted if the applicants possess a certain amount of equity
capital. The municipalities differ strongly from each other regarding their
willingness to assume risk.

EVALUATION AND NEED FOR ACTION

The poor incentives to attract new companies and to create jobs are at the
root of the problem that affects the municipalities in the region. Potentials for
regional cooperation would play a major part, especially where the motives

for locating in the region considered by the respective companies are concerned. It needs to be added, however, that skilled employees, who would strengthen the advantage of the location, are scarce in the region. For instance, there is a demand for employees skilled in wood processing. This domain would offer a potential for education and training initiatives in schools, or for media campaigns, conducted with the aim of counteracting the shortage of skilled employees. Similar potentials would lie in providing affordable land for construction, business premises or tax incentives for entrepreneurs.

4.3.9.9 Communication policy and creating a supraregional image

SITUATION

The municipality was one of the first in Slovenia to be present on the internet. The municipal government at that time was quick to see the importance of an interactive platform for its companies and tourist facilities. The local tourism offices organize congresses and symposia, e.g. on the topic of alpine flora. Moreover, theme paths were established, and an archaeological park is currently in the planning stage. The municipality also presents itself in supplements to a regional paper. Recently, it published an article on the occasion of the 100th anniversary of the local railway, which marked the beginning of the development of tourism in the region. The regional development agencies also strive to assist the municipalities of the region in image building, for instance, by means of a culinary festival, which features regional specialities.

In fact, the municipality also benefits from the positive image of tourism associated with internationally known attractions in the region. These include, in particular, a city with a lake situated in the region, a nature reserve and a winter resort. This effect is enhanced by the municipalities in the region mutually advertising each other, which does not always rest on a coordinated strategy for tourism. In contrast to the city mentioned, the municipality has not yet been developed for mass tourism, but can still offer unspoiled nature to its visitors, which constitutes an additional attraction in the tourism market.

EVALUATION AND NEED FOR ACTION

The municipality focuses its efforts to build an image on tourism and is guided by an already existing regional image. Basically, the municipality would meet the requirements necessary to position itself in the segment of "sustainable" tourism (i.e. tourism agreeable with the natural and social environments). However, this would necessitate paying even more attention to measures of environmental protection in the future, while increasing the capacity for accommodation. Tourism advertising could focus more on unique attractions situated in its surroundings. One example is provided by the Golitski waterfalls, which are even more spectacular than the well-known Savica waterfalls in the Triglav national reserve, when water supply is high. Moreover, it would be important to integrate companies from other sectors into a comprehensive concept for building a unique image of the municipality.

Other municipalities in Slovenia also draw on their historical traditions when positioning themselves as tourist destinations. For instance, Preseren emphasizes its image as a university town, while Kranj focuses on textiles and Trzic on the shoemaking craft. Others aim to establish a new identity, especially when traditional industries become extinct. The town of Jesenice offers an example of the latter approach: it used to be an important centre of the steel industry and is now trying to establish an image as a culinary tourist destination.

4.3.9.10 *Promoting new businesses in industries not yet well established*

SITUATION

There are plans to erect a regional centre for innovations, which is intended to promote the incorporation of new businesses in the region, e.g. by providing appropriate premises. In this capacity, it is to work alongside the already established regional development agencies. In all likelihood, the municipality will contribute to its financing together with other municipalities. At present, it is hardly the municipality itself that provides services related to start-ups; rather, such services are generally offered by the regional development agencies. In any case, the entrepreneurs need to take the initiative. The municipality also promotes the construction of an industrial zone on its territory, which could also house new industries. However, the price of land will be relatively high. The mayor states that he tries to assist the entrepreneurs when they need to take out loans or obtain necessary permits.

EVALUATION AND NEED FOR ACTION

At present, there is too little demand for attracting companies active in new industries to the municipality. Moreover, skilled young specialists move away from the rural areas, which presents a further difficulty. The mayor criticizes the poor transport connection, which constitutes a disadvantage for the municipality as a company location, but, at the same time, the municipality is too passive where the necessary extension of the road and rail networks is concerned. Furthermore, it hardly offers any incentives destined to actively attract new industries, for instance, in the form of affordable land or rental property. The still comparatively bad internet connection constitutes a further disadvantage, both for new companies and for already established enterprises. All the more so as, besides tourism, it is industries that particularly focus on the use of new media that offer potential for a positive economic development in rural areas.

4.3.9.11 Competitive products by virtue of local origin

SITUATION

The high-quality agricultural products from the region are competitive and successful on the market. This applies in particular to dairy products, especially an established regional brand of cheese, which fetches higher selling prices than comparable types of cheese owing to its popularity. In addition, meat and sausage products are also known for their good quality.

Moreover, the wood manufacturing industry, which predominantly caters to market niches, has become known beyond the region. The products range from furniture made of solid wood to hand-carved tobacco pipes. Diverse natural resources on the municipal territory also add to its brand value for tourism. A case in point is a large lake within the boundaries of a nature reserve. One flagship of the region is the internationally known sports manufacturer Elan based in Begunje, which produces approximately 550,000 pairs of skis with 1,100 employees at this location.

EVALUATION AND NEED FOR ACTION

The business structure of small and medium enterprises, which lies behind the branded products of the region, must also be supported by the municipalities, which need to create appropriate general conditions. It is only in this way that products of regional origin can be marketed authentically to tourists, the local residents and beyond the region. The quality cheese products are still produced regionally, but no longer on the municipal territory proper. This example illustrates the need for action on the part of the municipal representatives so that local flagship companies can be kept.

In future, the alpine municipalities of the region need to work more closely together in order to establish regional brands for food and tourism, but also for crafted products. In cooperation with the regional development agencies, the small and medium enterprises need to be assisted in building internationally competitive structures for business and cooperation (e.g. creating standardized quality criteria in production and sales, personalized marketing, cooperation with local gastronomic venues). Moreover, working together more closely would also make it easier for the municipalities to acquire necessary financial support from the EU Structural Funds for regional development. Ultimately, production must be profitable for the numerous small companies in the region, otherwise business succession can no longer be ensured, especially in rural areas.

4.3.9.12 Freeing town centres by relocating businesses that generate high emissions

SITUATION

As the municipality focuses on tourism, there are hardly any industrial enterprises with high emissions on the municipal territory. Still, the spatial planning concept of the municipality provides for a separate industrial zone, which is intended to keep emissions, especially by major companies, away from the village centres. These centres are to be reserved for shopping areas comprised of stores and service companies. However, it cannot be ruled out that trade companies (e.g. artisanal businesses) or agricultural enterprises can also remain there, as long as they do not expand too much. The regional development agencies try to coordinate the location of trade and industry together with the municipalities.

EVALUATION AND NEED FOR ACTION

Within the framework of municipal spatial planning, the fact that tourist facilities and larger farms can also generate emissions is ignored. Uniform regulations are either completely missing, or barely binding, in this region of Slovenia. The discussion of this measure also reveals that the municipality lacks a well-thought-out spatial development concept that regulates the location of industry, trade, tourism facilities and agricultural enterprises and thereby also facilitates specifically designing the town centre. In conclusion, it can be stated that newly arriving industrial companies tend to locate at the outskirts, but that at present there is no uniform regulation for separate industrial zones.

4.3.10 The municipality located in southern Slovenia

The municipality is situated in the downs in the south of Slovenia, which are known for their good wine, among other things. Within the region, the municipality can be considered average in terms of number of inhabitants and level of economic development. Châteaux, castles and churches dominate the landscape and bear witness to the rich cultural heritage of the region, which dates back to the times when Illyrians and Celts settled in the area.

4.3.10.1 Strengthening social cohesion by creating meeting places

SITUATION

Associations and societies are very active in the municipality and offer possibilities for social meetings and activities to the younger residents in particular. These associations include, firstly, the very active sports clubs (alpine associations, football and basketball clubs) and the local fire brigades associations. Secondly, the numerous music and folk groups that exist in the individual villages need to be mentioned, in particular with a view to their value for tourism. The level of activity of a given club or association is predominantly determined by the interests of the young generation, from whose ranks additional members are recruited.

The activities of these clubs and societies also provide a setting that encourages the residents to informally exchange information and ideas on various topics. By contrast, bars and inns play a rather subordinate role as social platforms in the municipality. The municipal government supports the activities of clubs and associations financially. However, the available resources are limited, which is why the financing of other municipal measures frequently has to be reduced.

EVALUATION AND NEED FOR ACTION

The active scenery of clubs and associations contributes to a pronounced sense of cohesion among the residents. Besides, participating in the activities of clubs and associations increases the individual's commitment both to his village and to the municipal territory as the centre of a person's life. Membership of a club or association encourages taking initiatives, which provides a good foundation for measures of endogenous municipal development. In this sense, the activities of clubs and associations can be interpreted as the driving force in municipal development. However, the danger of increasing social disintegration exists for those residents that are not actively involved in the local clubs or associations. They have fewer possibilities for including their interests in the development of the municipality.

The budget expense that the support of clubs and associations incurs for the municipality could be kept within limits if the members of clubs and associations contributed themselves and if company sponsoring were increased. The local entrepreneurs are interested in sponsoring activities, as this might serve to raise the solidarity the residents feel towards the local businesses. Sports clubs, in particular, but also singing associations, fulfil an important function for municipal and regional development, as they act as effective vehicles for marketing and communicating image beyond the region. For instance, awareness of the municipality increased internationally because one of its singers gave a successful performance at an international competition.

4.3.10.2 Democratic and pluralist decision-making processes

SITUATION

The present municipal government aims to delegate the major part of discussions about measures of municipal policy to the respective municipal council committees (e.g. committees for economic or cultural affairs).

Officially, party politics do not play a part in the decision-making process. With regard to the measures planned, the mayor himself explores the position towards which the opinions of the majority evolve, both in the committees and in discussions with local residents. Consequently, he personally endorses the opinion of the majority in the municipal council. However, when issues are put to the vote, rational discussion among the individual political groups is frequently neglected.

EVALUATION AND NEED FOR ACTION

In discussions and decision-making processes, the mayor should take a leading role after all and should not merely confine himself to the role of an observer. Particularly where a measure is agreed on, he should rely more on rational arguments and show less personal preferences. Otherwise, it comes as little surprise that the opposition describes his position on certain matters as opportunistic and stubborn. At any rate, in this municipality the following applies to suggestions put forward by the population: the more professional the presentation and the stronger the lobbying activities targeted at the municipal representatives, the higher the likelihood that the respective issue will be considered in the municipal council.

In some cases, the technical competence of those in charge is poor, which negatively affects the quality of rational discussion in the municipal council. The municipality lacks the resources necessary to prepare technically sound foundations for decision-making and to implement measures competently. In this context, establishing inter-communal structures, or using already existing structures more intensively, could contribute to improving the quality of measures of municipal policy.

4.3.10.3 Integrating the individual measures into a comprehensive development concept of the municipality

SITUATION

The municipality surveyed does not possess an integrated concept for municipal development. The budget is considered the central steering tool for the development of the municipality, with the focus predominantly on financial resources available for individual measures. At any rate, the mayor aims to optimize the state subsidies granted for infrastructure projects, such as the construction of a school and a kindergarten, which cannot be financed by municipal sources. Apart from these projects, it appears that the municipality predominantly tackles initiatives according to the principle of urgency, which is frequently determined by subjective criteria.

The local entrepreneurs are prepared to become involved in the process of planning municipal projects that also affect the business community in order to coordinate the different interests involved as early as possible.

At the regional level, pluralist decision-making structures have already been established. These are oriented towards inter-communal cooperation, e.g. within the framework of initiatives of the EU Structural Funds (e.g. regional forums). At the regional level, the municipality has been involved in planning for the domains of economy, tourism, environment and rural areas from the very beginning.

EVALUATION AND NEED FOR ACTION

The municipality lacks a proper and comprehensive development concept. This cannot be compensated for by the budget, binding as it is. Rather, the budget should represent one of several inter-related planning tools relevant to the development of the municipality. The municipal government should use the already established structures of regional cooperation as guidance and aim to implement similar instruments at the municipal level. As in the region, in the municipality it also takes external impulses for the decision-makers to acquire the necessary awareness of central issues and instruments of municipal development.

4.3.10.4 Consulting services provided for businesses willing to locate in the municipality

SITUATION

The regional chamber of commerce acts as the central point of contact for entrepreneurs willing to locate in the area. It is responsible for two municipalities and is financed by the membership fees paid by the businesspersons. At the chamber of commerce, the (potential) entrepreneur can obtain sound information about land available for business operations and the appropriate approval procedures, but also about financing possibilities and subsidies available for his business idea. In addition, the superordinate administrative units, as well as the regional development agencies, provide information about approval procedures.

Officially, the municipality provides initial information, which basically amounts to referring the entrepreneur to the chamber of commerce. Particularly when public projects are put up to tender (for instance, in the official bulletin), interested entrepreneurs and municipal representatives frequently come together in an informal setting and exchange further information.

EVALUATION AND NEED FOR ACTION

The municipality is aware of its limited expertise in counselling entrepreneurs willing to locate in its territory and, consequently, confines itself to acting as an intermediary. Nevertheless, the contact persons responsible at the municipal level do need to have certain specialist know-how in order to be able to offer basic initial counselling in the first place. Moreover, the content of such counselling needs to be aligned with the consulting services provided by the chamber of commerce.

Activities also need to be coordinated with the neighbouring municipality, which also falls within the scope of responsibility of the regional chamber of commerce. One case in point would be inter-communal industrial zones, the establishment of which the municipality aims to promote in the future. Entrepreneurs interested in such industrial zones should encounter one competent contact person each on the regional and the municipal levels, respectively. In addition, in line with the wishes of the entrepreneurial community, the municipality should hold official events where it gives information about planned measures of economic policy.

4.3.10.5 Resolving conflicting goals of municipal development through involvement of all interest groups

SITUATION

Generally, the mayor is open towards suggestions raised by the population, and by individuals who are not members of the municipal bodies. Still, he considers discussions in the municipal council and the corresponding specialist committees decisive for developing concrete strategies of implementation. He always reserves the right to make the final decision for himself.

When measures are launched, frequently interest groups emerge that reach across parties and villages. These aim to influence the formation of opinions in the specialist committees and in the municipal council. As the personal constellation in the municipal council has changed only recently, the newly elected municipal councillors, in particular, find this form of decision-making problematic. They frequently have the impression that decisions are not sufficiently discussed in a rational manner and that opinions and decisions have already been determined and are to be approved by the municipal council without further ado.

As municipal development is almost exclusively discussed in the official bodies, outsiders, such as entrepreneurs, can only put forward their interests and concerns and influence decision-making via informal channels. Consequently, many companies and also clubs or associations refer their questions more frequently to the regional development agencies than to the municipality itself.

EVALUATION AND NEED FOR ACTION

The decision-making bodies in the municipality lack an element of pluralism. For one thing, it is necessary to involve representatives of the opposition and of local citizens' initiatives seriously in decision-making processes. This is largely a question of the attitude of those involved, as the corresponding structures in the municipality are used insufficiently. The same applies to the entrepreneurial community, which is presently only informally connected with the municipality, if at all. For instance, it could be invited to sessions of the municipal council's economic committee at regular intervals. Besides, functions and events that provide information about municipal development should be more decentralized and accessible to everybody, so that decisions can be anchored more strongly in the local communities.

External impulses are called for in the municipality so that the structures of communication and decision-making can be improved, and the attitudes of municipal representatives can be changed. The mayor may encounter competent contact persons in the regional development agencies, but also in neighbouring municipalities, where the actors possess far-reaching experience in planning and implementing instruments of municipal development.

4.3.10.6 Actively securing land for construction

SITUATION

Approximately two years ago, the municipality constructed business premises and offered them at favourable rental fees. This measure served to attract several entrepreneurs – also from neighbouring municipalities. Other municipalities in the region have already followed this example in the context of their respective location policy.

The municipality lacks the financial resources necessary to acquire land on a large scale, or to exercise rights of first refusal. Still, there is the intention to increasingly act on such options in the future in order to secure affordable land for the construction of housing and business premises. The future zoning strategy is also intended to further this aim.

EVALUATION AND NEED FOR ACTION

The municipality is not yet fully aware of the necessity of a sustainable policy of securing land. Aggressive short-term location policy can negatively affect neighbouring municipalities and, consequently, needs to be viewed with criticism in the light of the objective of positive regional development. The municipalities should coordinate their respective measures and should not adopt a strategy of mutually enticing entrepreneurs away from each other.

As, at present, the legal conditions applicable to spatial planning are changing frequently, this limits the scope for implementing these measures. However, this also applies to other Slovenian municipalities. If a new programme of regulations for spatial planning becomes effective, it can conflict with the zoning plan existing in the municipality. This situation hinders the necessary long-term planning for land designated to housing and business also in the municipality surveyed.

4.3.10.7 Joint financing of inter-communal projects

SITUATION

In the past, the municipality was merged with a neighbouring municipality. Since that time, the two municipalities have shared infrastructure, such as the landfill or the kindergarten, which are still used by both municipalities today and are financed jointly according to the share of population. Besides, the municipality aims to take an active role in the mayors' council of the local area, where projects of inter-communal relevance are discussed and adapted to the special needs of individual municipalities. For instance, the construction of a large casino in the valley is currently being debated there. The mayors' council also undertakes to ensure that cooperation projects meet the requirements for eligibility for subsidies. In this capacity, it works together with the regional development agencies. To give an example, this challenge presents itself in connection with the project of establishing a shared system of sewage treatment and irrigation plants.

The mayors' council tries to organize the distribution of subsidies, which the region manages to acquire for its projects, e.g. from the EU Structural Fund, in such a way that financial means not expended in one period can be used for projects in neighbouring municipalities. The regional development agencies also provide important impulses for inter-communal cooperation – for instance, they assist the municipalities with expert counselling in establishing a wine route in the region. This cooperation project is also relevant for the municipality because it wants to position itself as the centre of viticulture in Slovenia.

EVALUATION AND NEED FOR ACTION

Where inter-communal projects are concerned, the municipal representatives fundamentally pursue a strategy that aims to avoid unnecessary duplication of structures in the region, but to identify and make use of synergies with neighbouring municipalities. As in other Slovenian municipalities, one incentive for inter-communal cooperation always lies in access to national or transnational subsidies. It appears that the crucial point in the context of cooperation between municipalities is financing and the concrete location of the individual projects.

It is evident that the municipality intends to establish itself as the centre of the region in tourism and administration once the regions in Slovenia are newly organized. This could lead to a potential conflict in inter-communal cooperation. At any rate, clear declarations of intent on the part of municipal politicians, as well as the construction of a large conference centre in the municipality, lend credence to this assumption.

It is also necessary to involve companies in projects of inter-communal cooperation so that know-how transfer can also be furthered in this field and competitive advantages can be generated. Owing to its previous cooperation activities, the municipal government could act as an important catalyst in this context.

4.3.10.8 Inter-communal coordination of efforts to attract new companies

SITUATION

When incentives are developed that aim to attract companies to the region, the predominant focus is on inter-communal competition. By taking proactive measures, the municipality has contributed to the competition among locations. It exempts new companies with at least 25 employees that locate in municipal territory from taxes and fees (e.g. sewage fees or electricity bills) for a certain period of time. The mayor states that this support in the start-up phase leads to a significant reduction in costs for the businesses concerned. In general, location policy has been made a top priority taken care of by the mayor personally. At any rate, this has resulted mainly in the municipality managing to lure companies away from the neighbouring municipalities and to induce them to move to the municipality's own industrial zone.

EVALUATION AND NEED FOR ACTION

The municipal representatives display opportunistic and short-sighted thinking in connection with measures designed to attract new companies. There is hardly anything left of the readiness to cooperate, which has been expressed in other contexts, when this measure is discussed.

At present, the municipality is painfully forced to acknowledge that its exaggerated competitive thinking is blocking new possibilities in municipal development: in the region, a system of educational grants has been established in order to promote young professionals. The municipalities, the business community and the state take over one third of educational costs each. While the neighbouring municipality has participated in this initiative from the very beginning, the municipality surveyed was not interested initially. However, after the initiative had been covered by all regional media and, consequently, several entrepreneurs from the municipality surveyed also enquired about the possibility of participating, the municipal representatives suddenly were under severe pressure. They started last-minute negotiations to participate in the scheme, but to no avail.

The example illustrates that, frequently, it takes external neutral parties to suggest the idea of cooperation to a municipality. As confirmed by representatives of a regional development agency, the process of convincing a municipality of the benefits of looking beyond its own backyard is laborious and time-consuming. The mayors' council would be the appropriate body for coordinating and fine-tuning the measure among the municipalities of the region.

4.3.10.9 Communication policy and creating a supraregional image

SITUATION

Given that it dominates the economic life of the valley, viticulture has become the supraregional hallmark of the municipality. What is more, the region, and in particular the municipality, was able to use active and well-coordinated communication to create a supraregional image as a culinary region that boasts producers of high-quality food products. By contrast, no such conclusive marketing concepts exist in other industries, such as tourism. One reason is that inter-communal cooperation is still too weak in this domain. First concepts for establishing a tourism network, e.g. by creating cultural and adventure hiking paths in the region, have already been prepared. They are intended as a first step towards establishing a regional destination for tourism within which the individual municipalities and local areas can position themselves, e.g. as culinary destinations.

EVALUATION AND NEED FOR ACTION

The regional image should be developed further in cooperation with other municipalities and under the guidance of experts in regional development. Under an appropriate regional brand, the municipality can position itself in certain areas. For instance, as well as its current positioning as centre of viticulture, it could also invoke the domains of culture and sport. Only regional cooperation will be capable of creating awareness for the municipality internationally, as one municipality on its own does not possess the necessary resources. Moreover, an image can only be communicated to customers, tourists and investors in an authentic manner if it is backed by the population. Consequently, the municipality should involve its residents more strongly in the process of image creation, in line with endogenous municipal development. Moreover, impulses that further regional cooperation between companies would also be important. The food industry can serve as an example in this context. The challenge in this context will definitely lie in ensuring smooth cooperation between the municipality's agricultural enterprises, manufacturing and processing industries, and tourism.

4.3.10.10 Promoting new businesses in industries not yet well established

SITUATION

Major companies in the municipality include a winery and a dairy, which both employ approximately 50 persons each. There are also smaller service companies with 15 to 20 employees, some of which also perform important upstream or downstream functions in the regional value chain corresponding to the food industry. It is not only in this segment that the municipality tries to attract smaller companies by means of a policy of granting specific incentives. As already mentioned, a new company is exempt from paying taxes and fees during the start-up phase. Moreover, the municipality cooperates with the regional chamber of commerce and offers low-interest loans to start-up entrepreneurs.

Entrepreneurs from neighbouring municipalities are targeted and invited to information talks, which aim to entice them to move their company operations to the municipal territory. The local entrepreneurs view this competitive location policy as clearly positive. The policy followed by the municipality becomes understandable if it is considered that, during the transition phase, privatization of large regional companies led to many municipal citizens losing their jobs. The mayor is now trying to compensate for this by establishing a structure of small and medium enterprises. He considers enticing companies from the region to locate in his territory one appropriate course of action.

Besides, the municipality invests in constructing or renovating property, which can wholly or in part be used for entrepreneurial purposes. One example is the construction of a conference centre in the municipality, which is also destined to house gastronomic venues. Apart from this, the municipality is hardly in a position to provide premises for entrepreneurial activity, as capacities are limited and financial resources are poor.

In contrast to this situation in the municipality surveyed, the neighbouring municipality established a centre for start-up companies and technology largely on its own initiative and without substantial financial backing from the state. This municipality also advertises a sponsorship award for innovative business ideas.

EVALUATION AND NEED FOR ACTION

Frequently, only inter-communal cooperation can ensure that measures intended to promote the start-up of companies are effective – in particular, where new industries are concerned. At present, the municipal representatives in the region are hardly prepared to cooperate in matters of promoting and attracting new companies. It is to be hoped that the start-up centre newly established in the neighbouring municipality will work for the entire region and also establish cooperations with educational and research institutions. The municipal representatives are called upon to abandon their mentality of parish-pump politics and to end their aggressive initiative to lure companies away from neighbouring municipalities, which is certainly not conducive to improving an atmosphere beneficial to cooperation.

However, like other regions in Slovenia, this municipality also lacks qualified skilled workers for whom manufacturing companies have particular demand. Besides, municipal residents who hold academic degrees commute or move to the capital of Ljubljana, because they do not find adequate job opportunities in the municipality surveyed.

4.3.10.11 Competitive products by virtue of local origin

SITUATION

Wines, in particular, have established themselves as products from the municipality that are competitive at the supraregional level. Business as well as political structures of cooperation are in place so that quality management and marketing in the region can be promoted and coordinated (e.g. producer groups, info points). The municipality's name is associated with other culinary products, including mainly meat and sausages as well as cheese. The producers resident in the valley and the municipal representatives are very much aware that a transparent proof of origin represents a competitive advantage in food production. In this manner, the municipality manages to differentiate itself from cheap own-label brands and to position the "original" in the premium segment of the market at a higher price. Moreover, the individual food products originating from the valley have already been assembled under a culinary umbrella brand and are advertised jointly by the producers from the municipality, e.g. at trade fairs.

EVALUATION AND NEED FOR ACTION

In future, the region needs to be established as a European culinary and tourist destination. In this context, the municipality could present itself as centre of viticulture. The food production in the region, which is already competitive across its boundaries, needs to be amended with high-quality tourist offerings. These include appropriate capacity of accommodation, high-level gastronomic venues, diverse sports offers and also cultural attractions. Other industries could also associate their quality products – manufactured in cooperative settings – with the regional brand and thus exploit synergies.

In order to establish a definitive tourist image, new producers must meet the specified quality standards and fit coherently into the regional marketing concept. This implies the need for effective tools of quality management as well as channels of communication and information between entrepreneurs and municipal representatives, but also citizens in the regional network.

The local residents – but also the official representatives of the individual municipalities – still need to develop their awareness of the region. This can only be communicated to national and international tourists in an authentic way if it has been fully recognized by the local actors first. In this context, the consulting services provided by the regional development institutions already bear fruit.

However, this development process is hindered by the fact that there are no proper administrative regions and corresponding institutions – a problem which applies to all of Slovenia. Moreover, the perception of consumers should always be considered when regional brands are established so that the needs of the market can be accommodated appropriately. For instance, it could prove more useful to establish the route of the cultural hiking path, one of the hallmarks of the region, not only through the low mountain range, but also from the Alps all the way to the Adriatic Sea. Moreover, synergies with already established socio-cultural structures should be sought. For instance, the activities of clubs and associations common to the municipalities in the region could also be emphasized specifically in the regional marketing strategy.

4.3.10.12 Freeing town centres by relocating businesses that generate high emissions

SITUATION

Business activities in the municipality have traditionally centred on the production and processing of food (e.g. wine, milk, meat) and have been strongly shaped by agricultural enterprises. This is why there are hardly any industrial enterprises that generate strong emissions in the municipal territory. The municipality generally tries to keep emissions away from the village centres as far as possible. For instance, it commissions landscaping of open space and aims to keep traffic within limits, e.g. by establishing car parks in the outskirts.

The municipal representatives hope that, once the motorway has been constructed, industrial companies will rather locate alongside the motorway and less in central town locations. The spacious office and industrial zone at the fringe of the municipality has been designated correspondingly. It is there that already existing companies can expand and land for construction is offered to those willing to locate in the municipality.

EVALUATION AND NEED FOR ACTION

When discussing this measure, it must not be overlooked that tourist facilities as well as agricultural enterprises and smaller trades operations generate emissions. These take not only the form of emissions of harmful substances, but also of possible noise exposure in the town centre. Conversely, from the point of view of tourism, it can appear to make sense after all to keep traditional crafts shops or farms in the town centre or its vicinity in order to offer an atmosphere of authenticity.

5 Conclusion

The transferability of the individual measures identified to the local areas surveyed have been analysed, and the results of the study are now broken down by topic, summarized and analysed for the whole region surveyed. Finally, suggestions for actions to be taken are derived and the scope of the statements formulated will be discussed.

Thesis 1: General development tendencies in the region surveyed – a functioning economic system involves more than just the free market.

In order to understand the structural conditions on a communal level, the focus of the survey has to be extended to development trends on the macro level. It is here, however, where municipalities have little influence. As a counter-reaction to socialist planned economies, which inhibited individualism as well as self-initiative of both population and businesses, the NCCE, based on an unwavering belief in the market's self-regulating powers, wanted to position themselves as star pupils in the transformation process by radically implementing the idea of laissez-faire. This effectively constituted a volte-face from the centrally planned economy to an extreme form of market economy. Neo-liberalism can thus be felt more intensely in the region surveyed than in Austria, as more widespread spheres of life were now subjected to the maxim of competition. Liberalism's problem-solving potential in a society, however, is – as the results of this study also show – generally overrated.

Curiously enough, the neo-liberal policies in the NCCE to a large extent actually prevented the emergence of functioning markets. The ideal market position for a business is as a monopolist. The more liberal the economic system, the easier it is for private entities to achieve a monopoly position in times of radical change accompanied by highly asymmetrical information. This also makes societal problems more likely. Therefore, the function of the state should be to safeguard functioning markets, and so counteract the coming into existence of (undesirable) monopolies, in order to maintain innovative activities by private entities and to reduce negative long-term effects for society.

The results of the study show that the companies, which now have liberties never experienced before, by no means satisfy the needs of the (rural) population sufficiently. On the other hand, the municipalities, because of a chronic lack of capital and botched administrative reforms, in many cases, are severely restricted in their actions more than two decades after the turnaround of 1989. This becomes particularly clear in view of the numerous statements in the regions under survey that bemoan the bad financial basis of the municipalities for the implementation of development measures – such as providing the appropriate infrastructure, making sure that there is land available for residential buildings and business premises, or government funding for local enterprises.

In the development of an efficient economic structure, the state – partly because it sees no alternative today – relies heavily on private (foreign) investors, for whom, however, the rural regions with their deficiencies in infrastructure are hardly attractive without massive state support. Due to the dumping strategy currently dominating the inter-communal rivalry between locations, municipalities with weak resources can hardly influence a larger company's decision where to locate itself. At the same time, the location is massively under threat once government support stops. This is a phenomenon that at the moment is a painful experience for traditional market economies, as, despite massive government support, they have to realize how little interest private (foreign) investors show in maintaining social cohesion at the location. The shutdown of the profitable Nokia works in Bochum (Germany) and the transfer of production for competitive reasons to Cluj (Romania), which resulted in the loss of roughly 2,000 jobs, all despite government support for the location in the amount of altogether roughly 88 million euros, shows how toothless location policy purely based on public support actually is.

Yet very little seems to have been learned from the mistakes made in "old Europe" during the period under survey. Rather, the (wrong) developments there were simply replicated. Based on the premise that it was necessary to make up for the deficit in development within a trend that was inaccurately assumed to be the same for all market economies, everybody looked for the fastest way towards achieving the status quo of the traditional market economies, without taking into account the circumstances in the respective country and the legacy from the planned-economy era. This conception of development, based on the Western examples, was reinforced by the EU's conditions in the pre- and post-expansion stages. In the NCCE, this resulted in a comprehensive and (too) fast liberalization of the economic system on the "drawing board".

On the other hand, it is exactly EU funds that stimulate activities in regional development more than national support instruments. They are, for instance, the main drivers for inter-communal cooperation in the region under survey. From the study, it can be clearly seen that, without the measures and incentives of regional and structural policy, there would be practically no cooperation between rural municipalities at all.

The results of the study also show that the bad experiences connected with coercive communities in real socialism have hardly any negative impact on the social cohesion in the municipalities surveyed. On the contrary, it seems to be rather strong today. The effects of centrally prescribed collectivism can rather be detected in the people's mistrust of communal policy. The (local) public sector is often seen not as a partner, but as a downright adversary of both populace and business community, who has to be outwitted whenever possible. From this understanding, both people and entrepreneurs use competitive rather than cooperative strategies *vis-à-vis* the municipality. Apart from outwitting, subverting and corrupting the authorities is another typical problem in former communist countries. In general, informally aligning the interests of the administration and the entrepreneurs and residence works as a barter transaction bordering on the legal. In this climate, people and businesses quickly see regulations and official norms as a reminder of the repression suffered from the authorities and not as a necessary system for living together in a society. This defensive attitude towards the public sector may also be ascribed to the command economy with its hostile view of any endogenous initiative. This also explains the population's frequently weak commitment regarding matters of municipality development.

The community spirit in the region under survey is occasionally swapped for an extreme type of individualism. So, even (pristine) nature – as a "public good" – is sometimes seen as an enemy and treated accordingly ruthlessly. Countermeasures against the dereliction of buildings and green spaces are only beginning to be taken. People's sense of responsibility for their own lives and the community is quite weak. They also perceive the public sector as a homogeneous whole. Instead of structural developments that make sense in the long term, such as infrastructure projects or revitalizing the environment, they often just demand cheaper food or fuel. The frequent attempts to create a tourism industry have made the municipalities' officials realize the importance of long-term strategies. Thus, a locality's nice appearance and a clean environment are absolute prerequisites for attracting the number of tourists hoped for.

Thesis 2: Relationship between municipality and business community – working with and for each other than next to and against each other.

For the whole area surveyed, it has been found that communication between municipality officials and local entrepreneurs is severely disrupted. Those few businesses hoping for support from the municipality feel mostly or totally neglected. The municipalities, on the other hand, seem to have little interest in the companies' situation and development. If a municipality actively tries to support a company, it quickly reaches its limits. At the same time, the entrepreneurs are expected to use their own initiative to solve problems that often have structural causes.

One central reason for the problematic relationship between municipality and businesses is the unwavering belief, adopted after the turnaround by everybody involved, in the self-regulative power of an extremely liberal market economy. Entrepreneurs, for instance, often do not even expect the municipality or politicians in general to be able to do something useful for them. They stay out of municipality development matters and want communal politicians to do likewise in matters of company development. The municipalities, on the other hand, have been exposed to free entrepreneurship for only 20 years and cannot handle their new role in the free market. The mayors therefore do not get involved in company matters, if at all possible.

Generally, businesses do see themselves as a part of the social community "municipality". Nevertheless, mentally, the business structure is little connected with the other areas of life in the municipality. On the contrary, there is a conscious separation between business and social spheres. In Hungary and Slovenia, where there was some form of quasi-free entrepreneurship even during communism, small differences can be detected: companies still tend to be seen as an important part of life in the municipality. Yet a real tradition of focused support for SME structures by the municipality is missing, as is the notion of social responsibility for the entrepreneurs.

The municipalities in the region under survey should try to signal their business competence to the entrepreneurs, in order to be seen as a reliable partner in business matters, and thus also company development. For instance, this could be achieved by training and employing competent contact persons for businesses, who in case of detailed questions can refer them to the appropriate institutions (e.g. regional chambers of commerce or regional development agencies). Subliminally, many municipality officials are associated with the (old) system, which is seen as the antithesis of the market economy and as hostile to business. To establish a new "view of the world" among the people involved, regular meetings between municipality officials and local entrepreneurs have to be organized, involving external facilitators. Without a reliable relationship between municipality and business community, it will be very difficult to solve the development problems in the rural area given the current macro-political circumstances.

Thesis 3: Tourism – creating target-group-specific offers and communicating them effectively.

Inspired by best-practice examples from the other EU countries and available support funds, rural tourism in the region surveyed has become a central area for the municipalities' economic policy. Tourism is, in fact, one of the few areas where cooperation between municipalities already works well.

Slovenia's rural municipalities are particularly well positioned for tourism, as – apart from the excellent conditions provided by nature – competitive structures had been developed even before the turnaround of 1989. The situation in the tourism industry can thus often be compared to that in the rural areas in Austria. As, in Slovenia, the municipalities are on average significantly larger than in the other countries surveyed, they often have a greater potential for tourism within their municipal boundaries. Because of the generally more favourable initial situation of the Slovenian municipalities in tourism, frictions in the cooperation of municipalities can result, as individual municipalities may not be willing to share what they have already achieved.

Only in the last few years has Hungary made efforts to develop effective tourism concepts for its structurally weak rural areas. Particularly in the east of the country, the scenery has little attractions for tourism and the infrastructure is patchy. Nevertheless, even in such regions, tourism features prominently in business promotion, and cooperation with neighbouring municipalities is welcome in order to broaden the resource base.

Likewise, in the Czech Republic and Slovakia, there is also a strong tendency towards tourism in the support for businesses on a municipality level. The rural areas in these countries have very attractive scenery, but even municipalities without any special attractions are trying to join in.

In the region surveyed, very few tourism destinations well known beyond the region have developed. While there are – mainly agricultural – high-quality products in many of the municipalities surveyed (sometimes after a long break), there are often deficiencies in compiling target-group-specific, regional tourism profiles and their effective communication both domestically and abroad.

In any case, for Western tourists, it might be attractive to explore regions that have not been fully developed for tourism yet. The potential of domestic holidaymakers has not been fully tapped so far, either. The municipalities often miss out on opportunities provided, for instance, by historical tourism or soft activity holidays. It would be a mistake to simply copy the projects of a neighbouring region. Such strategic monocultures lead to a mutual weakening in the market position and cannibalize the market potential between the municipalities. Ambitious plans for big projects (e.g. conference centres) are usually confronted with a rudimentary tourism infrastructure in the countries surveyed (e.g. hotel capacity, traffic connections), which is yet to be developed. Frequently, the current look of the localities does not meet the requirements of (international) tourists.

Thesis 4: Pollution – ecological awareness and regional identity are mutually beneficial.

Within communal economic policy, avoiding pollutant emissions has no priority at the moment. Occasionally, municipality officials state that considerations regarding possible pollution are part of location planning. In fact, municipalities accept pollution readily whenever jobs are to be created and there is no great resistance on the part of the populace.

Emissions and environmental pollution generally remain a poorly perceived problem, as long as they do not directly affect the quality of life. It appears that pronounced ecological awareness correlates with people's living standards. Currently, there are more important issues in the countries surveyed. Companies are – in most cases, wrongly – suspected as the main polluters. People burning household waste, for instance, are a common cause of the bad air quality in town centres. Together with the emissions caused by agricultural producers, which is not really noticed as such, this is problematic for the establishment of (soft) tourism programmes aimed for by many municipalities.

Potential emissions of companies should, in any case, be taken into account more explicitly in future projects. In general, a public debate initiated by neutral observers can increase environmental awareness of decision-makers and the population. Regional political cooperation, in turn, facilitates the alignment of ecological with economic/tourism interests. In particular, the discussion on climate change and its effects could be favourable for regional thinking, as a variety of options for positioning themselves become available for municipalities (e.g. climate-friendly region or regional products in local restaurants). Nature, the important resource, has to be maintained at all costs especially for the rural municipalities, as well as in view of the – partly irreversible – industrial pollution in the last few decades.

Thesis 5: Creating an image – becoming well known beyond the region through focused communication of regional characteristics and the municipality's strengths.

The municipalities surveyed in this study all use regional newspapers for communicating events and present development plans to the local population. However, comprehensive communication strategies making use of several media at the same time, such as the internet and regional television, are still nowhere to be found. Communication is still predominantly regional and not tailored to target groups. Therefore, the current web presence looks unprofessional, although the necessary content to be communicated would have been well prepared. Particularly for small municipalities, creating a stable image is, in view of the limited resources, only possible by means of intercommunal cooperation. Regional brands would also enable the municipalities to create individual emphasis when creating an image.

As well as regional papers, the use of regional or national radio and television in order to communicate local characteristics should be taken into consideration. Today, international target groups can also be reached by means of the tourism channels in the hotels in larger cities. A municipality's own home page has already become a minimum requirement of communication policy. What is often missed, though, is that this low-cost medium can only be fully effective in its multiplier effect beyond the region if the content has been professionally prepared. This includes, among other things, presentation in several languages, an appealing layout, contact details, regular updates, as well as links to other web pages in the regional network. It also seems necessary to develop periodical newsletters and to establish physical info points in the local areas in order to provide advice on local features more professionally.

Regarding the contents to be transported when creating an image, it would be best if a "regional story" were told that is based on historical and natural events, as well as including the regional products on offer. Additionally, "ambassadors for the region", i.e. leading companies, artists or sportsmen known beyond the region, should be recruited for the regional marketing. Only if the local population authentically represents all that told in the "regional story" will it be possible to create the image successfully. At the same time, the "regional story" has to realistically reflect reality in the region as experienced by the tourists. The impact of their word of mouth must not be underestimated as regards the image effects in the local area, particularly in a time of web logs and virtual discussion forums on travel impressions, and municipalities should take it into consideration as a comparatively cheap advertising medium.

Improving the communication policy of rural municipalities could turn into a central area for know-how transfer from Austria or other EU member countries.

Thesis 6: Public infrastructure – aligning the infrastructure with the region's needs.

The massive infrastructure deficit in the rural area is a relic and burden from the era of real socialism. Former prestige projects in the areas of transport routes, buildings and communications facilities were not developed in line with the population's needs and do not meet the requirements of a modern technical infrastructure. The rural municipalities also show similar deficits regarding utility and disposal infrastructure. Due to budget restrictions, this can be remedied only slowly.

In the NCCE, particularly on the private-household level, a modern communications infrastructure – especially the internet – has not yet become as widespread as in Austria or other Western European countries. This translates into a severe competitive disadvantage for the municipalities, but also and foremost for the companies located there. It is possible, though, that the stage of establishing a fixed infrastructure can be skipped in full by pushing flexible solutions such as mobile internet or UMTS.

Through an extensive provision of modern communications and information technology, an important success factor for corporate innovation in the rural area is created. At the same time, the internet is a decentralized communications platform for regional development and also a "window to the world" for the local population. Improving transport routes would give the companies located in the rural areas a better connection to the outside world, and thus would ameliorate disadvantages arising from their location.

Public funding for renovating buildings and improving neglected areas in the municipalities is of great importance. In order to show initiative in this area, it is particularly important that people and businesses identify themselves with the municipality.

At the same time, modern technical infrastructure and a nice overall appearance of the locality help establish an identity for the population and business community. By improving the technical infrastructure, an indirect impulse for the local economy can be given.

In addition, modern social infrastructure aligned with the people's needs is a major factor in order to position the municipality as an attractive place to live and thus keep the young in the community and win over new families with children. To achieve this, attractive child care, educational and spare-time facilities have to be provided on a communal level or together with other municipalities in the local area.

Thesis 7: Social cohesion – actively strengthening the sense of community and utilizing it for initiatives.

Social cohesion in the municipalities of the region surveyed is strong. There are a large number of places for social get-togethers, which tend to be popular and are also supported generously by the municipalities. Plans for long-term social development on the municipality level, though, have hardly been designed yet.

In the Czech Republic and Slovakia, the strong sense of community rests, among other things, on a successful tradition in club sports, with football and ice hockey the most popular. Already as youngsters, people are strongly integrated into the community via these clubs and have a strong connection with their homeland. In this context, the tradition of sports clubs that helps establish a national identity in the Slavic countries under survey should be mentioned.

In Slovenia and Hungary the "houses of culture" – municipal centres often established in the era of real socialism – are a centre of municipality life. It seems important to renew these facilities, make them more attractive and actively use them to strengthen the municipality. For instance, public internet access has given many municipal centres a new function as a social meeting place. As in Austria, in Slovenia, inns play a significant role in maintaining social cohesion. People go to the inn together and discuss matters of municipality development there.

Beyond the era of real socialism with its own politically-oriented club structures, an active club tradition (maintaining national culture) has been kept up and is partly consciously being revitalized today. In this context, sponsorship by local companies should be considered an important source of funding, as well as members' contributions and support from the municipality. The presence of sports and culture clubs beyond the region, in turn, produces an advertising effect for companies and also the local region.

Thesis 8: Young population – keeping the young in the municipality by providing attractive accommodation and spare-time activities.

In contrast to earlier generations, youngsters today are not just rooted locally, but they are much more internationally oriented. Like their peers in Austria, they are frequently drawn to the cities, but, due to the generally bad educational and job situation, increasingly to other European countries, too. As a result, they are (permanently) lost to their home municipalities.

Apart from jobs, the young population in many places lacks social infra-structure, such as cheap accommodation and appropriate educational, cultural and spare-time facilities, with the sports clubs from the communist past still fulfilling an important integrative function. The flagging interest of many young people in actively participating in the municipality's development is often homemade, as the youngsters have not been integrated into political and cultural life and club activities in time.

Whether the effects of the migration to the cities, which can be observed in all regions surveyed and mainly concerns the young population, are actually addressed in the municipalitics depends on the development status of the respective regions. If there are morc pressing problems, structural changes, which currently are not registered and whose negative effects only become apparent in the long term, are hardly noticed by decision-makers and the general populace alike.

The political and cultural life, as well as social cohesion, suffers from the drift to the cities, which also concerns young families, as they cannot see attractive living conditions in a structurally weak area. From the entrepre-neurs' point of view, the low supply of skilled workers represents a significant disadvantage for the location, which effectively creates a vicious circle as regards the job market.

The municipalities are trying to integrate the young population better, mainly by improving the cultural and sports activities offered. However, regarding the construction of social housing and getting companies to locate in the area, municipalities' hands are tied. Whether the school reform cur-rently taking place across the rural areas in Hungary has positive or negative effects on the living conditions of the young people there will only become apparent in the next few years.

Thesis 9: Regional products – infusing high-quality products with a regional identity.

In order to boost the economy in the municipalities surveyed and establish a competitive image, the promotion of regional agricultural and crafts products, in particular foods, has come to be seen as a panacea of communal policy. Frequently, however, this strategy is applied without much thought and lacks the necessary structural foundations. Currently, there is neither sufficient consumer awareness nor purchasing power. Therefore, the market potential for high-quality regional products is not yet high enough. The current range of regional specialities on offer is thus mainly targeted at (foreign) tourists with the necessary funds.

In the next few years, however, a local market for regional products is likely to develop. As a reaction to the sheer ubiquity of international discount markets with their product range that is not very transparent regarding quality, a consumer movement for products with identifiable origin and careful production methods seems to emerge. Accordingly, consumers' current superficial affinity with Western products could well recede in the next few years.

In order to support this trend, action clearly must be taken by political institutions on a national level as well. It is necessary (e.g. through media campaigns) to hone consumers' awareness of products of domestic origin and, thus, to stimulate local demand. Here, know-how transfer of regional policy measures from Austria to the region surveyed might be useful – take, for example, the media campaigns conducted by AgrarMarkt Austria. However, businesses in the rural areas of the NCCE are to learn from the experience of their colleagues in the EU15. The retail chains dominating the market will probably try to spearhead a trend towards regionality in the area surveyed too. To counter this, measures of economic policy have to be taken early in order to strengthen the competitiveness of SMEs in agriculture and trade through regional cooperation initiatives (Rößl et al. 2006). A barrier to this can certainly be found in the experience the actors had with state-run cooperatives during the era of real socialism.

Currently, the marketing of regional products is definitely not professional enough. Likewise, production criteria and quality assurance tools have not been sufficiently developed yet. Regional products should be linked more strongly with well-known region names or positively associated regional characteristics (e.g. nature, history) in order to create long-term positive associations in the customer's mind. This marketing strategy also includes revitalizing traditional regional raw materials and products, which often already possess positive image attributes beyond the region.

In order to bundle resources in production and marketing, it will be important in future to make use of regional umbrella brands, which, however, can only realize their full synergy potential based on a cooperation of strong local firms. Despite the relatively small market, for instance, in Slovenia, there are already several examples of high-quality food and craft products known beyond the region, which are produced in rural municipalities. Here, positive synergy effects with the growing tourism market can be detected, which makes the regions better known internationally and so opens up new markets for the local companies.

Thesis 10: Consulting for businesses – municipalities and regional consultants become effective together.

The dynamic development within the administrative structures set in motion with the turnaround and, especially, the membership in the EU, as can be clearly seen in the examples of Slovenia and Hungary, makes consulting for businesses more difficult. The municipality often does not know which institutions are responsible for which questions concerning the company, or which person might have a competent answer to a specific question from the entrepreneur willing to locate his company in the area. Frequently, more than one institution at different administrative levels at once is responsible for getting companies to locate in the area.

What makes matters more difficult is that entrepreneurs and the municipality cooperate little. Contact is made only in acute cases. For example, the municipality approaches the local businesses when it needs money, e.g. for clubs and charities. If mayors suggest regular meetings to improve inter-communal communication, the entrepreneurs react rather surprised.

Despite the little financial and partly even legal wiggle-room they have, it is often the mayors themselves that personally get involved with business consulting. They accompany the entrepreneur to the authorities, survey land for construction with him and negotiate the conditions for locating. In their consulting activities, they occasionally exceed their actual authority, although this is not clearly defined transparently for all parties involved.

Such ambitious individual initiatives of municipality representatives are foiled by the heavy competition between the municipalities in the whole area surveyed. This is especially true when new businesses are to locate in the area. Willing investors have long realized that mayors can easily be played against each other. Here, it will be necessary to rethink on both local and higher territorial levels. The inter-communal coordination of such projects must be defined as a prerequisite for allocating public money.

But what can a municipality actually do within the framework of business consulting? Its core competencies are zoning, communal taxes and construction permits. Beyond that, it mainly refers entrepreneurs to the appropriate regional authorities, chambers or consulting institutions for specific questions. Wherever such institutions are active regarding location consulting, they – instead of the municipality – are the first point of contact for founders and companies interested in locating there. Thus, they become important cooperation partners for the municipalities in advising (young) entrepreneurs and in matters of public support payments. The consulting procedure, of course, should be organized as simply and cheaply as possible.

In order to achieve this, better coordination between those administrative units competent in company matters and the governmental and non-governmental institutions providing advice has to be arranged. The division of competencies has to be settled in advance. Furthermore, there should be an internet page or a physical service point that provides information on the relevant legal situation for both the municipalities and the companies on a daily basis.

In future, the municipality leaders in any case have to position themselves as competent partners for the local businesses, but certainly cannot be responsible and competent for the whole range of questions and requests coming from the businesses. The entrepreneurs should find a local area whose municipalities coordinate location policy on a regular basis and bundle their consulting resources. It would be useful, for example, to have a common contact for locating companies in the local area.

As contacts for companies and municipalities, the various organizations involved in regional consulting play a central role in municipality development.

They are the main driver behind implementing endogenous development tools (e.g. citizens' forums), which can increase the pluralism and democratic co-determination in the municipalities. In addition, regional development agencies also act as contacts for businesses, further the preparation of sustainable agricultural and tourism concepts, and try to acquaint the municipalities with tools for finding and implementing strategies in various policy areas.

Apart from government support programmes, it is mainly the EU's LEADER programme that makes these important consulting structures for the rural development in the NCCE possible and defines major consulting contents. Therefore, through their Europe-wide network, the regional developers have conducted an avid know-how transfer from the EU15 and the new EU member countries. Within the INTERREG network, for instance, there is increased cooperation in Austria's regions bordering on the NCCE between regional consulting institutions on both sides of the border. On a municipality level, such know-how transfer has not been institutionalized yet, but takes place on an informal level, if at all.

It has to be noted that regional consultants – with their expert competence, their tendential political independence and their young teams of consultants – have become important partners for the municipalities in many development issues. It is only occasionally that municipality officials generally oppose external consulting, as these institutions are not primarily associated with governmental administration. The consultants themselves see the main barriers primarily in insufficient budgets and bureaucracy.

Thesis 11: Land for construction and dwellings – securing plots in time and enabling municipality development.

Municipalities in the area surveyed basically do not secure land for construction in any organized manner. Strangely enough, the same reasons why land should be secured for construction are often stated as reasons why it does not take place, e.g. no funds or no sites are available. In this context, the question of ownership, which is still unsolved in many areas, poses a massive structural problem. It also makes the overdue restoration of many buildings using public funds more difficult; additionally, the rural population is broadly unaware that this constitutes a problem in the first place.

In Slovakia, many sites are jointly owned, as after the turnaround state-owned property was privatized at high speed. In the Czech Republic, too, there is substantial legal uncertainty regarding the ownership of sites. The comparatively slow privatization process in Slovenia, from this point of view, has brought better results. Here, however, there is some contradictory legislation regarding spatial development, which impedes municipalities in actively securing sites. It is necessary to settle the question of ownership for sites in the municipal area fast, in order to prepare the zoning plans required for strategic municipality development.

Foreigners from the EU15 mainly buy properties in areas interesting for tourism and in economically successful regions. However, based on the results of the study, this can hardly be called a trend (any more), as investors have already begun to dispose of properties again. Where prices are expected to increase, there is, of course, property speculation, including property from restitution. This boosts prices and is thus an overall barrier to municipality development.

In the discussion on the municipalities' securing land for construction, the defects of neo-liberal policy become particularly apparent. In the turbulent phase after the turnaround, the sweeping privatization of formerly public property, which was socio-politically imperative within the framework of restitution but implemented hurriedly, was seen as a panacea. As a result of this, municipalities today have hardly any chance of acquiring property in favourable locations, because of private speculation. When land was still cheap, they neglected to do so. Securing land seems to be necessary not only for the advance planning of industrial zones, but also to safeguard reasonably priced accommodation for the young population and so to keep them in the municipality in the long term.

Thesis 12: Pluralistic municipality development – motivating the citizens to participate in politics and to show initiative.

The results of the study suggest that positive municipality development in the region surveyed is closely connected with the mayor. Particularly in small municipalities, he makes many of these decisions autonomously and is also, for instance, in direct contact with entrepreneurs willing to locate there. Differences in terms of level of activity, attitude to democracy, entrepreneurial thinking and also the courage to think outside the box mainly depend on whether a local politician was already politically active before 1989, or started his career or even his education only after the turnaround.

Addressing municipality development in the region surveyed as a generational problem also looks relevant because the young generation of politicians tends to be more open to the exchange of know-how, external consulting for the region and so the application of new political concepts. Apart from measures to attract businesses, this mainly concerns the establishment of pluralistic and also transparent decision structures in the municipality. Young mayors and councillors are much more likely to realize the need for this than politicians from the old system. It is for this reason that it seems important to reignite young people's interest in municipality development in general, and in communal politics in particular, in the whole region surveyed.

Disenchantment with politics does not just result from a general dissatisfaction with living conditions, but often also comes from the negative examples politicians on various institutional levels set for young people. Municipality politicians should be aware of their function as role models for the next generation of politicians. Room for external consulting and also cross-border exchange of know-how between municipal representatives from Austria and the NCCE can definitely be found in the fields of political education, social competences and management skills.

Many activities in regional and municipality development take place top down and are not backed by the local population. In the era of real socialism, endogenous development, personal commitment and regional cooperation were frowned upon, as the central government feared the critics of the systems and dissidents assumed to be involved in these activities. The effects of the passivity people fell into back then are additionally augmented by cultural aspects, which results in different variants of "passivity" of the population in municipality development.

The civil society, however, in many places, is much livelier than history would let us believe. Still, it often lacks more permanent organization, which hampers large-scale integration into regional political processes. Furthermore, the results of the study show that party politics on a communal level is of little importance for the actors involved.

In order to strengthen the civil society, citizens' meetings on specific subjects should take place on a regular basis, among other things. Decisions on municipal policy have to become more transparent and the people have to be integrated more actively into development processes. This might not necessarily improve the results, but they would be accepted more readily and interest in politics, particularly by young people, would be raised.

The municipalities often wait for the people to make suggestions, but do not further the emergence of such bottom-up initiatives. There is still a distinct lack of endogenous regional development, such as establishing regular and substantial citizens' forums or village regeneration societies. Where they exist, their quality needs some improving. Communication channels between municipality officials and the population have to become more institutionalized, with the LEADER programme again achieving progress in this respect.

Decision-makers pay too little attention to the fact that the people have pronounced self-organization skills, which could be used for regional development tasks if they are properly activated. Some of the reasons for this can be found in the informal, opaque networks that were commonplace in the era of real socialism. At that time, this form of informal, decentralized organization was necessary in order to make up for the inefficiencies of the planned economy in rendering typical public services, but also services of the private sector. Even today, it seems easy to conclude that self-organized groups with strong promoters can indeed fulfil tasks in individual areas of regional development (e.g. village renewal, social activities) better and faster without the involvement of the municipal administration.

The successful implementation of democratic and pluralistic decision processes is closely connected with the mayor and the generation of politicians he comes from. This is all the more relevant, as in the municipalities in the region surveyed there is almost always one dominant political party. It depends on his political position and view of the world, as well as his social leadership skills, whether the mayor strikes the right balance in including opposition, citizens' parties, businesses and the general population in decision processes, but, at the same time, makes important decisions autonomously and enforces them against outside influences.

Pluralistic and democratic attitudes of actors in the municipalities are, in turn, closely linked with the generations involved. The establishment of a young generation of communal politicians especially is to be promoted more intensively, as they contain a lot of creative potential for solving current problems. This will only work if it becomes interesting again for young people to get engaged in municipal policy, which can be effected, for example, by integrating them into the municipality's decision-making processes early on.

If a democratic and open attitude among decision-makers exists, a number of measures for improving transparency in municipal policy can follow. This includes the regular citizens' forums mentioned above, an open-door policy in the municipal offices, municipal publications including diverse points of view of municipality development, a transparent information policy regarding intentions and decisions of the municipality, individual talks with citizens or discussion platforms on the internet. A broader involvement of the people in decision-making processes is to be enabled.

As in "old Europe", failure of the state and the market results in the search for new cooperative structures in municipality and regional development. These initiatives lead to cooperation of state actors with businesses (public–private partnerships) and civil society organizations (public community partnerships). The hope that the current political debate will actually result in establishing new democratic and pluralistic governance structures must be taken with a grain of salt, not just regarding the region surveyed, but also the EU in general. If this is the case, the municipality or local area will be the most likely levels of candidates for such governance structures, due to the lower complexity. In contrast to Austria, the countries surveyed have no tradition of a liberal corporatism, as represented, for instance, by Austria's social partnership. On the other hand, there is a strong tradition of civil society movements.

Thesis 13: Establishment and innovation of businesses – enabling corporate innovation and regional cooperation between businesses.

When municipality officials in the region surveyed talk about companies and their problems, they generally refer to the local enterprises active in agriculture rather than in trade and industry. While the latter are structurally less pronounced in the rural areas, all of the municipalities surveyed have a strong agricultural sector.

The municipalities hardly support the establishment of new SMEs in any focused manner. Therefore, new entrepreneurs get assistance mainly from regional consultancies. Additionally, there are incubators and industrial parks, primarily around the urban areas, though. What are missing are regional strategies for promoting the establishment of new enterprises and innovations that take the peculiarities of the rural region into consideration.

A strategy that is misinterpreted as the panacea for creating innovations and jobs in local areas often results in the attempt to attract large companies and link them to the local producers, also in agriculture. The necessity of a diversified local economic landscape is not realized as such, nor is the problem, created by this strategy, of becoming dependent on individual large companies and sectors. In Hungary, it is primarily the renewable-energy sector where such strategies are being followed and have already entered the implementation stage. This has to be criticized insofar as the future prospects in this industry are becoming less and less clear due to current developments (e.g. the food crisis).

For people employed in dying industries and large companies, there is hardly any economic protection, as the economic structures still have not been diversified. If a large company is lost, the redundant workers do not find alternative jobs in the region. Apart from promotional measures in agriculture, and in recent years increasingly in rural tourism, there are no activities on a communal level that focus on establishing other industries.

Businesses see raising capital as a major obstacle to corporate innovation (including high interest rates on and securities for loans). In addition, the way public monies for companies are distributed is (e.g. in Hungary) described as inefficient.

Another major barrier to an active policy of municipalities and regional consultants attracting businesses is the drift of qualified workers to the cities and abroad. Additionally, the poorly developed and aged traffic infrastructure makes location in rural areas much less attractive. In Slovenia, newly established companies are also frightened off by the high property prices, particularly in tourist areas.

A particular problem is that there are no coordinated strategies in economic policy within the local areas. What is more, decision-makers often show absolutely no understanding for the need for inter-communal cooperation in economic policy, such as the development of inter-communal industrial zones. If there are such zones that function well, they are situated close to urban areas. Such projects, however, are not developed on a local level and do not strive for solutions beyond the municipality. In rural areas, industrial zones are often insular solutions, which, due to the lack of integration into surrounding structures, are not fully accepted by the businesses. Moreover, the extreme competitiveness of municipalities in matters of location policy gives investors great negotiation power. The opportunity to play municipalities against each other in negotiations damages the local area as a whole.

The results of this study show that the role of agriculture – simply because of the general structural situation – will also be decisive for municipality development in the future. In this context, cooperative strategies have to be developed in order to maintain a competitive agricultural sector consisting of small farms. For instance, it might be useful to establish cooperation across sectors that aims at producing regional food and craft specialities, which might give the enterprises involved a better competitive standing *vis-à-vis* foreign retail chains.

In setting up inter-business cooperations, in coordination with regional consultants already active in this field, municipalities could indeed play a key role. Cooperations between regional entrepreneurs should be supported. Appropriate measures for doing so include the organization of information events, the referral to competent cooperation advisers or the promotion of local sales outlets, as they can occasionally already be found in the region surveyed. Entrepreneurs, on the other hand, still tend to be mentally inhibited by the negative connotation of terms like cooperation or cooperative from the communist era and frequently show a sceptical attitude towards some of the actors involved (e.g. regional politicians, chambers, trade unions).

Finally, educational policy should be another starting point for regional innovation, by creating enthusiasm for entrepreneurship among the young population. Education was regarded as very important in the NCCE even in the communist era. Schools as the centres for local know-how have to be utilized also in questions of entrepreneurship and innovation. The exchange between local companies and local educational institutions should be pushed. Entrepreneurs can introduce the schools to local business traditions. On the other hand, educational institutions could infuse the entrepreneurs' practical experience with topical knowledge. The aim should be to provide a sense of modern entrepreneurship based on local business traditions that sees the local situation as a business opportunity and can communicate these special characteristics as a competitive advantage. In this context, business simulation games on the topic of "sustainable regional development" could be used. Nevertheless, strategies in business education will only succeed if cooperation between municipalities on a regional level works out.

Thesis 14: Inter-communal cooperation – more solidarity and less rivalry between municipalities benefit the local area and region.

Decision-makers publicly profess the need for inter-communal cooperation in municipality development. This idea, however, is implemented only in the field of tourism. Here, the persons responsible realize the advantages of bundling resources, and any progress or success can be discerned relatively quickly. First steps towards inter-communal cooperation have also been taken in the areas of infrastructure, welfare, education and culture. Yet every positive example of cooperation is still based on monetary incentives from promotional programmes and strong promoters. Furthermore, subliminally, inter-communal cooperation also involves the municipalities' and mayors' prestige.

Apart from that, especially when promoting businesses and in matters of location policies, municipalities fight on their own as well as together. The competitive idea is employed excessively. While the traditional market economies in Europe integrate more cooperative elements into regional policy again, in the region surveyed, competition is an almost purely positive maxim for action in practically all areas of policy – including municipality development. This excessive competitive thinking between municipalities is also the result of the real socialist regime's arbitrary distributional policy that went on for decades.

In matters of inter-communal cooperation, consolidating administrative units in the region surveyed also seems necessary. The expert know-how of municipal councillors and staff is often insufficient to make sound decisions for sustainable municipality development (e.g. locating businesses, social and educational measures). The regional potentials for establishing the required expert competences (e.g. business, law) should thus be bundled. Larger administrative units have the resources necessary to safeguard the quality of their decisions and advice given. However, this entails increased levels of bureaucracy.

Increased administrative consolidation also makes sense for efficiency reasons. The municipalities in the region surveyed have constant budgetary problems. Inter-communal municipal offices and school centres could help save budgetary funds. Unless the quality of the regional services offered is improved, however, there is the danger of a lower living standard of the people in the individual communities, as they lose the infrastructure referred to above. Moreover, the jobs lost through consolidation place a burden on the local job market.

When infrastructural facilities are concentrated in such a manner, mayors often try to secure them for their own municipality, which again furthers competitive thinking. Consolidation can only be enforced if regional development is still centralized. Once the municipalities are more autonomous, such a reform is hardly possible. Apart from the decrease in bureaucracy desired and more flexibility, on closer inspection, such a decentralized governance approach reveals an underlying neo-liberal regional policy. The municipalities are exposed to increased competition, as everybody wants to offer the best location with the most attractive conditions for companies. Their autonomy and the public money available will then be practically exclusively used for this purpose. In important matters of the local people's quality of life (e.g. social security, affordable properties for housing), the municipality and the governmental institutions will no longer be capable of acting.

In order to anchor inter-communal cooperation in the region surveyed in the long term, it is important to institutionalize the interaction between officials from the individual municipalities in a region. A positive example is the regular event of the mayors' council in Slovenian local areas. Public funding as the central incentive for cooperation has to give way to a real awareness of the advantages of regional cooperation. Only then will everybody involved see the continued existence of the cooperation, the cooperation partners and the aims of the cooperation as a personal objective.

How can such an impulse be given from outside in such a way it enables further impulses from within (e.g. strengthening the people's own initiative in matters of municipality development), without inducing a feeling of being coerced among the population and the businesses? The restructuring of regions in Hungary and Slovenia prescribed by the state has a strong flavour of the politics of the real socialist era and does not really create regional cooperation cultures, as there is no commitment at the grass-roots level.

Creating commitment that can also be relied upon within the framework of regional project implementation can most likely be achieved through a regionally anchored project management that all participants accept as independent. This implies an intensified know-how transfer from the regional consultants to municipality officials. The regional consultants, for their part, in this case, need the necessary financial as well as expert know-how resources. As a result, regional bodies should work out transparent projects embedded in municipality development plans that must be coordinated on an inter-communal level.

The hope remains that the externally motivated cooperators realize the advantages of cooperation and internalize this principle. This area is also clearly suitable for an international exchange of experience, as best-practice examples from neighbouring countries might provide new insights into the problems of cooperation for the municipalities in the NCCE.

Thesis 15: Planning municipality development – designing integrated development plans professionally.

Although awareness often exists in the countries surveyed that comprehensive development planning is absolutely necessary, there is, on the one hand, insufficient know-how for designing such plans and, on the other hand, no commitment for consequent implementation. Existing municipality development concepts thus lack an integrative character (i.e. connecting several areas of policy) and long-term orientation. Instead, in the municipalities' plans, a short-term view prevails, often specifically focusing on particular tendering procedures or, at the most, one legislative term. Short-term changes just before elections are quite common. Additionally, there is some overlap and inconsistency of individual plans on the communal, regional and national levels.

When there are sound development programmes for local areas, such as in Slovenia, these are mostly the work of regional consultancies and their expertise. For inter-communal planning, the municipalities themselves appear to be too passive in development and implementation. The bottom line is broadly disconnected development planning throughout the region surveyed showing little consistency.

The reasons for flawed development concepts can partly be found in the centralist planning tradition, which, in Hungary, has continued to this day. Objectives are thus broadly prescribed by the next level in spatial hierarchy level and not adjusted to the situation in the individual regions. In addition, the lack of professionalism of the municipality officials' strategy development is also the result of structural problems in administration. For instance, there is a dearth of adequately trained specialists on the municipality level, while parallel capacities have been built up on the regional and national levels.

In future, strategic planning tools have to be used more in municipality development. In order to improve the municipality officials' competence in this respect, an intensive know-how transfer from the national and regional to the communal level is necessary, and equally between municipalities across national borders. At the same time, communication channels must be institutionalized to provide information on the conditions and needs of the individual local areas to decision-makers on the regional, national and EU levels. Incidentally, such a knowledge management may also be needed in Austria. Regional consultants active in this field should be supported more substantially by regional research and educational institutions as well as by international cooperation programmes.

Thesis 16: The Central European perspective – similar challenges in municipality development as a potential for mutual learning.

The findings of the study show that, on a communal level, Austria and the NCCE show greater similarities in economic policy than one would expect. The local areas surveyed in this study have always been engaged in social, cultural and economic exchange with Austria. A central result of the study is that, throughout history, the interaction – which has not always been without friction – has also had a significant impact on communal structures, which has resulted in fairly similar behavioural patterns and institutional settings. For instance, even today, German, Slavic and Hungarian influences can be detected in the social and cultural life in the municipalities all across the region surveyed.

The European integration process and the EU's expansion to the East have reactivated interaction on the political, cultural and primarily economic levels. Similar needs and habits of the people also have to be seen in the context of the creation of a new European, if not even a global, societal structure, whose members have also found a common language in English. In contrast to former times, the hegemonic aspirations of particular ethnic groups are hardly a barrier to the cross-border exchange in the region surveyed any more.

It is globalization, in particular, that poses quite similar challenges for rural municipalities in the Central European area in creating adequate conditions for SMEs. Infrastructural problems (e.g. communications and traffic infrastructure) as a result of the centralized regional policy of the planned economy are still characteristic for most municipalities in the NCCE. The rural municipalities today suffer from a modernization backlog built up over decades. This is one of the significant differences to the challenges for Austrian municipalities.

The negative effects of an increasingly neo-liberal economic policy, on the other hand, can be felt everywhere, as public services are starved and civil society organizations are only seemingly integrated. The dependence on private investors in local development matters additionally raises the issue of democratic policy, as the people are only rarely able to choose the actual decision-makers. Nor are they are integrated in the decision-making process. Through the public sector's withdrawal from various areas of financing communal tasks, a culture following the principle of "he who pays the piper calls the tune" emerges that endangers social structures and exacerbates people's frustration and lack of interest in municipality development.

There are many arguments in favour of treating Central Europe more like one common development region, in which the local areas are connected due to similar problems and also develop cross-border development strategies. In spatial development, several levels are involved, on which specific bundles of measures to establish a Central European regional development programme have to be implemented. One example would be the INTERREG programme, a common initiative of the European Regional Development Funds (EFRE) to promote cooperation between EU regions.

Internationally active companies have long spotted the common elements of the Central European region through their marketing strategies and have incorporated them mostly successfully. It is time that politicians in Europe and the nation states involved adapt this point of view, too, and develop common strategies for economic development on a communal level. To make this possible, national egocentrism and the parish-pump politics of regional and communal decision-makers have to be left behind. Each municipal leadership should see their own actions in a greater context. Not the differences to other regions, but the similarities should build identities. This calls for further incentives on the European and national levels to promote cross-border links between the rural municipalities in Central Europe.

Thesis 17: Mutual know-how transfer – critical analysis of one's own situation as the foundation for adopting successful models

Based on the arguments just outlined, there should be mutual know-how transfer between municipalities in Central Europe, which should not simply focus on the mere transfer of development concepts from one local area to another. Particularly problematic is the practice in the NCCE of uncritically transferring development strategies from the EU15.

It appears highly questionable to equate "positive development" per se with the practice of regional policy that takes place in economically "more developed" countries. The main point is that local areas individually define their development strategies in line with their situation and needs and do not – e.g. because of guidelines for funding – adapt to ratios from comparable regions and so uncritically adopt their structures.

Especially in the NCCE, the negative consequences of standardized, purely theoretical regional-policy concepts can be observed. These concepts were simply applied to the regions without including the local population in the development processes. Instead of just copying measures that were successful in other municipalities, what is needed is an inter-European, and again specifically Central European, know-how transfer, which primarily familiarizes the municipalities in the region surveyed with the range of options in economic policy on a communal level. What is important is conveying knowledge by means of various instruments of communal economic policy and their application. This know-how transfer is not to prescribe a development path to the target municipalities, but to show them ways each municipality can find its own specific development path and follow it subsequently.

Here also Austrian municipality officials can learn from their counterparts in the NCCE, e.g. how municipality policy can be conducted under difficult structural conditions. Municipality officials in the era of real socialism and later in the years of transition were particularly confronted with the problem of scarce resources. Experiences from the transitional process can also provide valuable insights for Austrian municipalities that face structural changes in the local economic structure.

In evaluating the transferability of individual measures of economic policy on a communal level that were successful in Austria, the general problem of embedding strategies into the context must not be forgotten. Both measures taken by the municipalities and the strategies pursued by local companies only become effective in their interaction with the specific context. The way different factors in the areas of administration, businesses and population – which especially in rural local areas overlap substantially – interlock, and which outside influences affect the local area in this respect, determines whether the development in the municipality is more or less successful.

Therefore, positive experiences must first be removed from their original context to make them transferable. In order to do so, the system of causes behind the developments observed has to be understood and the requirements for the specific measures to unfold their desired effect have to be isolated. In reality, however, social systems are not easily predictable, which may cause individual measures to fail in their implementation, even if the requirements identified have been met. The effects and the way they are interconnected are much too complex to include all variables and the relationships between them. Each measure must thus only be understood as an abstract type of strategy that first has to be made specific by the actors in the local area. Only in this way can entrepreneurship be made community based in the sense of being embedded in the social context (Polanyi 1978 [1944]). Seen in this way, international knowledge transfer between municipalities represents a critical analysis of successful models (e.g. from Austria). Embedding a measure in the specific context is the responsibility of the decision-makers and those concerned.

Which measures look attractive for rural municipalities in the region surveyed, in order to establish favourable conditions for SMEs, and thus provide positive impulses for the local economic structure, can be seen from the results of this study. By doing so, we offer, on the one hand, municipalities in the NCCE a qualified selection of potential measures and, on the other hand, Austrian municipalities and SMEs valuable information on the situation in neighbouring municipalities in Central and Eastern Europe. This provides starting points for future initiatives in Central European municipality development.

Bibliography

Abrhám, Josef (2007): "Regional Differentiation of the New Member States of the European Union", CAP Working Paper.

Arzeni, Sergio (1996): "Entrepreneurship in Eastern Europe: A Critical View", in: Horst Brezinski; Michael Fritsch (eds): *The Economic Impact of New Firms in Post-Socialist Countries. Bottom-up Transformation in Eastern Europe*. Cheltenham u.a.: Edward Elgar; 52–8.

Atherton, Andrew; Hannon, Paul D. (2006): "Localised Strategies for Supporting Incubation. Strategies Arising from a Case of Rural Enterprise Development", *Journal of Small Business and Enterprise Development* 13 (1), 48–61.

Bagatelas, William T.; Oravec, Ján; Sergi, Bruno S. (2004): "Slovakia's Achievements and Prospects", in: Bruno S. Sergi; William T. Bagatelas (eds), *The Slovak Economy and EU Membership*. Bratislava: Lura; 31–45.

Baláž, Vladimír (2007): "Regional Polarization under Transition: The Case of Slovakia", *European Planning Studies* 15 (5), 587–602.

Baldridge, D.C.; Floyd, S.W.; Markoczy, L. (2004): "Are Managers from Mars and Academics from Venus? Toward an Understanding of the Relationship between Academic Quality and Practical Relevance", *Strategic Management Journal* 25 (1), 1063–74.

Bank Austria; Reuvid, Jonathan (2004): "Foreign Direct Investment", in: Jonathan Reuvid (ed.): *Doing Business with Slovakia*. London: Kogan Page.

Barta, Györgyi (2005): "The Role of Foreign Direct Investment in the Spatial Restructuring of Hungarian Industry", in: G. Barta; E. Fekete; I. Kukorelli Szörényiné; J. Timár (eds): *Hungarian Spaces and Places: Patterns of Transition*. Pécs: Centre for Regional Studies; 143–60.

Bateman, Milford (2000): "Neo-liberalism, SME Development and the Role of Business Support Centres in the Transition Economies of Central and Eastern Europe", *Small Business Economics* 14 (4), 275–98.

Bauer, J. (1979): "Quantitative Entwicklungsplanung für ländliche Regionen", in: P. Klemmer (ed.): *Beiträge zur Struktur-und Konjunkturforschung*. Bochum: Brockmeyer; Vol. 10.

Baum, Sabine; Weingarten, Peter (2004): "Interregionale Disparitäten und Entwicklung ländlicher Räume als regionalpolitische Herausforderung für die neuen EU-Mitgliedstaaten". Discussion Paper No. 61 des Institut für Agrar-entwicklung in Mittel-und Osteuropa (IAMO).

Benáček, Vladimir (1995): "Small Businesses and Private Entrepreneurship during Transition", *Eastern European Economics* 33 (2), 38–75.

Bender, Klaus W. (1997): "Entrepreneurship and Local Development in Countries in Transition", in: *Entrepreneurship and SMEs in Transition Economies. The Visegrad Conference.* Paris: OECD; 167–74.

Berko, Lili; Gueullette, Agota (2003): "Policy for Support of Small and Medium-size Enterprises in Hungary: The Case of the Central Region", *Post-Communist Economies* 15 (2), 243–57.

Bezemer, Dirk J. (2002): "De-collectivization in Czech and Slovak Agriculture: An Institutional Explanation", *Journal of Economic Issues* 36 (3), 723–45.

BFAI (n.d.): Branche kompakt. Tschechische Republik. Kfz-Industrie und Kfz-Teile. Bundesagentur für Außenwirtschaft.

Bohatá, Maria; Mládek, Jan (1999): "The Development of the Czech SME Sector", *Journal of Business Venturing* 14, 461–73.

Bouckenooghe, D.; De Clercq, D.; Willem, A.; Buelens, M. (2007): "An Assessment of Validity in Entrepreneurship Research", *The Journal of Entrepreneurship* 16 (2), 147–71.

Brenner, Y.S. (1993): "What Went Wrong with Communism?", *International Journal of Social Economics* 20 (5/6/7), 103–16.

Brezinski, Horst; Fritsch, Michael (1996): "Introduction: The Scope for Bottom-up Transformation in Post-Socialist Countries", in: Horst Brezinski; Michael Fritsch (eds): *The Economic Impact of New Firms in Post-Socialist Countries. Bottom-up Transformation in Eastern Europe.* Cheltenham u.a.: Edward Elgar; 1–6.

Bryson, Phillip J.; Cornia, Gary C. (2004): "Public Sector Transition in Post-communist Economies: The Struggle for Fiscal Decentralisation in the Czech and Slovak Republics", *Post-Communist Economies* 16 (3), 265–83.

Bukhval'd, E.; Vilenskii, A. (2003): "The Development and Support of Small Business. The Experience of Hungary and Lessons for Russia", *Problems of Economic Transition* 45 (11), 39–50.

Bukvic, Vladimir; Bartlett, Will (2003): "Financial Barriers to SME Growth in Slovenia", *Economic and Business Review for Central and South-Eastern Europe* 5 (3), 161–81.

Busenitz, L.W.; Page West III, G.; Shepherd, D.; Nelson, T.; Chandler, G.; Zacharakis, A. (2003): "Entrepreneurship Research in Emergence: Past Trends and Future Directions", *Journal of Management* 29 (3), 285–308.

Chandler, C.; Lyon, D. (2001): "Issues of Research Design and Construct Measurement in Entrepreneurship Research: The Past Decade", *Entrepreneurship: Theory & Practice* 25 (4), 101–13.

Crevoisier, Olivier (2004): "The Innovative Milieus Approach: Toward a Territorialized Understanding of the Economy?", *Economic Geography* 80 (4), 367–79.

Csatári, Bálint (2005): "Criteria of Rurality for the Hungarian Micro-regions. Major Problems Facing Rural Areas in Hungary", in: G. Barta; E. Fekete; I. Kukorelli Szörényiné; J. Timár (eds): *Hungarian Spaces and Places: Patterns of Transition.* Pécs: Centre for Regional Studies; 466–82.

Cziráky, Dario; Sambst, Jože; Rovan, Jože; Puljiz, Jakša (2006): "Regional Development Assessment: A Structural Equation Approach", *European Journal of Operational Research* 174, 427–42.

Dallago, Bruno (1997): "The Economic System, Transition and Opportunities for Entrepreneurship", in: *Entrepreneurship and SMEs in Transition Economies. The Visegrad Conference.* Paris: OECD; 103–24.

Damijan, Jože P. (2004): "Reentering the Markets of the Former Yugoslavia", in: Mojmir Mrak; Matija Rojec; Carlos Silva-Jáuregui (eds): *Slovenia. From Yugoslavia to the European Union.* Washington: World Bank; 334–49.

DeFillippi, Robert (1995): "Small Business Development in the Czech Republic", *Review of Business* 16 (3), 3–8.

Diekmann, A. (2000): *Empirische Sozialforschung. Grundlagen, Methoden, Anwendungen.* Reinbek bei Hamburg: Rowohlt.

Divila, Emil; Sokol, Zdeněk (1994): "Transforming of the Agricultural Sector. Conceptual Questions of Forming New Entrepreneurial Entities in Czech Agriculture", *Eastern European Economics* September–October, 52–64.

Dövényi, Zoltán (2001): "Development and Spatial Disparities of Unemployment in Hungary", in: Peter Meusburger; Heike Jöns (eds): *Transformations in Hungary. Essays in Economy and Society.* New York/Heidelberg: Physica; 207–24.

Drgona, Vladimir; Turnock, David (2000): "Policies for Rural Eastern Europe in Transition: The Case of Slovakia", *GeoJournal* 50 (2–3), 235–47.

du Plessis, Valerie; Beshiri, Roland; Bollman, Ray D.; Clemenson, Heather (2002): "Definitions of 'Rural', Agriculture and Rural Working Paper Series". Working Paper No. 61, Ottawa: Statistics Canada (Agriculture Division).

Dujmovits, Robert (1996): "Eigenständige Entwicklung in ländlich-peripheren Regionen. Erfahrungen", Ansätze und Erfolgsbedingungen, Frankfurt/Main u.a.: Peter Lang.

Duke, Vic; Grime, Keith (1997): "Inequality in Post-Communism", *Regional Studies* 31 (9), 883–90.

Duponcel, Marc (1998): "The Collapse of the CMEA and Hungary's Agro-Food External Trade", *Communist Economies & Economic Transformation* 10 (1), 119–28.

Dusek, Tamás (2006): "Regional Income Differences in Hungary – A Multi-Level Spatio-Temporal Analysis", paper submitted to the 46th Congress of the European Regional Science Association, Volos (Greece), 30 August–3 September 2006.

Ebel, Horst (1990): *Abrechnung. Das Scheitern der ökonomischen Theorie und Politik des "realen Sozialismus".* Berlin: Die Wirtschaft.

European Commission for Europe (n.d.): Statistical Standards and Studies – No. 49. Recommendations for the 2000 Censuses of Population and Housing in the ECE Region, New York/Geneva.

Enyedi, György (2005): "Processes of Regional Development in Post-socialist Hungary", in: G. Barta; E. Fekete; I. Kukorelli Szörényiné; J. Timár (eds): *Hungarian Spaces and Places: Patterns of Transition.* Pécs: Centre for Regional Studies; 18–27.

Erjavec, Emil; Rednak, Miroslav; Volk, Tina; Turk, Jernej (2003): "The Transition from 'Socialist' Agriculture to the Common Agriculture Policy: The Case of Slovenia", *Post-Communist Economies* 15 (4), 557–69.

Erjavec, Emil; Turk, Jernej; Rednak, Miroslav (1995): "The Economic Transition and Structural Changes of Slovene Agriculture", International Research Project: Long-Term Agricultural Policies for Central Europe: Country Draft Report.

Essmann, Hans (1980): *Zur Entwicklung des Ländlichen Raumes in Österreich. Ergebnisse einer Strukturuntersuchung und Folgerungen für die Raumordnungspolitik.* Salzburg: Salzburger Institut für Raumforschung.

European Commission (1998a): *Agricultural Situation and Prospects in the Central and Eastern European Countries. Czech Republic.* Working Document of the European Commission.

——(1998b): *Agricultural Situation and Prospects in the Central European Countries.* Slovak Republic. European Commission.

——(1998c): *Agricultural Situation and Prospects in the Central European Countries.* Hungary. European Commission.

——(1998d): *Agricultural Situation and Prospects in the Central European Countries.* Slovenia. European Commission.

Fassmann, Heinz; Meusburger, Peter (1997): *Arbeitsmarktgeographie. Erwerbstätigkeit und Arbeitslosigkeit im räumlichen Kontext.* Stuttgart: B. G. Teubner.

Ferrao, Joao (1995): "Enhancing Human Resources in Remote and Intermediate Rural Areas – Towards an New Understanding", in: OECD (ed.): *Creating Employment for Rural Development.* New Policy Approaches, Paris: OECD; 93–110.

Fink, M. (2005): *Erfolgsfaktor Selbstverpflichtung bei vertrauensbasierten Kooperationen – Mit einem empirischen Befund.* Frankfurt/Main: Lang.

Fink, Matthias; Lang, Richard; Harms, Rainer (2011): "Local Responses to Global Technological Change – Contrasting Restructuring Practices in Two Rural Communities in Austria", *Technological Forecasting and Social Change*, doi: 10.1016/j.techfore. 2011.10.001.

Fink, Matthias; Harms, Rainer (2012): "Contextualizing the Relationship between Self-commitment and Performance: Environmental and Behavioural Uncertainty in (Cross-border) Alliances of SMEs", *Entrepreneurship and Regional Development* 24 (3–4), 1–19.

Fischer, Holger (1999): *Eine kleine Geschichte Ungarns.* Frankfurt/Main: Suhrkamp.

Fischer, Stanley; Sahay, Ratna (2001): "The Transition Economies After Ten Years", in: Lucjan T. Orlowski (ed.): *Transition and Growth in Post-Communist Countries. The Ten-year Experience.* Cheltenham: Edward Elgar; 3–47.

Fogel, Georgine (2001): "An Analysis of Entrepreneurial Environment and Enterprise Development in Hungary", *Journal of Small Business Management* 39 (1), 103–9.

Forst, Martin (1996): *Helping Small Business in Eastern Europe*, The OECD Observer 198, 51–4.

Fox, William (1995): "Designing Infrastructure Policy to Create Jobs in Rural Areas", in: OECD (ed.): *Creating Employment for Rural Development.* New Policy Approaches, Paris: OECD; 111–29.

Freshwater, David (1995): "The Contribution of Direct Aid to Reducing Unemployment in Rural Areas", in: OECD (ed.): *Creating Employment for Rural Development.* New Policy Approaches, Paris: OECD; 51–71.

Gapinski, James H. (1993): *The Economic Structure and Failure of Yugoslavia.* London: Praeger.

Gibb, Allan A. (1993): "Small Business Development in Central and Eastern Europe – Opportunity for a Rethink?", *Journal of Business Venturing* 8, 461–86.

Glaser, Roman; Toros, Jani (2004): "Agriculture and Food Industries", in: Jonathan Reuvid (ed.): *Doing Business with Slovenia.* London: Kogan Page; 115–21.

Gligorov, Vladimir (2004): "Socialism and the Disintegration of SFR Yugoslavia", in: Mojmir Mrak; Matija Rojec; Carlos Silva-Jáuregui (eds): *Slovenia. From Yugoslavia to the European Union.* Washington: World Bank; 15–31.

Goglio, Alessandro (2007): "Encouraging Sub-National Government Efficiency", in: OECD (ed.): *OECD Economic Surveys.* Hungary, Paris: OECD.

Gopinath, C.; Hoffman, R.C. (1995): "A Comment on the Relevance of Strategy Research", in: P. Shrivastava; A.S. Huff; J.E. Dutton (eds), *Advances in Strategic Management: Challenges from within the Mainstream.* Greenwich, CT: JAI Press, 12(B): 93–110.

Gorton, Matthew; Davidova, Sophia; Banse, Martin; Bailey, Alistair (2006): "The International Competitiveness of Hungarian Agriculture: Past Performance and Future Projections", *Post-Communist Economics* 18 (1), 69–84.

Gow, James; Carmichael, Cathie (2000): *Slovenia and the Slovenes. A Small State and the New Europe*. London: C. Hurst.

Grichnik, D. (2006): "Die Opportunity Map der internationalen Entrepreneur-shipforschung", *Zeitschrift für Betriebswirtschaft* 76 (12), 100–125.

Gwóźdź, Zdzisław Piotr (2002): *Zentraleuropa Almanach Ungarn. Daten, Fakten & Informationen*. Wissenswertes über Ungarn, Molden Verlag.

Hahn, Herwig; Preuß, Hans-Joachim A. (1994): *Regionalplanung in der ländlichen Entwicklung. Materialien des Zentrums für regionale Entwicklungsforschung der Justus-Liebig-Universität Giessen*. Bd. 31, Giessen: Zentrum für regionale Entwicklungsforschung.

Ham, John C.; Svejnar, Jan; Terrell, Katherine (1998): "Unemployment and the Social Safety Net During Transitions to a Market Economy: Evidence from the Czech and Slovak Republics", *The American Economic Review* 88 (5), 1117–42.

Harms, R.; Kraus, S.; Schwarz, E. (2009): "The suitability of the configuration approach in entrepreneurship research", *Entrepreneurship and Regional Development* 21 (1), 25–47.

Hegedüs, József (2002): "Decentralization and Structural Adjustment in Hungary", 2nd International Conference on "Decentralization: Federalism: The Future of Decentralization States?", Manila, 25–27 July.

Henkel, Gerhard (1993): *Der Ländliche Raum. Gegenwart und Wandlungsprozesse in Deutschland seit dem 19. Jahrhundert*, Stuttgart: Teubner.

Hilde, Paal Sigurd (1999): "Slovak Nationalism and the Break-up of Czechoslovakia", *Europe-Asia Studies* 51 (4), 647–65.

Hill, Lewis E.; Magas, István (1993): "Requiem for Communism: The Case of Hungary", *International Journal of Social Economics* 20 (5/6/7), 35–43.

Hisrich, Robert D.; Fulop, Gyula (1995): "Hungarian Entrepreneurs and their Enterprises", *Journal of Small Business Management* 33 (3), 88–94.

Hitt, M.A.; Ahlstrom, D.; Dacin, M.T.; Levitas, E.; Svobodina, L. (2004): "The Institutional Effects on Strategic Alliance Partner Selection in Transition Economies: China vs. Russia", *Organization Science* 15 (2), 173–86.

Holzhacker, Hans (2004): *Wer produziert was in der erweiterten Union*. Bank Austria Creditanstalt AG Volkswirtschaft und Marktanalysen.

Horváth, Gyula (2005): "Decentralisation, Regionalism and the Modernization of the Regional Economy in Hungary: A European Comparison", in: G. Barta; E. Fekete; I. Kukorelli Szörényiné; J. Timár (eds): *Hungarian Spaces and Places: Patterns of Transition*. Pécs: Centre for Regional Studies; 50–63.

Hösler, Joachim (2006): *Slowenien. Von den Anfängen bis zur Gegenwart*, Regensburg: Verlag Friedrich Pustet.

Hovorka, Gerhard (1998): *Die Kulturlandschaft im Berggebiet in Österreich. Politiken zur Sicherung von Umwelt-und Kulturleistungen und ländliche Entwicklung. OECD Fallstudie (Forschungsbericht Nr. 43)*. Wien: Bundesanstalt für Bergbauernfragen.

Hunya, Gábor (2001): "International Competitiveness: Impacts of Foreign Direct Investment in Hungary and Other Central and East European Countries", in: Peter Meusburger; Heike Jöns (eds): *Transformations in Hungary. Essays in Economy and Society*. New York/Heidelberg: Physica; 125–56.

Hutchinson, John; Xavier, Ana (2006): "Comparing the Impact of Credit Constraints on the Growth of SMEs in a Transition Country with an Established Market Economy", *Small Business Economics* 27, 169–79.

Huw, D.; Nutley, S.; Walter, I. (2007): "Academic Advice to Practitioners – the Role and Use of Research-Based Evidence", *Public Money & Management* 27 (4), 232.

IHS (1994): *The Slovak Republic After One Year of Independence*. Vienna.

Illeris, Sven (1993): "An Inductive Theory of Regional Development", *Papers in Regional Science* 72 (2), 113–34.

Illner, Michal (2001): "Regional Development in the Czech Republic Before and After the Accession. Some Speculative Scenarios", *Informationen zur Raumentwicklung* 11, 751–56.

Indruch, Rainer (1994): *Der Übergang zur sozialen Marktwirtschaft in den Ländern des ehemaligen RGW am Beispiel der ČSFR und Ungarns.* Konstanz: Hartung-Gorre.

Ivy, Russell L. (1997): "Entrepreneurial Strategies and Problems in Post-Communist Europe: A Survey of SMEs in Slovakia", *Journal of Small Business Management* 35 (3), 93–7.

Jakoby, Mark (2002): "The Economic Development: A Country in Transition", in: Ján Figel; Wolfgang Roth (eds): *Slovakia on the Road to EU Membership. Schriften des Zentrum für Europäische Integrationsforschung.* Baden-Baden: Nomos; 59–74.

Janáček, Kamil (1994): "Unemployment and the Labor Market in Czechoslovakia and the Czech Republic, 1990–92", *Eastern European Economics* July–August, 55–70.

Kessler, Alexander (2003): *Unternehmensgründungen in europäischen Transformationsländern. Dargestellt am Beispiel der Tschechischen Republik.* Lohmar/Köln: Eul Verlag.

Kindleberger, Charles P. (1965): *Economic Development. 2. Aufl.* New York u.a.: McGraw-Hill.

Kirschbaum, S.J. (1993): "Czechoslovakia: The Creation, Federalization and Dissolution of a Nation-State", *Regional Politics and Policy* 3, 69–95.

Kornai, János (2001): *Highways and Byways. Studies on Reform and Post-Communist Transition.* Cambridge: MIT Press.

Kosta, Jiří (2005): *Die tschechische/tschechoslowakische Wirtschaft im mehr-fachen Wandel.* Münster: Lit.

Kovács Pálné, Ilona (2005): "Hungary of the Regions: Utopia or Ultimatum?", in: G. Barta; E. Fekete; I. Kukorelli Szörényiné; J. Timár (eds): *Hungarian Spaces and Places: Patterns of Transition.* Pécs: Centre for Regional Studies; 92–105.

Kovács, Teréz (2005). "Restructuring Agriculture", in: G. Barta; E. Fekete; I. Kukorelli Szörényiné; J. Timár (eds): *Hungarian Spaces and Places: Patterns of Transition.* Pécs: Centre for Regional Studies; 259–71.

Kremser, Iztok (1991): "Partnerships for the Renaissance of the Small Business Sector in Central and Eastern Europe – ININ Business Incubator Network Case", in: H.J. Pichler (ed.): *Partnerships for the Renaissance of Small Business in Central and Eastern Europe.* Wien: Fachverlag der WU Wien.

KSH (2007a): *Hungary, 2006.* Hungarian Central Statistical Office

——(2007b): *Economy and Society, January–August 2007. Statistical Report 8/2007.* Hungarian Central Statistical Office.

——(2007c): *Hungary in Figures, 2006.* Hungarian Central Statistical Office.

——(2007d): *Statistical Yearbook of Hungary 2006.* Hungarian Central Statistical Office.

Kuhar, Aleš; Erjavec, Emil (2007): "Implications of Slovenia's EU Accession for the Agro-Food Sectors", *Economic and Business Review* 9 (2), 147–64.

Kukorelli Szörényiné, Irén (2005): "Micro-regional Co-operation as a Hungarian Example of Local Development", in: G. Barta; E. Fekete; I. Kukorelli Szörényiné; J. Timár (eds): *Hungarian Spaces and Places: Patterns of Transition.* Pécs: Centre for Regional Studies; 343–58.

Lagemann, Bernhard; Friedrich, Werner; Döhrn, Roland; Brüstler, Alena; Heyl, Norbert; Puxi, Marco; Welter, Friederike (1994): *Aufbau mittelständischer Strukturen in Polen, Ungarn, der Tschechischen Republik und der slowakischen Republik*. Essen: RWI.

Laimer, Peter; Smeral, Egon (2004): *Ein Tourismus-Satellitenkonto für Österreich. Methodik, Ergebnisse und Prognosen für die Jahre 2000 bis 2005*. Studie von Statistik Austria und dem Österreichischen Institut für Wirtschaftsforschung im Auftrag des BMWA.

Lajh, Damjan (2004): "Responses to the Processes of Europeanisation and Regionalisation: Domestic Changes in Slovenia", *Perspectives* 23, 36–60.

Langosch, Rainer (1994): *Theoretische Grundlagen für die Analyse von innovationsbedingten Unterschieden des wirtschaftlichen Wachstums in ländlichen Räumen*. Frankfurt/Main u.a.: Peter Lang.

Laski, Kazimierz (1992): "Transition from Command to Market Economies in Central and Eastern Europe: First Experiences and Questions", in: Sandor Richter (ed.): *The Transition from Command to Market Economies in East-Central Europe*. The Vienna Institute for Comparative Economic Studies Yearbook IV. Boulder: Westview Press; 33–55.

Lorentzen, Anne (1996): "Regional Development and Institutions in Hungary: Past, Present and Future Development", *European Planning Studies* 4 (3), 259–77.

——(1999): "Industrial Development, Technology Change, and Regional Disparity in Hungary", *European Planning Studies* 7 (4), 463–82.

MARD (Ministry of Agriculture and Regional Development) (2003): "Agriculture, Forestry and the Food Industry", in: Jonathan Reuvid (ed.): *Doing Business with Hungary*. London: Kogan Page; 131–8.

Marot, Bozidar (1997): "Small Business Development Strategy in Slovenia", in: *Entrepreneurship and SMEs in Transition Economies. The Visegrad Conference*. Paris: OECD; 51–64.

Mayring, P. (2002): *Einführung in die qualitative Sozialforschung; Eine Anleitung zu qualitativem Denken*. Basel: Weinheim.

Mencinger, Jože (2004): "Transition to a National and a Market Economy: A Gradualist Approach", in: Mojmir Mrak; Matija Rojec; Carlos Silva-Jáuregui (eds): *Slovenia. From Yugoslavia to the European Union*. Washington: World Bank; 67–82.

Mertlík, Pavel (1997): "Czech Privatization. From Public Ownership to Public Ownership in Five Years?", *Eastern European Economics* 35 (2), 64–83.

Meusburger, Peter (2001): "Spatial and Social Disparities of Employment and Income in Hungary in the 1990s", in: Peter Meusburger; Heike Jöns (eds): *Transformations in Hungary. Essays in Economy and Society*. New York/Heidelberg: Physica; 173–206.

Miller, D. (1986): "Configurations of Strategy and Structure: Towards a Synthesis", *Strategic Management Journal* 7, 233–49.

——(1996): "Configurations Revisited", *Strategic Management Journal* 17, 505–12.

Mlčoch, Lubomír (1998): "Czech Privatization: A Criticism of Misunderstood Liberalism (Keynote Address)", *Journal of Business Ethics* 17 (9/10), 951–9.

Moulaert, Frank; Sekia, Farid (2003): "Territorial Innovation Models: A Critical Survey", *Regional Studies* 37 (3), 289–302.

Mugler, Josef (1998): *Betriebswirtschaftslehre der Klein- und Mittelbetriebe*. Bd. 1. Dritte, überarbeitete Auflage. Wien/New York: Springer.

——(2005): *Grundlagen der BWL der Klein- und Mittelbetriebe*. Wien: Facultas.

Mugler, Josef; Fink, Matthias; Loidl, Stephan (2006): *Erhaltung und Schaffung von Arbeitsplätzen im ländlichen Raum. Gestaltung günstiger Rahmenbedingungen für Klein- und Mittelbetriebe*. Wien: Manz.

Müller-Eschenbach, Gordon P. (1995): *Die Zukunftsperspektive der Tschechischen Republik und der Slowakei zwei Jahre nach Spaltung der CSFR. Eine volkswirtschaftliche Analyse.* Weiden: Eurotrans.

Murray, Michael; Dunn, Larry (1995): "Capacity Building for Rural Development in the United States", *Journal of Rural Studies* 11 (1), 89–97.

Myant, Martin (2004): "Economic Development in a Czech Region", paper presented at Europe at the Margins: EU Regional Policy, Peripherality & Rurality, 15–16 April 2004, Angers, France.

Myant, Martin; Smith, Simon (2006): "Regional Development and Post-Communist Politics in a Czech Region", *Europe-Asia Studies* 58 (2), 147–68.

Myrdal, Gunnar (1957): *Economic Theory and Under-Developed Regions.* London: Duckworth.

Nagy, Erika; Turnock, David (2000): "Planning Regional Development: Promoting Small Settlements in a Trans-Frontier Situation", *GeoJournal* 50: 255–71.

Nagy, Gábor (2005): "Changes in the Position of Hungarian Regions in the Country's Economic Field of Gravity", in: G. Barta; E. Fekete; I. Kukorelli Szörényiné; J. Timár (eds): *Hungarian Spaces and Places: Patterns of Transition.* Pécs: Centre for Regional Studies; 124–42.

Nemes-Nagy, József (2001): "New Regional Patterns in Hungary", in: Peter Meusburger; Heike Jöns (eds): *Transformations in Hungary. Essays in Economy and Society.* New York/Heidelberg: Physica; 39–64.

Niederlaender, Elodie (2006): *Die Todesursachen in der EU, Statistik kurz gefasst.* Bevölkerung und Soziale Bedingungen. Eurostat.

Nižňanský, Viktor (2005): *Verejná správa na Slovensku.* Bratislava: Government of the Republic of Slovakia, Office of the Minister for Decentralization of the Public Administration.

O'Dwyer, Conor; Kovalčík, Branislav (2007): "And the Last Shall be First: Party System Institutionalization and Second-Generation Economic Reform in Post-communist Europe", *Studies in Comparative International Development* 41 (4), 3–26.

OECD (1993): *Welche Zukunft haben unsere ländlichen Räume? Eine Politik der ländlichen Entwicklung.* Paris: OECD.

——(ed.) (1993): *Welche Zukunft haben unsere ländlichen Räume? Eine Politik der ländlichen Entwicklung.* Paris: OECD.

——(1995): *Creating Employment for Rural Development.* New Policy Approaches, Paris: OECD.

——(1996): *Small Business in Transition Economies.* OECD Working Papers IV, Paris: OECD.

——(2001): *OECD Territorial Reviews.* Hungary. Paris: OECD.

——(2004): *OECD Territorial Reviews.* Czech Republic. Paris: OECD.

——(2006): *Economic Surveys.* Czech Republic. Paris: OECD.

Ohral, Jan (1991): "Partnerschaft für die Renaissance der Kleinen und Mittleren Unternehmen in Mittel und Ost-Europa. Wo sind wir und was brauchen wir in der Tschechoslowakei", in: H.J. Pichler (ed.): *Partnerships for the Renaissance of Small Business in Central and Eastern Europe.* Wien: Fachverlag der WU Wien.

OIR (2000): *Danube Space Study. Regional and Territorial Aspects of Development in the Danube Countries with Respect to Impacts of the European Union.* Final Report. OIR.

Oláh, Judit (2001): *Die Situation der ländlichen Entwicklung in Ungarn am Beispiel der statistischen Planungsregion Nagykálló, Tagung der Österreichischen Gesellschaft für*

Agrarökonomie, February. Summit of the Austrian Association for Agricultural Economics, Graz, Austria.

Oplotnik, Zan; Brezovnik, Bostjan (2004): "Financing Local Government in Slovenia", *Post-Communist Economies* 16 (4), 483–96.

ÖROK (1992): *Österreichisches Raumordnungskonzept 1991*. Wien: ÖROK.

Pampillón, Rafael; Jiménez, José Luiz (1997): "The Czech Republic: A Review of the Eastern European Economy with the Lowest Unemployment Rate", *Management Research News* 20 (1), 61–72.

Pavlínek, Peter; Smith, Adrian (1998): "Internationalization and Embeddedness in East-Central European Transition: The Contrasting Geographies of Inward Investment in the Czech and Slovak Republics", *Regional Studies* 32 (7), 619–38.

Pavlínek, Peter (1995): "Regional Development and the Disintegration of Czechoslovakia", *Geoforum* 26 (4), 351–72.

Petrakos, George C. (1996): "The Regional Dimension of Transition in Central and East European Countries. An Assessment", *Eastern European Economics* 34 (5), 5–38.

Petrakov, Nikolai (1993): "The Socialist Idea and the Economic Failure of Real Socialism", *Problems of Economic Transition* 6–24.

Pfeil Somlyódyné, Edit (2005): "Balancing Between Transition and Modernity: Principles and Institutions of Regional Planning in Hungary", in: G. Barta; E. Fekete; I. Kukorelli Szörényiné; J. Timár (eds): *Hungarian Spaces and Places: Patterns of Transition*. Pécs: Centre for Regional Studies; 106–23.

Pieper, Karin (2005): "Die Europäisierung der Regionalpolitik in Ungarn und Polen. Zur Umsetzung regionaler PHARE-Programme", in: Cyrus Salimi-Asl; Eric Wrasse; Gereon Schuch (eds): *Die Transformation nationaler Politik. Europäisierungs-prozesse in Mitteleuropa*. Deutsche Gesellschaft für Auswärtige Politik, Berlin.

Pissarides, Francesca (1999): "Is Lack of Funds the Main Obstacle to Growth? EBRD's Experience with Small- and Medium-sized Businesses in Central and Eastern Europe", *Journal of Business Venturing* 14, 519–39.

Polanyi, Karl (1978 [1944]): *The Great Transformation. Politische und ökonomische Ursprünge von Gesellschaften und Wirtschaftssystemen*. Frankfurt: Suhrkamp.

Porter, Michael E. (1990): *The Competitive Advantage of Nations*. London and Basingstoke: Macmillan.

Radice, Hugo (1996): "The Role of Foreign Direct Investment in the Transformation of Eastern Europe", in: H.J. Chang; P. Nolan (eds): *The Transformation of the Communist Economies. Against the Mainstream*. Stadt: St. Martin's Press; 282–310.

Rao, Hayagreeva; Hirsch, Paul (2003): "'Czechmate': The Old Banking Elite and the Construction of Investment Privatization Funds in the Czech Republic", *Socio-Economic Review* 1, 247–69.

Reuvid, Jonathan (2003): "Foreign Direct Investment (FDI)", in: Jonathan Reuvid (ed.): *Doing Business with Hungary*. London: Kogan Page; 19–24.

——(2004): "Foreign Direct Investment", in: Jonathan Reuvid (ed.): *Doing Business with Slovenia*. London: Kogan Page; 17–22.

Rößl, Dietmar; Berger, Gerda; Fink, Matthias; Lang, Richard (2006): "The Evolution of Co-operation and Co-operatives between Agricultural and Commercial Enterprises: Implications of Empirical Findings"; International Conference on "European Challenges to Co-operative and Family Business" der UNWE and CCU; Sofia, Bulgarien.

Roth, Wolfgang (2002): "Conclusive Evaluation of the Last Decade", in: Ján Figel; Wolfgang Roth (eds): *Slovakia on the Road to EU Membership. Schriften des Zentrum für Europäische Integrationsforschung*. Baden-Baden: Nomos; 115–26.

Rothacher, Albert (1999): *Die Transformation Mittelosteuropas: Wirtschaft, Politik und Gesellschaft in Tschechien, Polen, Ungarn, Slowenien, Kroatien und Litauen*. Wien: WKO.

Rovan, Jože; Sambt, Jože (2003): "Socio-economic Differences Among Slovenian Municipalities: A Cluster Analysis Approach", *Developments in Applied Statistics* 19, 265–78.

Rudolph, Annette (1997): *Die Bedeutung von Handwerk und Kleinunternehmen für die Regionalpolitik. Eine theoretische und empirische Betrachtung*. Duderstadt: Göttinger Handwerkstudien Nr. 51.

Rust, H. (1981): *Methoden und Probleme der Inhaltsanalyse*. Tübingen: Narr.

Růžička, Richard (1996): "Small Entrepreneurs in the Society of Employees", in: Horst Brezinski; Michael Fritsch (eds): *The Economic Impact of New Firms in Post-Socialist Countries. Bottom-up Transformation in Eastern Europe*. Cheltenham u.a.: Edward Elgar; 217–26.

Schmalhaus, Stefan; Stember, Jürgen (1993): "Schaffung gleichwertiger Lebensverhältnisse im ländlichen Raum. Möglichkeiten und Grenzen der Raumordnung", in: Stefan Schmalhaus; Jürgen Stember (eds): *Entwicklungsprobleme im ländlichen Raum*. Münster/Hamburg: Lit, 3–24.

Schön, Helmut (1997): *Regionalpolitische Konzepte und Strukturwandel ländlicher Räume. Eine Analyse am Beispiel des oberen Altmühltals*. Berlin: Duncker & Humblot.

Schönfeld, Roland (2000): *Slowakei. Vom Mittelalter bis zur Gegenwart*. Regensburg: Verlag Friedrich Pustet.

Schütze, F. (1987): *Das narrative Interview in Interaktionsfeldstudien*. Fernuniversität Hagen.

Senn, Lanfranco (1995): "Indirect Policies for Rural Area Development", in: OECD (ed.): *Creating Employment for Rural Development. New Policy Approaches*, Paris: OECD: 73–91.

Silva-Jáuregui, Carlos (2004): "Macroeconomic Stabilization and Sustainable Growth", in: Mojmir Mrak; Matija Rojec; Carlos Silva-Jáuregui (eds): *Slovenia. From Yugoslavia to the European Union*. Washington: World Bank; 115–31.

Skalnik Leff, Carol (1997): *The Czech and Slovak Republics. Nation Versus State*. Boulder: Westview Press.

Sládek, Kamil (2002): "Slovenia on the Way to Independence", in: Ján Figel; Wolfgang Roth (eds): *Slovenia on the Road to EU Membership*. Baden-Baden: Nomus; 31–74.

Smallbone, David; Welter, Friederike (2001): "The Role of Government in SME Development in Transition Economies", *International Small Business Journal* 19 (4), 63–77.

Smith, Adrian (1996): "From Convergence to Fragmentation: Uneven Regional Development, Industrial Restructuring, and the 'Transition to Capitalism' in Slovakia", *Environment and Planning A* 28, 135–56.

——(2003): "Territorial Inequality, Regional Productivity, and Industrial Change in Postcommunism: Regional Transformations in Slovakia", *Environment and Planning A* 35, 1111–35.

Soós, Gábor (2002): "Local Government Reforms and the Capacity for Local Governance in Hungary", paper presented at the Joint International Conference on "Reforming Local Government: Closing the Gap Between Democracy and Efficiency", Stuttgart, 26–27 September.

SOSR (2006): *Statistical Yearbook of the Slovak Republic 2006*. Bratislava: VEDA.
———(2007): *Slovenia in Figures 2007*. Ljubljana: Statistical Office of the Republic of Slovenia.
Šuster, Martin (2004): "Developments of Slovakia's Economy since 1990", in: Bruno S. Sergi; William T. Bagatelas (eds): *The Slovak Economy and EU Membership*. Bratislava: Lura; 47–86.
SVLR (*Slowenisches Ministerium für lokale Selbstverwaltung und Regionalpolitik*) (n.d.): White Paper on the Regional Development in Slovenia.
Swain, Nigel (1999): "Agricultural Restitution and Co-operative Transformation in the Czech Republic, Hungary and Slovakia", *Europe-Asia Studies* 51 (7), 1199–219.
Tomass, Mark (1999): "A Decade of Conflicts in Czech Economic Transformation", *Journal of Economic Issues* 33 (2), 315–24.
Töpfer, Armin (1996): "Unternehmensführung beim Transformationsprozeß in die Marktwirtschaft: Anforderungen und Probleme. Befunde einer empirischen Studie", in: K. Schweickart; R. Witt (eds): *Systemtransformation in Osteuropa. Herausforderungen an Unternehmen beim Übergang von der Planwirtschaft in die Marktwirtschaft*. Stuttgart: Schäffer Poeschel; 29–51.
Tsang, E.; Kwan, K.-M. (1999): "Replication and Theory Development in Organizational Science: A Critical Realist Perspective", *Academy of Management Review* 24 (4), 759–80.
Uhlíř, David (1998): "Internationalization, and Institutional and Regional Change: Restructuring Post-communist Networks in the Region of Lanš-kroun, Czech Republic", *Regional Studies* 32 (7), 673–85.
UNDP (2007): *Human Development Report 2007/2008. Fighting Climate Change: Human Solidarity in a Divided World*. New York: United Nations Development Program.
UNICEF (2004): *The Situation of Children and Young People at the Regional Level in Slovenia. MONEE Country Analytical Report*. Florence: UNICEF.
Van de Ven, A.H. (2002): "Strategic Directions for the Academy of Management: This Academy is For You", *Academy of Management Review* 27 (2), 171–84.
Veliyath, R.; Srinivasan, T.C. (1995): "Gestalt Approaches to Assessing Strategic Coalignment: A Conceptual Integration", *British Journal of Management* 6 (3), 205–19.
Vernon, Raymond (1966): "International Investment and International Trade in the Product Cycle", *The Quarterly Journal of Economics* 80 (2), 190–207.
Vértesi, László (1991): "Die Wiedergeburt der Kleinunternehmen in Osteuropa", in: H.J. Pichler (ed.): *Partnerships for the Renaissance of Small Business in Central and Eastern Europe*. Wien: Fachverlag der WU Wien.
Weber, Max (2000 [1905]): *Die protestantische Ethik und der "Geist" des Kapitalismus, 3. Aufl.* Weinheim: Beltz.
Weltbank (2003): *Slovak Republic – Joining the EU. A Development Policy Review*. Washington: Weltbank.
Welter, Friederike (2002): "Small and Medium Sized Enterprises in Hungary", in: O. Pfirrmann; G.H. Walter (eds): *Small Firms and Entrepreneurship in Central and Eastern Europe. A Socio-Economic Perspective*. Heidelberg/New York: Physica-Verlag; 139–55.
Wiklund, J.; Shepherd, D. (2005): "Entrepreneurial Orientation and Small Business Performance: A Configurational Approach", *Journal of Business Venturing* 20 (1), 71–91.
Williams, Allan M.; Baláž, Vladimir; Bodnárova, Bernadina (2001): "Border Regions and Trans-border Mobility: Slovakia in Economic Transition", *Regional Studies* 35 (9), 831–46.

Wostner, Peter (2002): *Regional Disparities in Transition Economies – The Case of Slovenia*, paper submitted to the European Regional Science Association Conference, Dortmund 27–31 August.

Zapalska, Alina; Zapalska, Lucyna (1999): "Small Business Ventures in Post-Communist Hungary", *Journal of East-West Business* 5 (4), 5–21.

Index

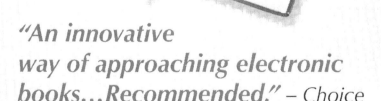

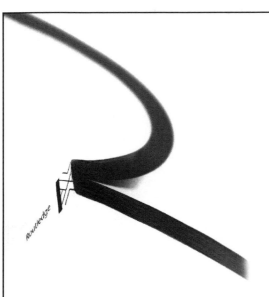